You Can't Write That

T0372692

People read and write diverse English every day, yet what counts as "correct" English has been narrowly defined and tested for 150 years. This book is written for educators, students, employers, and scholars who are seeking a more just and knowledgeable perspective on English writing. It brings together history, headlines, and research with accessible visuals and examples, to provide an engaging overview of the complex nature of written English, and to offer a new approach for our diverse and digital writing world. Each chapter addresses a particular "myth" of "correct" writing, such as "students today can't write," or "the internet is ruining academic writing," and presents the myth's context and consequences. By the end of the book, readers will know how to go from hunting errors to seeking (and finding) patterns in English writing today. This title is also available as open access on Cambridge Core.

Laura Aull is an Associate Professor and Writing Program Director at the University of Michigan, USA, where she teaches English linguistics and writing pedagogy. Her previous books include *How Students Write: A Linguistic Analysis* (2020) and *First-Year University Writing* (2015).

You Can't Write That

8 Myths About Correct English

Laura Aull

University of Michigan

CAMBRIDGE
UNIVERSITY PRESS

Shaftesbury Road, Cambridge CB2 8EA, United Kingdom

One Liberty Plaza, 20th Floor, New York, NY 10006, USA

477 Williamstown Road, Port Melbourne, VIC 3207, Australia

314–321, 3rd Floor, Plot 3, Splendor Forum, Jasola District Centre,
New Delhi – 110025, India

103 Penang Road, #05–06/07, Visioncrest Commercial, Singapore 238467

Cambridge University Press is part of Cambridge University Press & Assessment,
a department of the University of Cambridge.

We share the University's mission to contribute to society through the pursuit of
education, learning and research at the highest international levels of excellence.

www.cambridge.org
Information on this title: www.cambridge.org/9781009231305

DOI: 10.1017/9781009231299

When citing this work, please include a reference to the DOI 10.1017/9781009231299

First published 2024

A catalogue record for this publication is available from the British Library

*A Cataloging-in-Publication data record for this book is available from the
Library of Congress*

ISBN 978-1-009-23130-5 Hardback
ISBN 978-1-009-23128-2 Paperback

Cambridge University Press & Assessment has no responsibility for the persistence
or accuracy of URLs for external or third-party internet websites referred to in this
publication and does not guarantee that any content on such websites is, or will
remain, accurate or appropriate.

To those who defy myths,
like Suzy Soto.

Contents

Figures

Tables

Acknowledgments

A stoplight parrotfish dramatically changes from one phase to another. As a young fish, it is deep red, army green, and muted beige. As an adult, it is impossibly bright, its tailfins yolky yellow and its body the aqua-pink of the sea at sunset. You would not guess one turns into the other.

Where I'm going with this: Colleagues, friends, and reviewers generously read this book and offered feedback, transforming it into something clearer and brighter – the remaining want of which is entirely on me. Thank you, Norbert Elliot, principal and principled reader, for your tireless support and feedback. Thank you, Dylan Dryer, for reading multiple chapters multiple times and for telling me when something worked. Thank you, Shawna Shapiro, for reading and sending emails with exclamation points. Thank you, Bethany Aull, for reading multiple drafts with your generous eye. Thank you, John Swales, for reading and telling me to read. Thank you to my writing group, Anne Ruggles Gere, Ebony Thomas, and Mary Schleppegrell, for helping me write more accessibly. Thank you, Sigrid Anderson, for a fresh take. Thank you, Julie Buntin, for the cover and the commiserations. Thank you, Monu Lahiri, for listening. Thank you, Liz Aull and Tammy Cantarella, for generously agreeing to read. Thank you, Kathleen Fleury, for believing. Thank you, James, for diving in all kinds of seas. Let me know if you find the endnote about you. Thank you, Little Cayman Divers, Dougie, Craig, Grace, and David, for boat breaks from this book, and for your morphologically savvy shirts.

Thank you to Andrew Appleton Pine for exciting discussions at the start of the project; thank you to Jason Godfrey for thoughtful and cheerful work at the end of the project. Thank you to Rosie Ettenheim for original continuum visuals. Thank you to Monu, Kile, Julie, Gabe, James, Sarah, Nika, Bethany, Randall, Paul, monét cooper, and my fall 2022 English linguistics students for feedback on the cover and title.

Thanks to all these and other family, friends, students, and colleagues for conversations and learning that keep me full of wonder.

Thank you to the excellent team at Cambridge University Press, especially my editor Becky Taylor for stellar support from the start of this project to the last. Thank you to the patient organizational guru Izzie Collins and the meticulous Charles Phillips. Thank you to Rebekah Johnston at Cambridge Assessment Archives for enthusiastic help. Thank you to proposal and manuscript reviewers who engaged so thoughtfully with this project. Thank you to the University of Michigan TOME fund and its dedicated committee for making it possible that this book be open access, so that anyone able and willing to read its digital version can do so.

This book is freely available in an open access edition thanks to TOME (Toward an Open Monograph Ecosystem) – a collaboration of the Association of American Universities, the Association of University Presses, and the Association of Research Libraries – and the generous support of the University of Michigan. Learn more at the TOME website: openmonographs.org.

Introduction: When Writing Means *Correct Writing*

It is easy to find what you can't, or shouldn't, write. An internet search for *you can't write that …* will lead to "grammar mistakes that make you look dumb" and news articles saying students can't write and college graduates can't write to get a job.[1]

My own students, whether brand new undergraduates or graduate students training to be professors, have all heard these messages. They learned them by having their writing corrected continuously. "Correct English was whatever my English teacher deemed correct and had written in red all over my writing assignments," said a college student this fall. "I learned that the language we used in school, particularly for written tasks, was the most ideal for all situations," noted another. They describe dreading timed writing tests, following rules such as "don't use I," and learning to avoid words they use with family and friends, like *ain't*.[2]

Most reveal that in the process they also learned they are bad writers, or not writers at all. When I tell them they write every day, crafting text messages, posting ideas and reactions, and sending emails, they say that doesn't count. "But that's not real writing," one said to me last year. "Anyone can do it." What I am getting at is that none of these messages actually mean people can't write. They mean writers aren't always using one kind of writing, the kind expected in schools and tests. That's why we understand the blog title "How to write a college application essay when you can't write" – because it is common to use terms like "write" and "writing" to refer only to what is so-called *correct writing*.[3]

As you can tell, I am using *correct writing* to refer to the formal, written English required in school, particularly in and after secondary education. By then, most students are expected to write formal sentences and paragraphs, and they are taught and tested according to only a small part of the writing they do every day. Accordingly, there are some things I don't mean by *correct writing*. I don't mean literary or fiction writing. Though admired, literary writing is not how most people have to prove their learning or gain employment, and it has more flexible norms than the norms we will see emerge in myth 1. I also don't mean all *standardized English*, since people can use standardized English and any other English dialect more and less formally, in speech or writing. *Correct writing* does vary across authors and audiences (e.g., general or specialist), genres (articles, proposals, essays), and fields (engineering, history); even so, *correct writing* entails some important overall ideas and language patterns we will see throughout this book.

i.1 The Writing We Actually Do

The actual writing most people do goes far beyond *correct writing*. In a single day, it is common to write a text message in one moment, an email in another, and a paper or report after that. Even these won't all be the same – your text to your friend may be more informal than one to your coworker, for instance.

Table i.1 shows a continuum of written English, beginning with informal, interpersonal, and personal texting and ending in formal, informational, and impersonal published writing. Remarkably, this whole diverse, dynamic continuum is possible in written English.

i.2 Language Regulation Mode

This continuum is not what most of us learn, at least not explicitly. In school, we learn about what we can't or shouldn't write, according to the far right of the continuum only. We don't learn what we can and do write – or might write in the future – across the full continuum.

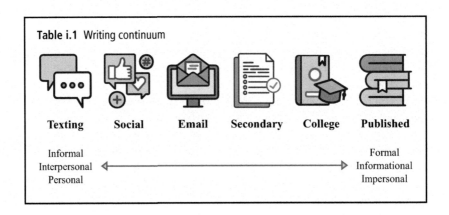

Table i.1 Writing continuum

| Texting | Social | Email | Secondary | College | Published |

Informal   ←—————————————————————→   Formal
Interpersonal   Informational
Personal   Impersonal

In other words, most people learn in language regulation mode, which means they actually learn less about language. They learn only to regulate, and be regulated by, *correct writing* rules and errors, rather than to understand a range of possible writing choices. The sociolinguist Geneva Smitherman calls this "linguistic miseducation," which is when "teachers be obsessed wit teaching 'correct' grammar, spelling and pronunciation rather than teaching students what language is and allows human beings to do."

In this quote, Smitherman describes and defies the limits of language regulation mode. She follows some norms on the far right of the continuum, including spelling choices dating back to Chancery English, as we will see in myth 1. She also follows some spelling and grammar norms used beyond the far right of the continuum, including *wit* and the continuous *be* verb (*be obsessed*) used in informal and formal Black English.

But many of us have learned only language regulation, rather than learning to understand the power of a full continuum of writing options. In the process, we've learned several myths about writing. In particular, we've learned eight writing myths addressed in this book:

1. Only one kind of writing is correct.
2. Schools must regulate writing.
3. Writing indicates natural intelligence.
4. Tests must regulate writing.
5. Most students can't write.
6. Writing should be mastered in secondary school.
7. College writing ensures professional success.
8. New technology threatens writing.

Some of these myths – for example, the first three – have been with us since English came to schools and tests 150 years ago, and all of them fuel one another. It is hard to even recognize that they are myths. Individuals such as Geneva Smitherman may see past them, but her view is the exception, not the rule.

Here's one way to think about this, if you are a sighted person: These myths are like a pair of shutter glasses we began wearing very early, before our eyes were trained without them. The myths don't give us a *true* (or unadjusted) view of writing, but that view is real – it is our perceived reality.[4]

We take the myths for granted, like glasses (bear with me) we never realized we put on. We trust the view, even when key facts don't make sense, such as the fact *correct writing* is not useful across the continuum in Table i.1 but is the writing considered *correct*. Or the fact that we

Figure i.1 Myths glasses

say every student should have a chance, but we only give *correct writers* credit and opportunity. Or the fact that tests call only the right side of the continuum "clear," as though informal writing cannot be understood. Through the myth glasses, we get used to these contradictions. We don't know how to see writing, or talk about it, any other way.

All the while, schools and tests automatically reward people with the most exposure to the right side of the continuum – most often middle- and upper-class families, white people, children of parents who went to college. As this goes on, writing myths limit everyone's knowledge of the actual writing people do.

If we are looking through the myth glasses, none of this appears to be a problem, or at least not a solvable one. It is impossible to use contrary evidence (such as writing variation) because that very evidence is treated as irrelevant, or as lowering standards. Put another way: Even when we see limitations and contradictions, we are likely to be told the problem is us, not the glasses.

So it is that with writing myths, we judge more, and we learn less.

i.3 What Should We Do Instead?

To judge less, and learn more, we need language exploration instead. We need to explore writing patterns across the continuum, instead of regulating one part of the continuum. To illustrate, we'll look at two examples my students often mention: first-person pronouns like *I*, and the word *ain't*.

In language regulation mode, many of us learn "don't use *I*" and "don't use *ain't*." In language exploration mode, instead, we learn how people tend to use first person pronouns and *ain't*.

For example: First-person pronouns are used across the writing contin- uum, but differently. On the informal, interpersonal, personal side of the continuum, writers tend to use first-person pronouns in "text external" ways, meaning they emphasize personal experiences and reactions in the "real world." In a recent tweet I saw, for instance, a new user introduced themselves using the first person *my* to emphasize personal experience, and informal punctuation and spelling norms to convey excitement and familiarity: *english is not **my** first language !!.*

On the formal, informational, impersonal side of the continuum, writers tend to use first-person pronouns in "text internal" ways, meaning they focus on information in the unfolding text or research. In this book, for example, I include text-internal first person and formal punctuation and spelling norms, like I just did: *In this book, for instance, **I** include text-internal first person.*

Ain't, on the other hand, is rarely used on the right side of the continuum. Historically maligned in upperclass conversation, *ain't* has been viewed with the myth glasses firmly on. As we will see in myth 1, early usage guides put *ain't* on the left side of the continuum and told writers it was always *incorrect*, even though it is grammatically possible and meaningful in English, used by writers of English, and very like the contraction *won't*. Today, *ain't* is regularly used on the left side of the continuum, often with negation and first- and second-person pronouns – for instance, in expressions like *if it ain't broke, don't fix it*, and usage such as *ain't no stopping me now*.[5]

What I've done here is pay attention to patterns in how people use written English, across the continuum. To say more about this, I'll address why we should do language exploration now, and why we shouldn't keep doing what we are doing, which is prioritizing *correct writing* only.

i.4 Why Language Exploration Mode?

Today, the gates to universities and other schools are much more open than they were 150 years ago, when myth 1 emerged. Black, brown, female, neurodivergent, and working-class students, people not welcome until relatively recently, pass through the gates. Even as more diverse writers are welcome, however, more diverse writing is not.

We have similar writing gatekeepers, no matter the wider gates, in other words. More than a century ago, we had the monocled eighteenth-century grammarian Lindley Murray (more on him later); today, we have the style guide *Eats, Shoots & Leaves* saying we live in a world where "Everywhere one looks, there are signs of ignorance and indifference." At universities, we had Harvard's Charles Eliot in the 1870s, ensuring entrance exams in all subjects were checked for *correct writing*; today, we have standardized writing exam scores used in college admissions. Writing gatekeepers demand *correct writing* before college; then they follow everyone inside, hovering about in writing courses and papers and playing a decisive role in college graduation and job applications. *Correct writing* gratekeepers have numerous tools to help them, from standardized writing exams to cover letter advice. They have trusted institutions, which give up on people who don't use *correct writing*.[6]

And yet we have had an alternative all along.

Patterns across the writing continuum are already part of our language knowledge. At minimum, we have unconsciously been paying attention to language patterns all our lives: in the womb, to sound patterns; as toddlers, to grammatical patterns; as teens, to texting punctuation and school-essay formats.

These patterns created a foundation for understanding and producing English. When we started writing English, for instance, we didn't memorize and regurgitate what we read. We relied on patterns, big and small:

- *happy birthday*, not *merry birthday
- **make** *a* **decision** (or: **make** *the right* **decision** or **make** *difficult* **decisions**), not **decision make a right*
- capitals as emphasis (AMAZING!!!) in informal text messages, but capitals at the start of a sentence in a formal chapter.

These are example patterns we recognize, consciously or subconsciously. They appear at all levels of writing, from phrase (*happy birthday*) to genre (text message or book chapter) to register (informal or formal). Sometimes, these patterns are obvious, and sometimes, they are subtle. But we can explore and learn about them if we know what to look for.

Since most of us learned by language regulation – instead of language exploration – many students, educators, and employers do not have conscious knowledge of writing patterns. Unfortunately, subconscious knowledge is less usable than conscious knowledge, and it makes it much easier to keep the myth glasses on.

i.5 But Shouldn't We Still Prioritize *Correct Writing*?

Most of us have learned that we have to prioritize *correct writing* in school, in the name of access to opportunity, or based on the idea that the alternative means having no standards at all. But language exploration is not the same as *anything goes*. Language exploration means we explore what people **can** and **do** write rather than limiting ourselves to what they **can't** or **shouldn't** write. Expanding our understanding of writing makes us more knowledgeable about what is already true. Diverse writing is correct in different contexts, already, even if it is not understood or studied as *correct writing*.

Furthermore, we haven't tried the alternative. We have never had a widespread English schooling model that explores diverse writing patterns for native and early learners of English. We've only ever had language regulation of one part of the continuum. This why throughout the myth chapters, you will see government policies, school reports, and news headlines that reinforce the myths, as they have for over a century.

On the one hand, this repeition reminds us not to take *correct writing* too seriously, seeing as we could go back to the nineteenth century and tell writing gatekeepers that written English did survive, and people kept right on complaining about it. It reminds us that some doomsayers will always believe that writing is going to hell on a Ferris wheel, no matter what this book says.

On the other hand, longevity doesn't make writing myths harmless – quite the contrary. Writing myths, benefit some people and not others, and their consequences are more dire for some than others. Some of the writing myths have been specifically used to erase Indigenous languages, to label Black and brown people *lazy* or *dumb*, and to pronounce women less capable of college. Many groups and individuals who have not used the far right of the continuum at the right moment – even as they write in many compelling and successful ways – have faced consequences that *correct writers*, perceived as *disciplined* and *intelligent*, have not.

Worse: We are still living with the myth glasses on. Writing myths are not a thing of the past. I still encounter them all the time, and I use *we* in this book because, like so many, I learned to write, and evaluate others' writing, with the myth glasses on.

The good news is that many of us are seeking better answers. Better answers for the student told they cannot write, and the employer who won't hire someone who uses *ain't* or a comma splice. Better answers to the claim that people don't write anymore, and the fear that English writing is doomed.

Regardless of prior training, this book is written for the many of us in this situation – educators, students, employers, scholars, parents – who regularly encounter English writing and writers, and want better ways to do so. I have accordingly tried to make this book accessible for a range of readers, by noting references at the end (organized by myth chapter and section) and avoiding the dense syntax customary on the far right of the continuum. I also focus on how historic, educational, and linguistic details come together in myths, though many of these details have their own stories beyond the scope of this book.

i.6 Chapter Outline

The book addresses eight writing myths in eight myth chapters. Each myth chapter is organized in three parts:

- **Context: how we got the myth**
  ○ An origin story
- **Consequences: why the myth matters**
  ○ Why we should care
- **Closer to the truth: how we move beyond the myth**
  ○ Exploring language patterns

The myths are summarized briefly below according to their opening scenes, leading characters, and key details. In the conclusion, I talk more about what to do next.

Myth 1 You can't write that
Or, Only one kind of writing is correct
Opening scenes: fifteenth-century spelling standardization
Leading characters: Chancery spelling, dictionaries, usage guides

This myth starts with early spelling standardization and continues with early usage guides. Its consequences include making enemies of formal and informal writing, and making people think *correct writing* means one thing – and means a capable and good person. Closer to the truth? Terrible writers can be good people, good writers can be terrible people, and all shared writing includes some fundamental similarities, and some differences. Formal writing fancies nouns more than verbs, for instance, and it likes informational subjects. Informal writing has more equal affection for nouns, verbs, pronouns, and adverbs, and it favors interpersonal subjects.

Myth 2 You can't write that in school
Or, Schools must regulate writing
Opening scenes: eighteenth-century schools
Leading characters: language policies, English literature, school curricula

This myth starts as English shifts to schools (away from home instruction), and schools shift to English (away from classical languages). Its consequences include making English regulation common and desirable, and making language variation a threat. Diverse ways of writing persist, but they aren't studied in school. Closer to the truth is that language diversity and language knowledge are human rights, but school writing focuses only on a narrow part of the writing continuum.

Myth 3 You can't write that and be smart
Or, Writing indicates natural intelligence
Opening scenes: mid nineteenth-century schools and tests
Leading characters: phrenology, IQ tests, writing scales

Myth 3 starts as *correct writing* becomes a tool for ranking students and innate ability. Consequences include limiting how we understand *intelligence*, trusting tests instead of teachers, and trusting test results without understanding tests. Closer to the truth is that uniform tests and scales are not fair, and they tell us a two-dimensional story about writing. Closer to the truth is that writing is three-dimensional – social, diverse, and unnatural – and on a continuum rather than a scale.

Myth 4 You can't write that on the test
Or, Tests must regulate writing
Opening scenes: late nineteenth-century expansion of higher education
Leading characters: college entrance examinations, standardized exam tasks

This myth starts as spoken and interactive exams end and written English exams begin. Its consequences include that every exam becomes an English exam, as *correct writing* gets evaluated in everything from history to geography to English composition exams. Its consequences also include that exam culture overshadows learning culture, and we prioritize efficiency and sameness over variation. Closer to the truth is that standardized test scores measure socioeconomic status, tests only test what is on tests, and exam tasks solicit a narrow continuum of writing.

Myth 5 Chances are, you can't write
Or, Most students can't write
Opening scenes: twentieth-century news
Leading characters: writing exam reports, standardized test results, news headlines, standardized exam writing

This myth begins when early college exam graders say students cannot write, then really emerges when headlines begin reporting standardized test results. Consequences include that test results define *writing* and *writing failure*, and we accept test-based claims and criteria. We make limited standards the same thing as excellent standards, and we think about writing in terms of *control* rather than practice. Closer to the truth is that early exam reports were sometimes inaccurate, errors are changing but not increasing, and tests and scoring criteria change. Standardized exam writing is limited, but most students write across a broad writing continuum when they are not writing standardized exams.

Myth 6 You can't write if you didn't write well in high school
Or, Writing should be mastered in secondary school
Opening scenes: twentieth-century secondary schools
Leading characters: standardized tests, composition courses, news headlines, secondary writing, college writing

Myth 6 starts at the same time as myth 5, but in this one, we learn that *correct writing* should be mastered by secondary school. As a result, this myth limits how we think about *writing development*, including who we think is responsible for it. Other consequences include that we ignore important differences between secondary and college writing, like the fact secondary writing tasks tend to be brief, persuasive, and rigidly organized, while college writing tends to be multistep, explanatory, and organized according to topic and genre. Closer to the truth is that writing development is a spiral rather than a line: It is ongoing, and not everything comes together at once. Also closer to the truth is that we can support the move from secondary to college writing by exploring writing continuum patterns.

Myth 7 You can't get a job if you didn't write in college
Or, College writing ensures professional success
Opening scenes: twentieth-century colleges and workplaces
Leading characters: magazines, university presidents, college papers, workplace email

This myth begins when popular magazines and university presidents start selling the idea that college education will lead to economic mobility. Consequences include that workplace writing is a "sink-or-swim" process for many new workers, while college assignments and courses are often limited to *correct writing* only. Closer to the truth is that college and workplace writing are different worlds, with different goals and tasks. Yet we can build metacognitive bridges between writing worlds, by exploring writing patterns within and across them.

Myth 8 You can't write that because internet
Or, New technology threatens writing
Opening scenes: late twentieth-century headlines
Leading characters: television, digital writing, news headlines, formal writing

The final myth brings us full circle to myth 1, because it keeps limiting *correct writing*. It puts *correct writing* at odds with informal digital writing, even when *correct writing* is critiqued for being stodgy. We get the idea that *correct writing* is controlled, whereas informal digital writing is careless, and we limit who reads *correct writing* and what writing is studied in school. Closer to the truth is that if you are alarmed by something – say, text message slang – you will notice it more, even if most written English is neither changing nor fundamentally different. Informal writing is not the same thing as careless writing, and it is both similar to and different from formal writing on the writing continuum.

Conclusion: Writing continuum, language exploration

The conclusion looks back over the myths to consider where we've come from and where we can go next. We already have language patterns, subconscious knowledge, and interest in language to help us. With awareness of timeworn myths, we can move to a new metaphor for writing: a continuum with shared purposes, as well as distinct patterns. A continuum enables us to recognize the range of informal and formal, personal and impersonal, interpersonal and informational writing our world demands. It allows us to see that all these types of written English are systematic, meaningful, similar, and distinct. It allows us to approach a full range of written English as fodder for knowledge and exploration.

CHAPTER ONE

Myth 1 You Can't Write That

Or, Only One Kind of Writing Is Correct

1.1 Pick a Century

See if you can tell which century each passage comes from: eighteenth, nineteenth, twentieth, or twenty-first.

1. Dear student, When you hold this essay in your hands, I know that you will look immediately at the mark I've written at the top of the first page. You will make assumptions about yourself, your work – perhaps even your worth – based on this number.
2. It is certain that if a child is not learning good English he is learning bad English, and probably bad habits of thought; and some of the mischief done may never afterwards be undone.
3. I recognize but one mental acquisition as an essential part of the education of a lady or a gentleman, namely, an accurate and refined use of the mother tongue.
4. Thus two essential qualities of usage, in regard to language, have been settled, that it be both *reputable* and *national.*

If you guessed that the passages appear most to least recent, you were right. First is a twenty-first-century passage, from a 2016 *Guardian* article written by a university lecturer. Second is a 100-year old statement from the 1921 Newbolt Report to the United Kingdom Department of Education. Third is a pledge from Harvard president Charles Eliot documented in 1883, and fourth is an excerpt from George Campbell's 1776 *The Philosophy of Rhetoric.*

Across four centuries, the passages declare there is one kind of *correct English*, which means a *correct* mind, character, and nation. Those who use any other English are careless – even doomed, their mischief never undone.

During these four centuries, writers and writing have changed dramatically, from a few writers with quills, to many writers, with smartphones and spellcheckers. What hasn't changed dramatically is myth 1: Only one kind of English is *correct.*

And yet there was a time when English existed but these associations did not. Our story begins in the centuries before the opening passages.

1.2 Context for the Myth

1.2.1 Spelling Becomes Uniform and Moral

Fourteenth-century England was a site of sundry spelling. (Try saying that five times fast.) Very few people had written literacy, but for them, English was not uniform. As an English scribe, you might spell the same word multiple ways on the same page.[1] Your spelling might be influenced by other languages, particularly French (the early language of Parliament) and Latin (the early language of bureaucracy). You might specifically choose Latin spellings, to be paid more for longer words.

Correct English spelling didn't exist yet, in other words. It wasn't "anything goes" – scribes were disciplined for wandering attention and haste, for instance. But readers and writers were accustomed to varied English spelling.

Things changed when English started becoming the national language. The Court of Chancery, which at the time was like England's courthouse and treasury in one, started issuing documents in English, and Chancery English became a guide for publishing houses.[2] As Chancery English spelling spread, so, too, did the idea of *Standard English*, which we can call *standardized English* to highlight that it is not an objective standard, but something made through an ongoing process.

Both the *what* and *how* of this process were important: What English was getting standardized, and how it was promoted, mattered. After Chancery clerks began writing in English in the early 15th century, the 1422 resolution of the London Brewers' Association labeled English the language of the king, the ruling class, and the law. It said English was acquired by diligent writing and "setting aside" other languages. Chancery English was not just one version of one language, adopted for specific correspondence, in other words. It was *correct writing*, the writing of careful study and powerful people.

As time passed and more official documents appeared in English, there was less and less official room for anything but *correct writing*. Regional English writers and printers left local varieties behind, lest they be labeled provincial. Scottish writers experienced added pressure after the 1603 Union of the Scottish and English crowns. British colonists began taking *correct writing* across the globe, carrying print materials and proclaiming English the language of *good, civilized* people.

In turn, texts printed in *correct writing*, and the idea that *correct writing* indicated morality and progress, circulated simultaneously. While a full writing continuum included regional varieties, the part of the writing continuum considered acceptable was shrinking.

1.2.2 *Correct English* Becomes Patriotic

In the eighteenth and nineteenth centuries, prominent writers presented *correct English* as a national duty. In 1712, Jonathan Swift published "A Proposal for Correcting, Improving, and Ascertaining the English Tongue" in the name of "all the Learned and Polite Persons of the Nation." In 1755, Samuel Johnson's *Dictionary of the English Language* aimed to fix "improprieties and absurdities" in English, including regional variation, which he described as "capricious."

On the other side of the Atlantic, Noah Webster took a similar stance while adding a heavy measure of US patriotism. His *American Spelling Book* in 1790 aimed to end regional US dialects and "purify" English, and his later *American Dictionary of the English Language* was written "for the continued increase of the wealth, the learning, the moral and religious elevation of character, and the glory of my country."

These early, prominent sources helped expand and circulate myth 1. They not only suggested there was one *correct English*. They also proposed that national unity depended on it. Upholding *correct English*, they implied, was part of upholding a refined and moral nation.

1.2.3 Usage Wardens Tell Grown People How to Use English

English usage guides (also called style guides) promoted *correct writing* even more comprehensively than spelling books and dictionaries. Several usage guides emerged in the eighteenth century and became even more popular in the nineteenth century, when a new middle class sought the social advantages of English associated with the upper classes. By then, we know, the message that *correct English* was the language of the ruling class had been around for centuries.

Early usage guides were written by especially devout writing gate-keepers. They tended to be educated, well-established writers themselves – of sermons, of legal texts – who began publishing their own usage preferences for other writers. Prominent examples included Bishop of London Robert Lowth (a man "inclined to melancholy"), British philosopher and dissenting clergyman Joseph Priestley (who allowed, "It is possible I may be thought to have gleaned too much from the Latin idiom"), British educator Ann Fisher (a rare non-Londoner and woman in the group), Scottish minister and philosopher George Campbell (who wrote *The Philosophy of Rhetoric* we encountered in the opening), and retired US lawyer Lindley Murray (who promised *Perspicuity in Speaking and Writing*). Usage guides by these authors were among the most widely circulating books of their time, which would be like if a usage guide today competed with *Harry Potter.*

George Campbell's *The Philosophy of Rhetoric*, for instance, was repeatedly printed, sold, and reviewed for broad audiences in periodicals like the *Critical Review* and *Monthly Review*. Campbell had no tolerance for variation and evoked a strict language caste system. "In the lower walks of life," he wrote, people misapplied the language of "superiors." They needed better understanding as soon as possible, so that they could "renounce their own [usage] immediately."

Like Swift, Johnson, and Webster, Campbell approached *correct English* as a nationalist project, but he fixated on *correct writing* in particular. Spoken English could be "negligent" if necessary, he wrote. But *correct writing* would keep English "reputable, present, and national," safeguarded from foreign incursion.

Other usage guides were infused with a similarly moralizing tone. One of Ann Fisher's books was *The Pleasing Instructor, or Entertaining Moralist.* John Ash's eighteenth-century *Grammatical Institutes*, a usage guide reprinted at least fifty times, opens with the platitude "The Knowledge of Letters is one of the greatest Blessings that ever God bestowed upon Man." Lest readers think variation was part of Knowledge of Letters, Ash included an activity entitled "Promiscuous Exercises of False Syntax."

Bishop Lowth, who appears to have been an unwitting gatekeeper,[3] praised writing – which he said was rare – that showed "correctness, propriety, and purity of English style." He also implied that his usage recommendations were not necessarily required for success, since "our best Authors have committed gross mistakes, for want of a due knowledge of English Grammar, or at least a proper attention to the rules of it." We'll see this same paradox in myth 2.

Correct writing regulation was especially championed by Lindley Murray, whose 1795 *English Grammar* defined rules and errors with unprecedented rigidity. Murray is seen as the father of what linguists call *prescriptivism*: prescribing what English *should* be like, rather than what it *is* like (which would be *descriptivism*). Murray's *English Grammar* became the most popular usage guide for decades in Britain and the United States, offering what the contemporary book *The Dictionary Wars* called "a lifeline to success and an improved social status." Today, Murray's legacy lives on in several inflexible rules for *correct writing*.

1.3 The Myth Emerges

So it was that between 1400 and 1800 the first myth emerged, along with popular reading to proclaim it. Only one kind of writing was *correct writing*. And *correct writing*, despite representing the preferences of only some texts and people, meant goodness, ability, and national progress.

1.4 Consequences of the Myth

1.4.1 We Limit *Correct Writing* (and *Correct Writer*)

With this myth, we limit *correct writing* – and the goodness and ability associated with it – to only a small part of the writing continuum. The rest of the continuum does not indicate goodness or ability; it might even threaten national safety and progress. Table 1.1 emphasizes the limited part of the continuum acknowledged in this myth, taken by many as the continuum itself.

Within this overall consequence, there are several more specific consequences, which appear in Table 1.2.

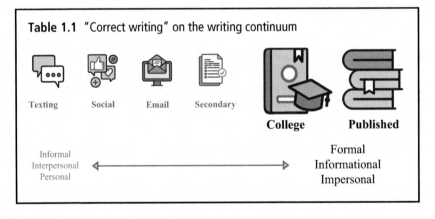

Table 1.1 "Correct writing" on the writing continuum

Texting   Social   Email   Secondary

College   Published

Informal
Interpersonal
Personal

Formal
Informational
Impersonal

Table 1.2 Consequences of myth 1

Once we believe **only one kind of writing is correct, then…**	… English spelling is a mess that matters
	… English variation is a national threat
	… Usage preferences of a few are usage preferences for all
	… Narrow standards are high standards
	… Formality and informality are enemies
	… We tolerate confusing references to *grammar*
	… We miss opportunities for learning and connecting

1.4.2 English Spelling Is a Mess that Matters

Since Chancery English spelling was standardized and moralized, we've been stuck with it. This means that spelling expected across much of the writing continuum, and certainly the spelling of *correct writing*, is characterized by lasting oddities.

Some oddities reflect the early influence of other languages. For instance, we write *quick* (versus *cwic*) because Old English *cw* was replaced by the French *qu*. Other oddities come from pronunciation: Pronunciation evolves over time as words are spoken, so a lot of spelling that was intuitive in the past is not intuitive today. If you were describing a *gnarly knight* in 1400, for instance, you'd have pronounced the *g* and *k*.[4] Even more confounding is that English has never had letters for all of its vowel sounds. For example, the letter "a" in *about* sounds different from the "a" in *apple*, but the same letter appears in the English spelling of those words.[5]

Basically, we've inherited spelling that has long been troublesome. Centuries ago, there were already complaints that Chancery English spelling didn't guide pronunciation. In the early twentieth century, English was described as "antiquated, inconsistent and illogical" by spelling reformist R. Zachrisson. By the late twentieth century, English spelling was described by linguist Mario Pei as "an awesome mess."

But here's the rub: since this start of this myth, English spelling has been a mess that matters. It is a mess linked with morality and capability. A 1900 entry in *The School Journal* proclaimed: "If a man is a slipshod speller it is because he is a slipshod thinker ... sure to act [on] inadequate moral ideals." A 2015 *Harvard Business Review* linked spelling and credibility, warning: "People jump to all kinds of conclusions about you when they read documents you have written."

1.4.3 English Variation Is a National Threat

In the many early sources that limited *correct writing*, variation within and beyond English posed a national threat. Campbell wrote about *correct writing* as something to be protected from foreign incursion. Johnson characterized English dialect variation as careless. Webster made *correct writing* tantamount to American freedom and national harmony. In these messages, *correct writing* more easily becomes a tool for discriminating against those who don't use or value it. We will see this consequence again in other myths, but we see it begin resolutely with this myth.

1.4.4 Usage Preferences of a Few Are Usage Preferences for All

Many preferences of the eighteenth- and nineteenth-century usage wardens have lasted. This means that the preferences of writers from a narrow population and set of experiences (mostly educated, Christian and religious, economically well-positioned, white men in England and the US) have been the usage preferences represented in *correct writing* for centuries. We will see a prominent illustration in a moment, in the contemporary example of Strunk and White's *Elements of Style*.

1.4.5 Narrow Standards Are High Standards

More important than particular rules or standards are what people believe about them. With this myth came the message that *correct writing* standards are not just narrow, or specific, standards; they are high standards. Josephine Baker's *Correct English*, published between 1899 and 1950, was written so adults could keep up "a high standard of expression" after their schooling and thereby avoid "bad English." Similar messages appeared in popular periodicals such as *The Spectator* and *The Rambler* in the UK and *Time* and *Harper's Magazine* in the US.

Likewise, nineteenth-century university leaders promoted *correct writing* as the highest standard for language and moral development. In 1828, University of London professor Thomas Dale said the aim of education was "to inculcate lessons of virtue, through the medium of the masters of our language." Charles Eliot, whom we met at the start of the chapter, linked *correct writing* to "the higher moral interest and greater promise" of English-speaking political and social institutions. At Harvard, Eliot established English entrance exams and courses that valued *correct writing* above other writing or languages. (More generally, Eliot objected to all kinds of diversity, as we will see in myth 3.)

The idea that narrow standards are excellent standards makes it hard to challenge or expand *correct writing*. A century after Eliot, critics denounced Webster's *Third New International Dictionary of the English Language* for including *ain't*, despite its widespread use and linguistic similarity to *won't*. The outcry highlighted the lasting idea that when English dictionaries and usage guides include diverse usage, they fail to be what applied linguist David Brown describes as "upholders of propriety." This is a good example of how myth 1 fuels language regulation mode: Propriety is associated with only one part of the continuum, and addressing a fuller continuum of English is not allowed.

For contemporary evidence of this myth, we can look to a particularly famous usage guide, Strunk and White's *The Elements of Style. The Elements of Style* sold more than 10 million copies between 1959 and 2009 alone, often as a gift for secondary graduates heading to college. Like earlier usage guides, *The Elements of Style* moralizes *correct writing*, equating written style with human character. *The Elements of Style* also illustrates the passing of language regulation from one generation to another: Strunk was White's college professor, and when White became an author, he expanded and published Strunk's usage rules in a new book.

The fiftieth anniversary celebration of *The Elements of Style* in 2009 included a *New York Times* article by a seasoned reporter, who opens by second-guessing his writing:

How does a professional writer discuss *The Elements of Style* without nervously looking over his shoulder and seeing Will Strunk and E. B. White (or thousands of readers of their book) second-guessing him? (Is "second-guessing" hyphenated or not? Is posing a question the same as using the passive voice?)

After several paragraphs of similar praise and paranoia, the article cites a University of Edinburgh linguistics professor who shows how *The Elements of Style* severely simplifies English. Strunk, however, had a gatekeeper's rejoinder for critiques such as these, which he passed on to White: "It is worse to be irresolute than to be wrong."

"It is worse to be irresolute than to be wrong" does not seem like great advice in many situations (flying a plane, performing an amputation), but it has particular consequences when it comes to writing. Being *irresolute* about *correct writing* leaves room for questioning and exploring. Being *wrong* means limiting writing despite pervasive language variation. Strunk and White's resolute boundaries around *correct writing* might especially impact those without their confidence – a confidence so complete that the two authors break their own rules in *The Elements of Style* without acknowledgment.

Yet the tone of *The New York Times* article is one of wistful appreciation for just that sort of rigid confidence, which upholds high standards: "Unless someone is willing to entertain notions of superiority," White is quoted as saying, "the English language disintegrates."

The Elements of Style has not been updated to account for new forms of communication, because, explains the publisher, its popularity shows that its advice is timeless. And so the guide continues to circulate widely, emphasizing the *correct writing* error, avoiding change and variation. Language regulation, The *Elements of Style* illustrates, can be at once limiting and well-loved.

1.4.6 Formality and Informality Are Enemies

Early usage guides separated formal and informal English, depicting *correct writing* as formal and careful and all other writing as informal and careless. Today, students continue to receive this advice from a range of sources.[6] The University of Southern California and the University of Melbourne, for instance, advise avoiding first person pronouns, phrasal verbs, and abbreviations in college writing. While personal correspondence with familiar audiences calls for informal usage, the advice suggests, college writing calls for formal writing no matter the task.

In consequence, informal and formal writing are enemies, not neighbors or friends, their respective writing patterns separate rather than mutually illuminating and sometimes overlapping. The formal end of the continuum is considered *correct*, and it is exclusively prioritized and tested in school despite the fact that most of the continuum is characterized by informal patterns. Even ongoing calls for Plain English don't always call for informality, but rather for less technical jargon.[7]

1.4.7 We Tolerate Confusing References to *Grammar*

Many claims about *incorrect* or *bad grammar* refer to one of two things: conventions or usage preferences. By conventions, I mean norms for spelling, punctuation, what is called "wrong word," and capitalization, rather than what is grammatically possible in English. And usage preferences are just that: preferences for usage, rather than what is grammatically possible in English.

For instance, a recent online list called "15 grammar goofs that make you look silly" emphasizes conventions rather than grammar. No fewer than ten of the fifteen concern words that sound the same but are different – for example, *it's* versus *its, your* versus *you're*, and *their* versus *there*. These homophones are impossible to note in speech, and readers can easily decipher the intended meaning. Often, they are interchangeably used in informal digital writing such as texting. Still, the use of "terrible grammar" to refer to conventions is common. We've seen some examples in this chapter, and we will see many more throughout the book.

1.4.8 We Miss Opportunities for Learning and Connecting

When we only value *correct writing*, we only value part of the continuum. We only reward those writers with exposure and practice with *correct writing.* We prioritize and moralize only the language use and culture of a highly limited mold. In the shady reality of this myth, in other words, the son of Bishop Lowth faced a life of presupposed opportunity and moral rectitude, no matter his capability or character.

We support unfair treatment, as a result, and we miss opportunities. We miss different values and ways of relating. We miss connections across a full continuum of writing and writers.

1.5 Closer to the Truth

1.5.1 Standardized Spelling Depends on Memorization and Practice

Correct writing spelling, expected on most of the writing continuum, is an awesome mess. To use this mess, you need practice and memorization. Still, spelling practice is not the same as writing practice: Spelling instruction appears to improve spelling skills but not writing skills. You can be a hardworking, capable writer, but you won't know how to write *gnarly knight* unless you have practiced its peculiar, outdated spelling.

The informal end of the writing continuum has more flexible spelling norms, meaning spelling can change more easily and intuitively. For example, text message spelling often includes *nite* for *night* or *u* for *you*, which approximate English sounds (or phonemes). Indeed, research shows that children who use textisms have enhanced language skills, which researchers attribute to awareness of English sounds and letters.

1.5.2 Grammar Is What Is Possible and Meaningful in a Language

The linguistic definition of *grammar* is what is meaningful and possible in a language – the norms for forming words, phrases, and sentences, regardless of usage preferences or conventions. Sound (or phonological) norms in English, for instance, prevent us from pronouncing the *p* sound in *pneumonia*. Word (or morphological) norms in English allow us to add *-ly* to change adjectives to adverbs (e.g., *quick* to *quickly*), and to use verb contractions like *ain't* or *won't* to express negation. In other words:

- English grammar does not mean "*correct writing* usage preferences" such as "do not use *ain't.*"
- English grammar does not mean "*correct writing* conventions" such as *correct writing* spelling, punctuation, and capitalization.
- English grammar is what is possible and meaningful, across the full writing continuum.

Table 1.3 English grammar

English grammar	Not English grammar
A writing continuum	* *continuum a*
The continuum	* *continuum the*
Writing is on a continuum	*Continuum on a is writing*
Writing be on a continuum	* *Continuum be a writing*
Idk	* *Kdi*

This definition means, for instance, that the formal phrase *a writing continuum* falls within English grammar, and the informal abbreviation *idk* (for *I don't know*) falls within English grammar.

In Table 1.3, the left-hand column follows what is grammatical (read: possible and meaningful) in English. The nouns follow articles *the* or *a*, and the sentences (including the abbreviation *idk*), use subject-verb-object order. The right-hand column (marked with *) includes ungrammatical (read: not possible) examples. In these examples, we can't decipher meaning.

Usage preferences and conventions are not grammar. When *correct writing* usage preferences or conventions are not followed on the left of the continuum, we might pause because we expect something different. But the full writing continuum is possible and meaningful within English grammar.

1.5.3 Terrible People Can Be *Good* Writers, *Terrible* Writers Can Be Good People

Correct writing is an indication of practice, not goodness. The US terrorist called the Unabomber wrote in *correct writing*. Civil rights activists who couldn't write English fought for equal opportunity and fair treatment for all races. Other examples are everywhere around us, from prominent leaders to unknown children. Producing the narrow version of English that became *correct writing* does not make a person good.

1.5.4 Diverse Usage Is Similar

Writing across the continuum, whether it is considered *correct writing* or not, shares several grammatical patterns like the ones we just saw.

The famous writer Maya Angelou describes this variation in her memoir *I Know Why the Caged Bird Sings.* Angelou offers two example sentences, one she associates with school and one she associates with meeting in the street.

At school, in a given situation, we might respond with "That's not unusual." But in the street, meeting the same situation, we easily said, "It be's like that sometimes."[8]

Angelou's two examples follow what is grammatical in English. For one thing, they follow the same subject-verb-object structure we've seen already, which has been in English for centuries. Using that structure, the first example uses the present progressive *be* associated with *correct writing* ("That **is** not unusual"), while the second example uses habitual *be* associated with African American or Black English ("It **be's** like that sometimes").

Angelou's examples also illustrate that diverse usage includes many of the same words – particularly pronouns, conjunctions, and prepositions (or *closed lexical categories*). For instance, both Angelou's examples include the pronoun *that*, a word that has been around for more than 800 years.

In a final example of similarities, writing across the continuum follows parallel morphological processes. Morphological processes dictate what is grammatical (read: possible and meaningful) for forming new words in English. If we've grown up writing English, we know the morphological process I mentioned earlier – adding *-ly* to make something an adverb – even if we don't consciously know we do. Here's another example. I scuba dive with a company, Little Cayman Divers, that has this phrase on the back of their staff shirts shown in Figure 1.1: *Okayest dive masters in the world.*

Figure 1.1 *Okayest* follows English morphology

If you are familiar with written English, you recognize *okayest* because it follows morphological rules that dictate what is grammatically possible and meaningful in English. According to English morphology, we compare adjectives with one or two syllables by adding *-er* (e.g., cool becomes cooler). We add *-est* to make something superlative (cooler now becomes coolest). This is how our knowledge of English morphology, consciously or not, makes *okayest* funny, since *okay* itself means mediocre.

The upshot is that not only is a full continuum of writing important in our lives, but also, the full continuum shares fundamental similarities. Only the myth glasses, as old as this myth, make *okayest* "not real English." It might be on the informal part of the continuum, but *okayest* is grammatically possible and meaningful in English. Meanwhile, Microsoft Word grammar checker, disciple of this myth, is alerting me to change *okayest*.

1.5.5 Diverse Usage Is Correct

While some grammatical structures and words are used across the writing continuum, some language patterns are distinct according to where they are on the continuum. Distinct does not mean *better*. Language regulation mode ignores the continuum, pretending *correct writing* patterns always apply. But language exploration mode looks across the continuum for overlapping and distinct patterns, all of which tell us something about written English.

To illustrate, we'll look at two patterns that differentiate informal and formal writing. One pattern – lots of nouns – appears in what is considered *correct writing*. The other pattern – fewer nouns, more verbs – appears on the rest of the writing continuum.

1.5.5.1 *Correct Writing* Hearts Noun Phrases … *Incorrect Writing* Totally Doesn't

Correct writing uses a lot of nouns. In particular, it uses a lot of noun *phrases*, which include prepositional phrases, adjectives, and other nouns. In other words, on the far right of the continuum, noun phrases tend to take up the stage, leaving less room for verbs, pronouns, adverbs, and adjectives that are not in noun phrases.

By contrast, most of the writing continuum, including informal digital writing, workplace emails, and secondary writing, doesn't use so many noun phrases. Instead, on most of the writing continuum nouns, verbs, adjectives, adverbs, and pronouns share the stage. We'll look at a set of examples.

- Example from left of continuum: *Correct writing is totally strange. It hearts nouns.*
  - Here, the nouns and verbs roughly share the stage. The sentence has two clauses, one with a noun (*correct writing*), a verb (*is*), and an adverb and adjective (*totally strange*). The other has a pronoun (*it*), a verb (*hearts*), and a noun (*nouns*).
  - If we are familiar with the words, this proportion makes it easy to tell the main subject, and what is happening, and how.
- Example from right of the continuum: *Relative to informal digital writing, formal academic writing contains a high proportion of dense noun phrases.*
  - Here, we get a single sentence dominated by noun phrases (all but one word of it!). In addition to these noun phrases, we have one verb (*contains*).
  - The noun phrases in this example contain several embedded phrases, including <u>nouns</u> and [prepositional phrases]:
    [Relative to <u>informal digital writing</u>*]*, *[*<u>formal academic writing</u>*]* *contains [*<u>a high proportion</u>*][of* <u>dense noun phrases</u>*].*

What this means is that *correct writing* often means "includes a lot of noun phrases." In turn, reading *correct writing* – such as academic books or articles – means parsing a lot of dense noun phrases.

What this also means is that what is considered *incorrect writing* often means "includes few noun phrases." Reading informal digital writing, which most people have a lot more practice with, means parsing a closer balance of nouns, verbs, pronouns, and adverbs, which tend to be a bit more obvious about who (or what) is doing what.

These are overall trends. Some workplace emails might use noun phrases, and some academic writing might use simple nouns and many verbs. But these are general trends, when it comes to noun phrases across the continuum. (For my part, I wonder if formal writing really needs to be so noun-dense all the time. But more on that in later myths.)

1.5.6 Linguistic Equality and Social Inequality Are for Real

As we can see in the writing continuum, closer to the truth is that we have a range of writing patterns that are grammatically possible and meaningful in English. Closer to the truth is that all of these patterns are linguistically equal: They are all rule-governed and responsive to different writing situations.

Even so, we have hundreds of years of the opposite message: that only spelling dating back to the fifteenth century is *correct*; that only usage-guide preferences are *correct*. Also closer to the truth, therefore, is that all language use is not *socially* equal, despite being linguistically equal. Many of us learned only language regulation mode: to judge writers and writing in terms of *correct* and *incorrect* usage. We did not learn language exploration mode: to observe writers and writing in terms of patterns accurate in different situations.

1.5.7 Writing Is on a Continuum of Shared Purposes and Distinct Patterns

Along with some grammatical norms, writing across the continuum shares five purposes that facilitate communication. In other words, there are five things all shared writing does, though how it does them depends on the writing. Here are the five purposes, with example patterns.

(1) Writing has **cohesion**
   • To signal new input or ideas, written English includes emojis, new paragraphs, or transitions such as *also* or *however*.
(2) Writing makes **connection**
   • To address writers and readers, written English includes specific uses of first- and second-person pronouns, and citations or other references.
(3) Writing shows **focus**
   • To emphasize different kinds of topics, written English includes a balance of nouns and verbs, or many noun phrases, and it includes active verbs, or passive verbs.
(4) Writing shows **stance**
   • To show doubt, certainty, or a positive or negative attitude, written English includes boosters, hedges, and generalizations.
(5) Writing follows **usage** norms
   • To follow norms, written English includes flexible and rigid spelling and punctuation conventions, and informal or formal usage preferences.[9]

Along with the fundamental similarities we discussed earlier, the five shared purposes help us understand and use a range of writing. Meanwhile, the different patterns allow us to use different writing for different ends. These different patterns are correct for different kinds of writing, and they distinguish the two ends of the continuum. On the left side near informal text messages, writing is more informal, personal, and interpersonal; on the right side near formal published books, writing is more formal, impersonal, and informational. For example, even

Table 1.4 Writing continuum purposes and patterns

	Texting	Social	Email	Secondary	College	Published

Continuum Patterns

Continuum Purposes	Informal Interpersonal Personal ⟷					Formal Informational Impersonal

Cohesion *Writers move between topics and language users*	• Pragmatic markers (*so, like, yeah*) • Emojis • Punctuation • Pacing, pauses, new posts or messages • Narrative moves such as orientation, complicating action, evaluation	• Transition words (*nonetheless, thus*) • Rhetorical moves such as given-new, introductory, or development moves • New paragraphs • Sections in research articles such as intro, methods, results, discussion
Connection *Writers address readers/writers*	• 2nd person pronouns, direct questions • Text-external 1st person, in relation to experiences and events (*I remember; We going to*) • Reactions, exclamations (*omg*) • References to people, events	• Directives (*Consider this; See table*), rhetorical questions • Text internal 1st person, in relation to text and process (*I will argue; we conducted trials*) • References to sources, citations
Focus *Writers emphasize priorities*	• Nouns, verbs, pronouns, adverbs • Simple sentence subjects emphasize people, experiences • More active verbs	• More noun and prepositional phrases • Dense phrase subjects emphasize ideas, phenomenon, and processes • More passive verbs
Stance *Writers show (un)certainty and attitude*	• More boosters (*totally*), fewer hedges • More generalizations and exaggerations (*everyone, no way*) • Strong evaluative adjectives (*amazing*) and adverbs (*ridiculously*)	• More hedges (*perhaps, suggests*), fewer boosters, few generalizations • Moderate evaluative adjectives, often before nouns (*important contribution*)
Usage *Writers follow grammatical and usage norms*	• Flexible punctuation and usage, conventions able to change	• *Correct writing* punctuation and usage conventions (from 18th c) and spelling (from 16th c)

Norms across the continuum	subject-verb-object construction open lexical categories (nouns, verbs, adverbs, adjectives) for new words closed lexical categories (e.g., pronouns, prepositions, conjunctions) that rarely change morphological rules of English

when informal text messages share information, they have more patterns focused on personal reactions and interpersonal connection with others. And though some academic books share personal anecdotes, overall they have more informational patterns than personal or interpersonal ones. This is why linguists say that "phraseology and epistemology are indissolubly interlinked," which is a formal, informational, impersonal way of saying that different language patterns support different goals and values.

Sometimes, the same feature is used differently, depending on where it is on the writing continuum. First-person pronouns are a good example, as we saw in the introduction. Writing on the left of the continuum tends to use first-person pronouns in text-external ways, emphasizing personal experiences and reactions, while writing on the right side of the continuum tends to use first-person pronouns in text-internal ways, emphasizing the information that the writers are writing about.

To capture purposes and patterns on the writing continuum, I've added rows in Table 1.4. We've already seen some grammatical norms shared across the continuum, and these appear at the bottom of the continuum.

In a full writing continuum, we have shared purposes and patterns, as well as important differences. And yet: From the Court of Chancery to *The Elements of Style*, this myth tells us only one kind of writing is *correct*.

Closer to the truth is that we are all limited by this myth, because we learn less about the full writing continuum. The far right of the continuum is treated as *correct* and wholly separate from other parts of the continuum. Those who do not practice or value that part of the continuum are told they are *bad writers*. They may have been told they are *careless* or *lazy* besides.

At least here, we have dwelled with *correct writing* a different way, as just one part of a full, connected writing continuum. As we address other myths, we'll keep exploring the full continuum, adding examples from written English over time. But we will continue to see *correct writing* refer to the narrow version of written English we get in this myth.

CHAPTER TWO

Myth 2 You Can't Write That in School

Or, Schools Must Regulate Writing

2.1 Pick a Century

More passages from the eighteenth, nineteenth, twentieth, and twenty-first centuries appear below. Can you put them in order?

1. We must help students master standard English.
2. We desire ... more attention to English composition and orthography [for students'] command of pure grammatical English.
3. The gentlemen of this nation ... are left utterly untaught ... they are not able to write or spell true English.
4. What we need to restore is the teaching of correct English as the essential craft through which all writing, whether creative or not, must be expressed.

The words "gentlemen" and "restore" might give away the last two examples. Otherwise, we get different centuries, but the same message: Schools need to regulate *correct writing*, for the sake of students and the nation.

The actual chronological order of the passages is: 3, 2, 1, 4. Passage 3 is the oldest, first appearing in Daniel Defoe's *The Compleat English Gentleman* in 1729. Passage 2 appeared in 1864, in a UK education report with the longest title ever: *Clarendon Report of Her Majesty's Commissioners appointed to inquire into the Revenues and Management of Certain Colleges and Schools, and the Studies Pursued and Instruction Given Therein.* Passage 1 appeared in the British newspaper *The Observer* in 1982, and the final passage appeared in the US *Chronicle of Higher Education* in 2018.

This myth brings myth 1 to schools and universities. Yet while there was a time when myth 1 didn't exist – a time when there wasn't such a limited version of *correct writing* – there was never a time when English writing in school meant something other than *correct writing*. By the time English writing was taught and tested, what counted as *correct* was already limited.

Still, there was a time when English writing was not the focus of education. That is where our second origin story begins, as English shifted to schools, and schools shifted to English.

2.2 Context for the Myth

2.2.1 English Shifts to Schools, and Schools Shift to English

Before the eighteenth century, a primary site for cultivating English literacy was at home, through family instruction and reading. School, on the other hand, was a site for studying classical languages, at least for the children able to go to school. *Grammar schools*, so named, focused on Latin and Greek grammar, not English grammar.

The slow shift toward English study began in the eighteenth century in UK and US universities. Inspired by the practical and nationalist ideals of the Enlightenment and the American Revolution, groups of Scots, Brits, and Americans began reforming education and promoting English-language study. Scottish universities were studying English in the 1730s; in England, dissenting academies had broken from the Oxford and Cambridge tradition and were providing secular English study by the mid-eighteenth century. Defoe, whose passage about *true English* opens this chapter, was one such dissenting academy student.[1]

The US shift to English was promoted by Princeton's Scottish president John Witherspoon, and many Americans considered it a welcome change. Puritans were suspicious of classical pagan writers and their threat to Christian scripture, and Quakers preferred practical curricular subjects. Prominent eighteenth-century thinkers promoted English as well: Thomas Paine, Enlightenment disciple and author of *The Age of Reason*, did not study Latin; Benjamin Franklin advocated English study in schools, with classical languages and even other modern languages for elective study.

Still, revolutionary as it was to call for English at the time, the English called for was not revolutionary. It was *correct writing* only. A usage warden we met in myth 1, clergyman Joseph Priestley, provides a good illustration. Priestley was an eighteenth-century tutor at Warrington Academy known for his radical ideas about education, politics, and religion. Yet his radicalism stopped short of his ideas about English: Priestley implied standardized English was inherently superior, while other varieties were "bad English."

Priestley's instructional materials also provide a good illustration of the early practice of using several languages in educational materials. When it came to English, Priestley tolerated only *correct writing*; at the same time, he did not confine his writing to English alone. His published lectures included examples from English, Hebrew, Latin, and Greek.[2] His examples for the "harmony of sentences," for instance, include Cicero's Fourth Oration against Catiline in Latin, then Milton's Treatise on Education in English. Later university materials, such as George Campbell's 1776 *The Philosophy of Rhetoric* and Hugh Blair's 1784 *Lectures on Rhetoric and Belles Lettres*, included multiple languages b *correct writing* in English, particularly in responses to English literature.

By 1866, Alexander Bain's textbook *English Composition and Rhetoric* used examples from Campbell's *Philosophy* but aimed to "methodize instruction in English Composition," and did not include regular references to Latin. The textbook's particular goal was to foster "the discrimination between good and bad in expression," by correcting written English.

For Bain, there was "no better method" than to amend "imperfectly worded" writing according to "the laws and the proprieties of style." Readers were tasked, for instance, with correcting figures of speech in these sentences:

- Many a youth launches forth on the journey of life with no fixed goal in view.
- Followers and friends, around the dying hero's couch, hold their breath, while the last spark of life is ebbing and the soul is preparing to take its heavenward flight.

These examples are all grammatically possible and meaningful in English. But they were not *correct* enough according to Bain, and it was the job of schools and students to correct them.

College entrance examinations showed similar changes by the end of the nineteenth century. The University of London regular entrance examinations in the 1830s and 1840s included Greek and Latin translation and did not include English composition, but by the 1870s and 1880s, they included timed English composition essays, often focused on literary texts in English.

Similarly, the first Harvard English exams in 1874 had students write timed essays "correct in spelling, punctuation, grammar, and expression," focused on "Shakespeare's Tempest, Julius Caesar, and Merchant of Venice; Goldsmith's Vicar of Wakefield; Scott's Ivanhoe and Lay of the Last Minstrel," and the Cambridge 1883 English exam asked students to write about dates and grammar in Shakespeare's writing. The 1883 Cambridge examiners were ultimately disappointed in student responses: "The grammatical peculiarities of Shakespeare's time were described by many candidates as 'bad grammar' without any explanation," the examiners complained. The students, it seems, were regulating language without language knowledge, thereby showing the combined success of myths 1 and 2.

Just like universities, primary and secondary schools were increasingly testing and teaching *correct writing* in English in the nineteenth century. Industrial revolutions in the UK and US brought rural families without written literacy to cities, and school legislation responded by expanding and focusing on English: The UK school curriculum was essentially defined by classical languages until the Grammar Schools Act of 1840, but by the 1850s, educational reports suggested speaking Latin was optional. By the 1861 Newcastle Report on popular education, English was a major focus. A school commissioner insisted:

[W]hat is commonly understood as an English education takes too low a place. I say this the more confidently as I find that scarcely a boy in the whole institution, in his written answers to my questions, more especially in the lectures which afford the greatest scope for it, has exhibited much power of English composition, and most have shown no power or facility at all.

In response, the report outlined compensation for teachers in order to promote "the study of the subjects proper to elementary [education]": History, English Literature, Geography, Physical Science, and Applied Mathematics. The 1864 Clarendon Report from the opening of the chapter likewise named Latin and Greek not as independent subjects, but as instruments for helping students learn "pure grammatical English."

Already supported by myth 1, this myth fueled the idea that *correct writing* in English was moral training needed for all of the nation's children. More and more people received this message through schools, because education levels were rising: While in 1870 adults averaged three to five years of education, by 1910 the same groups averaged closer to six to seven and a half years. In the process, educational institutions became dominant spaces for cultivating and defining English literacy.

2.2.2 Language Policies Privilege English and English Literature

In these developments, English became the language of schools, after already being a language of law and commerce. Other native UK languages did not receive the same emphasis. Welsh and Gaelic use declined in part because opportunity was increasingly yoked to English, and in part because of explicit, narrow language policies.[3] In Scotland, the Napier Commission of 1883 made English literacy the core of the curriculum, even as Gaelic was sometimes used in classrooms. In Ireland, the British government's 1831 National System of Education only made provisions for English, and textbooks from the National Board were written in English and promoted English literature. In Wales, government reports disparaged the Welsh language. As the nineteenth century continued, official UK documents conflated the English language with progress.

In the US, the nineteenth century was mixed: There were no explicit English-only policies (yet), but English was used to subjugate and discriminate. Prominent examples included Native American schools and literacy requirements for non-European immigrants. Native American children were sent away from their homes and families to English-only boarding schools with the goal of forcefully assimilating them to English and Anglo settler cultural traditions. And in just one example of policies affecting non-European immigrants, the children of Chinese and Japanese immigrants were ineligible for citizenship and often kept out of mainstream education.

At the same time, certain nineteenth-century immigrants joined a US society where linguistic diversity was viable and reflected in policy. Schools in multiple states provided instruction in English as well as the languages of other local immigrant families. German communities and language programs, for instance, were so prevalent that knowledge of German was deemed "essential to a finished education" by the US Commissioner of Education in 1870. For a time, selective policies like this emphasized multiple languages. At the same time, English was already the language of US law and commerce, and *correct English* was the English of schools.

2.3 The Myth Emerges

By the end of the nineteenth century, this myth had emerged, ensuring schools regulated one kind of English. *Correct writing* began its reign in schools, at the expense of other language use.

2.4 Consequences of the Myth

2.4.1 We Limit *Writing in School*

In this myth, *correct writing* in English starts to count more than other languages in school, and more than literacy outside of school. Schools, in turn, become places for hunting down errors in students' written English.

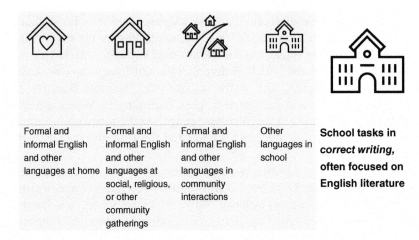

Formal and informal English and other languages at home	Formal and informal English and other languages at social, religious, or other community gatherings	Formal and informal English and other languages in community interactions	Other languages in school	**School tasks in correct writing, often focused on English literature**

Figure 2.1 Continuum of language contexts

Figure 2.1 depicts a continuum of language contexts, from language use at home to restricted language at school.

The 1883 book *Speech and Manners for Home and School* modelled what said error hunting should be like: extensive, and no fun whatever. In a chapter called "Correcting Composition," Miss Blank (perhaps not the most inspiring name for a teacher) has the following exchange.

STUDENT: I wish you'd read us some nice compositions, Miss Blank, and not just all the mistakes.
TEACHER: So I would if you had come together for an hour's amusement, Nina, but if you want to improve your style and learn to write correctly, the only way is to have your faults pointed out, and if we do that there is no time for anything else.

After Miss Blank clarifies that learning *correct writing* should not be amusing, she further specifies that it should not explore students' natural English knowledge. As she points out errors, the student Penelope Piper offers a revision according to what she calls "good grammar." In Socratic fashion, Miss Blank presses Penelope.

TEACHER: Isn't all grammar good, Pen?
STUDENT: Good English, I suppose I ought to say, but it will never seem natural.
TEACHER: It will seem natural if you say it often enough.

Such is Miss Blank's approach: Error-hunting, unnatural and unamusing as it is, defines writing. This leaves "no time for anything else."

The overall consequence of this myth is that we limit writing in school. Between this myth and the last, we narrow both the part of the writing

Table 2.1 Consequences of myth 2

Once we believe	... English regulation becomes "manifestly desirable"
Schools must regulate writing, then...	... Writing in school means hunting for errors rather than exploring patterns
	... *Correct writing* is a bond while other language use is a threat
	... Language difference comes at a double cost
	... We have limited options amid mass migration
	... We miss opportunities for language knowledge

continuum, and the contexts, that define *correct writing*. We can see the contexts left behind in Figure 2.1.

Narrowing writing in school comes with several more specific consequences.

2.4.2 English Regulation Becomes "Manifestly Desirable"

This myth takes for granted that one form of writing – not diverse language use – is best for students. In the eighteenth century, Priestley championed English as a more egalitarian language, but he did not champion egalitarian usage of English. More than a century later, the Harvard examiner Byron Satterlee Hurlbut described the requirement of *correct writing* as "simple," suggesting that "no demand could be more reasonable, more legitimate."

A similar tone appeared in the 1921 Newbolt Report commissioned by the UK Board of Education. The report argued that *correct English* – the "language spoken at the Court, and in Oxford and Cambridge" – was not better than other language use. But it was "manifestly desirable" that all English people learn it, because it was necessary for people "to be fully intelligible to each other" and because not using it was "a serious handicap in many ways." This restriction was not avoided by everyone learning about multiple kinds of English, but by everyone learning and regulating *correct writing*. Table 2.1 identifies the shortfall of a constrained view.

In turn, regulating *correct writing* is necessary, because *correct writing* is associated with success and mutual understanding. Language regulation mode is therefore neutral, as though it doesn't interfere with students' other language use or identities, or it is necessary, even if it does. Error hunting becomes a key part of what people believe schools do, and beliefs about *correct writing* overshadow experiences in which varied writing is useful. These beliefs inform the predominant culture of schooling in English, and they make it very hard to change institutions.

Likewise, regulating *correct writing* is manifestly desirable because it upholds high standards, whether or not students agree. The passage at the start of this chapter from *The Observer* illustrates this presumption. Titled "The Decline and Fall of English Grammar," the article was by John Rae, headmaster of the prestigious Westminster School, who argued *correct writing* is best for students, especially those who were not "middle-class children from literate homes." The way to regulate "decline" in *correct writing*, Rae argued is to use a thirty-year-old usage guide, which would "restore correct English and clear thinking to the curriculum." In this solution, Rae brings us right back to myth 1, and no matter how narrow his ideas were, he was in the position to enforce them.

Why privilege one kind of English rather than facility with diverse language use? This myth not only means that we don't have a good answer to this question, other than the self-fulfilling desirability of *correct writing*. It also means that the question is unlikely to be asked, because the job of schools is to regulate *correct writing* in English.

2.4.3 Writing in School Means Hunting for Errors rather than Exploring Patterns

A consequence of this myth is that teachers and students have abundant incentive to hunt for errors in *correct writing*. They do not have incentive to explore what is grammatically possible and meaningful in a full writing continuum.

This consequence persists even as specific usage conventions change. For example, until recently, English usage guides said "split infinitives" were errors: Writers were told **to write** *definitely this way*, rather than **to** *definitely* **write** *this way*. This advice was based on what is grammatically possible in Latin (recall the Latin-loving gatekeepers we met in myth 1), rather than what is possible in English.

Today, this usage prescription has changed. Split infinitives are not usually considered errors. Still, because they learn in language regulation mode, students are more likely to learn they can or cannot split infinitives than to explore how writers use infinitive verbs.

Few native-speaking writers of English receive explicit opportunities to explore language patterns across the writing continuum in school, and so even writers with a lot of formal writing practice often have subconscious, rather than conscious, writing knowledge. They have learned to hunt for errors, rather than to explore what is variously possible and meaningful in English.

2.4.4 *Correct Writing* Is a Bond while Other Language Is a Threat

We saw earlier that the Newbolt Report placed *correct writing* in opposition to all other usage. All non-standardized usage was mislabeled as *dialect* (even though standardized English is also a dialect), and non-standardized usage was only permitted outside of schools and workplaces: "Side by side with standard English," the report described, "dialect will probably persist and be used in the playground and the street." Narrow as that is, the report did not stop there: "In many cases, indeed, it will deserve to persist, on account of its historic interest." Here, the report commissioners (and through them, schools) decide which kinds of language "deserve to persist" (and even then, as tolerated historic artifact).

The same report framed English as a national bond and answer to class conflict. "A feeling for our own native language would be a bond between classes and would beget the right kind of national pride," the report states. The report praised national literature along the same lines: "even more certainly should pride and joy in the national literature serve as such a bond."

UK and Commonwealth language policy after the Newbolt Report showed a similarly paternalistic bent, primarily supporting English monolingualism modelled on southern British usage preferences. In Australia, legislation between 1937 and 1973 justified neglect of Australian Indigenous languages and other non-English language teaching in the name of "protecting" and "advancing people's welfare." Bilingual Indigenous-English education policies improved after the 1970s, but still often treated language diversity as something to be contained rather than prioritized.

More recent UK and Commonwealth policies include counterexamples, particularly since the 1990s. Contemporary Australian language policies have been described as progressive and pluralistic, and they have added an incentive for students to study non-English languages. In New Zealand, late twentieth-century reforms implemented Māori-medium education, though advocates argue that more needs to be done. In Canada, attention to Indigenous languages, in addition to Canada's two official languages of English and French, has recently grown. Scotland, Northern Ireland, and England all require foreign language study alongside English in primary school, and Wales includes a bilingual English/Welsh education curriculum.[4] In educational requirements such as Scotland's "Mother tongue plus 2," language diversity is framed as an asset. Sometimes, these provisions appear in one country but not another, leaving uncertainty, on one hand, but local flexibility, on the other.

In the US, language policies have prioritized English and *correct writing* since World War I, when the country began crafting a national identity that equated English with patriotism. In 1917, the pointedly named Trading with the Enemy Act declared non-English printed matter unmailable without a certified English translation. In 1918, Iowa Governor William Harding banned the use of any foreign language in public – in church, in schools, and on the telephone, still public at the time. Theodore Roosevelt, then the US president, endorsed the ban a few days later in a speech, insisting "There can be but one loyalty – to the Stars and Stripes; one nationality – the American – and therefore only one language – the English language." Five years later, the Supreme Court prohibited foreign-language bans in *Meyer* v. *Nebraska*, but by then, non-English programs, including many in German, French, and Spanish, had been dropped from school curricula.

In the late twentieth century, the idea that US unity depended on English monolingualism appeared in public media, proposed legislation, and the English-Only movement. In 1977, the president of Boston University, John Silber, linked bilingual voting ballots with declining standards and equated English with US stability – unlike "Canada, Belgium, and other nations with explosive linguistic problems." In another narrow equation, Silber linked *correct writing* with communication, insisting all students should learn to write with "middle-class proficiency" to be able to "communicate fully." He made no mention of the alternative, that teachers could learn their students' diverse dialects to be able to communicate fully.

In the 1980s and 1990s, the US English-Only movement equated English monolingualism with national unity and upward mobility. In Congress, a 1981 constitutional amendment attempted to make English the official language of the US and, in schools, to restrict other languages to instruction toward English proficiency only. In the mid-1980s, the English Language Amendment (ELA) argued that "unquestioned acceptance of [English] by immigrants" ensured US unity, to the "envy" of other, "fractured" societies. These federal amendments did not pass, but state-level policies like them did. In the process, the English-Only movement implied that English use was the primary measure of a successful education, echoing the manifest desirability of English in earlier educational policies.

English-Only efforts continue in the US in the twenty-first century, as do counterefforts. Support for bilingual education has grown somewhat over the past decade, and immersive Indigenous language and cultural education have shown consistently positive results. Simultaneously, many US schools continue to frame language difference as a threat. In 2007, attempting to ban the use of languages other than English on school buses, a superintendent evoked the same paternalistic reasoning we saw in the 1921 Newbolt Report: "[It may be] more comfortable for many to speak their native language … but what is always more comfortable is not always what is in their best interest." The bus ban was eventually overturned, but today, more than thirty US states have passed policies that emphasize English as a source of unity and assimilation.[5]

In short, while language policies can support language exploration and knowledge, many have instead upheld the first two myths. Teaching English to Speakers of Other Languages (TESOL) educators have put it this way: Most language policies prioritize one language and culture, regardless of how that impacts student learning, even as learning is meant to be the primary job of schools.

2.4.5 Language Difference Comes at a Double Cost

Because schools reward and regulate it, those who practice and identify with *correct writing* are rewarded in school. Those who practice and value other writing face a double cost. Their usage is not rewarded in school, and their use of other parts of the writing continuum can have a confessional effect, betraying an identity or origin whether they like it or not. In this way, different language users face different costs. Each speaker or writer, observed author James Baldwin, "has paid, and is paying, a different price" for what is considered *correct*.

Meanwhile, the judgments of the writing gatekeepers are widely accepted, viewed as manifestly desirable and appropriate. The result, in the words of linguist Rosina Lippi-Green, is that language discrimination remains "the last widely open backdoor to discrimination." Students can go to school and university with practice in multiple parts of the writing continuum. But if they don't practice the *correct writing* at the right time, their language use will not be recognized or rewarded in school.

2.4.6 We Have Limited Options amid Mass Migration

Language directly impacts access and opportunity for migrants, and we live in a time of mass migration. Global estimates suggest there were 281 million international migrants in the world in 2020, and those estimates preceded important migration events such as the war in Ukraine, beginning in 2022.

Language regulation mode, which rewards English and specifically *correct* English, means some migrants will have more opportunity and aid than others in English-medium nations. But mass migration necessitates an approach like English as a lingua franca – an approach that seeks practical, positive points of understanding amid inevitable language diversity, rather than only one kind of English.

Here's an example cautionary tale, of mass migration and artificial intelligence (AI). Immigration language AI varies – some, such as Finland's Kamu and the US Mona, provide immigration and legal advice in real time to immigrants and refugees. In several cases, these technologies can save time and facilitate rapid access to aid. However, in cases of *correct writing* regulation, AI can go wrong, particularly in high-stakes educational situations without human verification. In one example from 2016, the UK Home Office erroneously deported 7,000 international students for cheating on English language tests needed to secure UK visas. The Home Office AI had mistakenly perceived cheating in 20 percent of the cases.

2.4.7 We Miss Opportunities for Language Knowledge

Many well-intentioned parents and educators regulate *correct writing* in the name of access. This is understandable, given the pervasiveness of language regulation mode. But a fixation on a highly limited mold of English can overshadow learning and mean missed opportunities for supporting diverse language knowledge and experiences.

For instance, it is common to see regulation of *correct writing* no matter what students are doing. They could be describing a historical event or chemical process unrelated to *correct writing*, for example, but their usage is regulated along with their chemistry or history information. This can make students feel less safe and more self-conscious, so that they use cognitive bandwidth to focus on *correct writing*, rather than on the intended focus of their learning.

In another example, people and policies often use deficit descriptions to refer to any language use that is not *correct writing*. Deficit terms focus on what English users do not know rather than what they do know, and they imply intellectual inferiority, such as by describing non-standardized usage as *broken* or *lazy*. This demeans most of the writing continuum, along with its many writers, identities, and values. Geneva Smitherman, the linguistics professor we met in the introduction, puts it this way: "See, when you lambast the home language that kids bring to school, you ain just dissen dem, you talking about they mommas!"

With all of this is missed opportunity: People miss out on all kinds of language knowledge outside of *correct writing* errors. Students learn deficit ideas and *not* additive ideas – ideas that affirm existing language values and practices that people already rely on every day. Students, and their teachers, miss opportunities for connecting with others and for understanding different kinds of language patterns.

2.5 Closer to the Truth

2.5.1 Language Diversity and Language Knowledge Are Human Rights

This myth makes it possible for schools to regulate social and geopolitical concerns through regulating language. Some policies prioritize English at the expense of other languages, and many evoke English, and literature in English, as essential national tools. Most policies to date use the terms English or writing when they mean *correct English* or *correct writing*. All policies we've seen reinforce schools as the site for literacy development and nation-building, but the worst of the lot appear in the US, where many policies, past and present, equate monolingualism with national unity despite the documented social, cognitive, and economic advantages of multilingualism.

As we saw in the last chapter, closer to the truth is that writing across the continuum is linguistically equal, and schools and homes and streets are full of writing that is possible and meaningful in English. Also closer to the truth is that language policies can support this diversity, by framing language variety as a valuable part of national and individual literacy and identity.

Such is the spirit of the 1996 Universal Declaration of Linguistic Rights, which showed international consensus on principles for language rights. Articles 9 and 10 note that "All language communities have the right to codify, standardize, preserve, develop and promote their linguistic system, without induced or forced interference," and state that "All language communities have equal rights." In other words, language diversity is a human right, including diversity of registers and dialects within a language.

Other Declaration articles concern language learning. Articles 27 and 29 note that "All language communities are entitled to an education which will enable their members to acquire knowledge of any languages related to their own cultural tradition" and "This right does not exclude the right to acquire oral and written knowledge of any language which may be of use to him/her as an instrument of communication with other language communities." In other words, language knowledge – of diverse language use, including diverse registers and dialects – is also a human right.

2.5.2 Language Diversity Persists but Isn't Studied in Schools

Even as language regulation prioritizes only a small part of the writing continuum, language difference offers knowledge and community across the continuum, with new chances to learn and relate based on authentic, up-to-date language use. Traditions like English as a lingua franca (ELF) already illustrate the productive use of pluralized English that accommodates diverse speakers' needs, norms, and values. In universities specifically, a small number of international institutions follow ELFA norms (English as an academic lingua franca), based on English used by millions of educators and students in hybrid and innovative forms considered *incorrect* according to this myth. In education that does not currently take an ELF approach, including most native English education, we can do more to resist this myth and see the full writing continuum as part of language knowledge.

2.5.3 School Writing Is on a Narrow Continuum

To add to the writing continuum in this chapter, we'll look at two student essays. These essays and their examiner commentary illustrate what characterized *correct writing* as universities began to regulate students' English.

The essays were written in response to a task on the 1887 Harvard English entrance exam, which appear below in Figure 2.2. The task emphasizes literature and *correct writing*, according to "correct spelling, punctuation, arrangement, and accuracy of expression."

The Harvard examiner for that year, L. B. R. Briggs, included the two essays in his report. Briggs had nothing positive to say about the first essay that appears below, but he used the second as an illustration of an average, passing (if disapointing) theme. Below, I've placed both essays on the continuum and described them in terms of (1) the five shared purposes of cohesion, connection, focus, stance, and usage, and (2) informal to formal, interpersonal to informational, and personal to impersonal writing patterns. In this case, the essay that especially disappointed the reviewer is the more informal, interpersonal, and personal one. Still, because we are looking at student writing after the start of myths 1 and 2, we are only looking at a small part of the wider continuum.

First, Table 2.2 shows continuum patterns throughout the students' sentences and paragraphs. Then, the full essays appear, with marginal notes

---

ENGLISH COMPOSITION. 1.

Write a composition — with special attention to clearness of arrangement, accuracy of expression, and quality rather than quantity of matter — on one of the following subjects : —

1. The Story of Viola.
2. Viola's Errand to Olivia.
3. How Malvolio was Tricked.
4. Sir Andrew Aguecheek's Challenge and What Came of it.
5. Mr. Darcy's Courtship.

Figure 2.2 1887 Harvard English entrance exam task

Table 2.2 1887 Harvard student exam writing continuum

Texting Social Email

Secondary   College

1887 Harvard Student Exam Writing Patterns

	Secondary	College
Continuum Purposes	Informal Interpersonal Personal	Formal Informational Impersonal

	Secondary	College
Cohesion	• **Hourglass organization:** Text moves from very general questions (*inconsistency*) to details about the novel (*Darcy's courtship*), back to general concepts (*pride, love*)	• **Pyramid organization:** Text moves from specific book examples following the book's plot, to general concepts (*frankness, independence*)
Connection	• **Interpersonal connection** Rhetorical questions, 2nd person pronouns 1st person is text-external	• **Informational connection** No direct address, rare 1st person references unfolding argument (*I think*)
Focus	• **Personal and interpersonal subjects** Mostly simple sentence subjects (*you, Darcy, he, love*) emphasize feelings and personal reactions Some passive verbs	• **Informational subjects** Sentence subjects are dense noun phrases about characters and abstract concepts Some passive verbs
Stance	• **Certain stance** Regular boosters and generalizations (*really, mere, merely, anyone, anything, every, surely*)	• **More neutral stance** No regular boosters or hedges No generalizations
Usage	• *Correct writing conventions and usage preferences*	• *Correct writing conventions and usage preferences*
Opening sentences	What a strange paradox of character Darcy at first seems ? You hardly can account for it. It may seem unnatural when first you think of it. But think. …	Mr. Darcy, a young man of distinguished birth and great wealth, with that peculiar pride in his character which young men of wealth generally acquire from the adulation paid to them by ignorant people, is surprised at and delighted with the independence and frankness of spirit with which a certain Miss Bennett receives him. This Miss Bennett he first saw at an evening party given by the sisters of a friend of his. …
Examiner comments	Vicious morality and fatal facility blight every line... None but a cynic can fail to sympathize with the writer of this theme for the agony that awaits him in Harvard College, the lashing that he must endure before he finds his true place in that hardhearted little world. If there is one thing that Harvard College will not tolerate, it is "gush," – "gush" in general, and moral or oratorical "gush" in particular.	A theme of average mark clearly above the passing line. … The boy does not dream that the story is full of life; to him it is something to go through – like statistics. Accordingly he tabulates it, and appends a moral duller than his tables.

and annotations showing examples of cohesion, connection, focus, and stance in the writing, with some sentence subjects underlined, transitional words **in bold**, connection markers [in brackets], *hedges* in italics, ***boosters*** and ***generalizations*** italicized and bolded, and passive verbs [[in double brackets]].

2.5.3.1 Poorly Rated 1887 Harvard Essay

What a strange paradox of character <u>Darcy</u> at first seems? [You] *hardly can* account for it. <u>It</u> *may seem* unnatural when first you think of it. But think. Know [you] not many of [your friends] whose actions *seem to be* inconsistent. Aye, look [you] at your own. [Think how often you astonish yourself, as well as those who know you, by your various actions and then look at Darcy.]

Pride and Prejudice — Darcy's character ***alone*** would have given the first part of the title of the book. But what is pride? Does it not ***continually*** display itself? Does it not *consist* (emphasis original) itself in display. How noticeable then when it occurs. ***Surely*** pride in itself is no tremendous fault, but its disagreeableness lies in this ***very*** characteristic — display.

But you wonder how this has ***anything*** to do with his courtship. Aye, in ***every*** way. [Do you not remember his pride, the very first time you saw him there in the ballroom? how he was above dancing? Do you not remember seeing Bingley go up to him to beg of him to dance? And can you not remember his reply, remarking that Elizabeth was only tolerable?] **But** that same Elizabeth in a few years is mistress of Pemberley. Mark how he ***only*** watches the second Miss Bennet, but he is too proud to court openly. **Also**, by way of remark, I

Hourglass organization and interpersonal opening: In this paragraph, the writer addresses the reader directly several times. The writer does so to introduce the topic of Darcy's character, and to propose that even the reader's own character may be inconsistent

A certain stance: Several boosters convey a sense of certainty in this paragraph

An interpersonal and certain stance: In this paragraph, the writer moves to connect the theme of inconsistency with the exam topic of courtship, and again addresses the reader directly throughout the paragraph. The

think I remember hearing him speak to Bingley about the Bennets' vulgar relatives. **Even** his love breaks not through his pride; his Pride and Love go hand in hand, if Pride does not lead the way. **But** his love is safe, for that love's bitterest enemy, pride, [[is overthrown]] by Elizabeth's disdainful rejection. [Could you not almost foresee this?] Would **any one** have been a wonderful prophet to have told that he was in love with Elizabeth, nay **even** that he would propose, (and why should he not for he, through his pride, was confident of acceptance?) that Elizabeth would scornfully refuse, and that his pride would [[be broken]]? What could more **surely** break one's pride than have a proposal, in assurance given, cast back in one's face, as Darcy's was?

There was something that made me love Darcy from the beginning. It shone through his pride, through his arrogance, and made me feel that, behind that unpleasant outside, there was a *true man*. I know not what it was, but it made me feel that I wished I had that man's character without his pride.

With Elizabeth's refusal his true courtship *really* begins. Before, he was courting his own pride; **now**, he courts Miss Elizabeth Bennet. His love, no longer smothered under the wet blanket of his pride burns unhindered; and to have Darcy's unhindered love was to have a most precious, most priceless thing. It was not a *mere* passionate affection, that lived *merely* for the pleasure of its existence. It was a love of tender regard, that lived *solely* for the being to whom it was directed and because of whom it came into existence.

Can it not be put this way Darcy had pride. Love crept in. That love grew and grew. That love startled his pride. It was too late for the love to be stifled, it *could only be* restrained. His pride was broken, and his love unrestrained filled his life. Pride can no more enter that heart of which true Love has full possession."

paragraph shows knowledge of the text and mainly countering transitions like *but*, along with strong stance markers including *only* and *surely*

Personalized paragraph: This paragraph emphasizes the writer's personal reactions and feelings

A certain stance: Here, the writer expresses a strong stance that after Elizabeth Bennett's refusal, Darcy puts aside his pride

Hourglass organization and interpersonal conclusion: To close, the writer addresses the reader directly and offers generalizations about pride and love

2.5.3.2 Passing 1887 Harvard Entrance Essay

<u>Mr. Darcy, a young man of distinguished birth and great wealth, with that peculiar pride in his character which young men of wealth generally acquire from the adulation paid to them by ignorant people,</u> [is surprised at and delighted with] the independence and frankness of spirit with which a certain Miss Bennett receives him. This Miss Bennett he first saw at an evening party given by the sisters of a friend of his. He afterwards saw her at the home of his friend where, contrasting the sharp, witty conduct of Miss Bennett towards him with the ignorant adulation of his friend's sisters, he falls in love with her.

> **Hourglass organization and informational opening:**
> In this introduction, the writer uses many dense noun phrases to emphasize information about Darcy and Bennett. The sentences favor nouns and phrases, with very few verbs, including passive construction

Miss Bennett [[is so influenced]] by the insinuations of a renegade ward of Darcy's father that she despises him. When, by chance, they meet at the country house of Darcy's aunt, Darcy proposes and [is rejected] by Miss Bennett who flaunts in his face the wrongs charged to him by his father's ward. Darcy is *so* incensed that he says nothing and leaves. After some consideration, he concludes to explain away these falsehoods and does so to the entire satisfaction of Miss Bennett who now begins to see many noble traits in Darcy and, after a while, falls in love with him.

> **Impersonal stance:**
> Here the writer offers details from the plot of the novel without using many boosters, hedges, or generalizations.

Darcy, after he has done many favors for Miss Bennett's family, again proposes to Miss Bennett and is **heartily** accepted. Darcy, when asked by Miss Bennett why he fell in love with her, admits that it was *principally* on account of her humbling his spirit of pride and teaching him the pleasure of treating one's supposed inferiors well.

Darcy finally marries Miss Bennett to the great chagrin of his friend's sisters (the Bingleys) who make great protestations that the match is pleasing to them.

> **informational stance:**
> Here, the writer offers information from the novel and a boosted and hedged stance about Darcy's courtship

The moral of **all** this, *I think*, is that slavish flattery will **never** attract the attention either of those who may deserve our praise or of those who do not to any qualities, either of mind or body, which we **may** possess.

> **General, interpersonal closing:**
> Here, the writer moves to close

While, **on the other hand**, <u>frankness and independence of spirit</u> will *always* obtain [for us], even among the greatest of men due consideration and respect.

> with a boosted
> and hedged stance
> about courtship
> more generally

Both of the essays use grammatically possible and meaningful English. They both answer the exam question, and they are both critiqued by the Harvard examiner. But the more informal, interpersonal, personal essay (appearing first) is evaluated more negatively than the more formal, informational, impersonal essay. The poorly evaluated essay falls further left on the continuum; its language patterns convey something akin to excited, conversational musing about the character of Darcy. The more positively rated essay falls further right on the continuum; its language patterns emphasize information in the text more than the reader's personalized reaction.

These two examples add to our writing continuum details, and they highlight the confounding limits of *correct writing*. In this case, students were told to write about "Mr. Darcy's Courtship" under timed circumstances, using *correct* spelling, punctuation, arrangement, and accuracy of expression. Both essays followed these instructions. Still, they did not both please the examiner, and additional, more particular preferences emerge in the examiner responses. We will see many more such examples in the chapters to come.

Closer to the truth is that to pursue the human rights of diverse language and language knowledge, we need more explicit, transparent exploration of the full continuum of writing. But first: To continue to understand the myths that have kept us from this approach, we turn to myth 3, in which *correct writing*, now regulated by schools, becomes an indicator of *intelligence.*Xime ressequas dolorehent asi officiae ditate con pres et reriorercil et et, aboremporro dolorpo sandit rerciis aut pa

CHAPTER THREE

Myth 3 You Can't Write That and Be Smart

Or, Writing indicates natural intelligence

This time, a freebie for *pick a century*. The passages below are identified for you and are betrayed by wording besides. Still, they show a consistent message over time.

1. **Nineteenth century** (1845, Horace Mann in *The Common School Journal*)
   [Writing exams offer] a transcript ... of the state and condition of the pupils' minds ... taken and carried away for general inspection.
2. **Twentieth century** (1925, Cyril Burt in *The Sub-normal School-child*)
   The reader... may deduce, both from the physiognomy and from the style of writing, spelling, and expression, what were the intelligence, the temperament, and the educational attainments of the several children.
3. **Twenty-first century** (2021, online, with an intelligence test that takes twenty to thirty minutes)
   Have you ever wondered how intelligent you are compared to your friends, your colleagues ... and the rest of the nation? The Great British Intelligence Test ... can reveal all.

Different though they are, these passages reflect the timeworn quest for a single way to measure and rank intelligence. Typing "how intelligent am I?" into Google in the year 2023, I get 454 million links in under 0.4 seconds. Most sources promise that I can "find out where I stand" in less than half an hour.[1] On the first page of results, I have eight options for taking an intelligence test or quiz. By the second page, I can read how to "make my writing sound more intelligent" and how "science explains why people who love writing are smarter."[2]

Here are easy some conjectures from this search:

- People are very interested in testing intelligence.
- Intelligence is something some people possess more than others.
- Intelligence can be tested easily.
- Formal written English is part of intelligence.

These ideas pair easily with our first two myths, which limit *correct writing* and writing in school.

In this myth, *correct writing* is further limited, and further empowered. *Correct writing* becomes testable, connected to innate ability, and used to decide who is *intelligent,* and who is not.

Before that happened, people were not all tested the same way. They were not subjected to the inspection described by Horace Mann in passage 1. They would be, however, thanks to an origin story that begins with nineteenth-century science.

3.1 Context for the Myth

3.1.1 *Correct Writing* Becomes a Tool for Ranking and Selecting

Horace Mann once sent a plaster head to his sister in the mail. He was sharing his fervor for phrenology, the nineteenth-century science of measuring head size and shape to determine ability and goodness. At the time, scientific developments were beginning to reach general audiences, and phrenology was fueling public interest in calculating intelligence and morality. By that time, too, we know, *correct writing* already dwelled in popular imagination as a sign of character and capability, thanks to myths 1 and 2.

Enter Mann, who was was a firm believer in myths 1 and 2. Mann merged these beliefs with his conviction that eugenic progress – the notion that racial improvement occurs through selective breeding – was possible through education. Education perfected human nature, he argued, and *correct writing* provided a way to examine where individuals were in that perfection process. Mann was among the first to bring phrenological ideas and *correct writing* together, in written English examinations.

Mann's first step was to blindside students with unexpected tests. In 1845, on a day when Boston primary and secondary students went to school as usual, they were greeted with unannounced, timed, individual tests of written English. Mann promoted the exams as "impartial" testing that avoided teacher "interference."

This approach to testing was new. Until then, US primary and secondary students demonstrated their learning in annual, interactive exhibitions open to parents and other community members, who could attend and ask questions. Mann's Boston area school exams, by contrast, were unexpected, externally designed, individual, and written.[3]

Mann's use of the tests was also new. He used overall exam scores as well as the number of *correct writing* spelling, grammar, and punctuation errors to publicly compare and rank Boston schools. For example, Mann showed that the "number of errors committed in Grammar" was 98, and the "number of errors committed in Spelling" was 97, for the students tested at the Adams School, while it was 199 and 91, respectively, for students at the Boylston School.

A few years later, Mann became president of Antioch College in Ohio, where he instituted the first college entrance exams in English composition in 1853. These, too, were evaluated for spelling, grammar, and punctuation errors according to the right side of the continuum.

In other words, first, Mann made *correct writing* errors the basis for public ranking and inspection of schools and students. Then, Mann used *correct writing* errors as the basis for college admission.

We've already seen where that went: Two decades later, *correct writing* entrance exams gained visibility when Charles Eliot began using them at Harvard. Eliot, whom we met in myth 1, really took to human ranking and hierarchy based on mythical ideas about *intelligence*. In particularly horrific examples, he called for racial purity and forced sterilization of the physically disabled as protection from "moral degeneracy." And he believed that only students with testable *innate ability* deserved excellent education. In his very first address as Harvard's president, Eliot made this clear:

The community does not owe superior education to all children, but only to the *élite*, – those who, having the capacity, prove by hard work that they have also the necessary perseverance and endurance.

For Eliot, similar logic meant Harvard could not consider admitting women. "The world knows next to nothing about the natural mental capacities of the female sex," Eliot declared. Accordingly, it would take "generations of civil freedom and social quality … to obtain the data necessary for an adequate discussion of women's natural tendencies, tastes, and capabilities."

Like Mann, Eliot implemented English writing exams for college admission based on the idea that *correct writing* usage, punctuation, and spelling indicated general aptitude. In particular, Eliot favored *correct writing* in response to questions about English literature. By this logic, in other words, *correct writing* of timed essays on "Mr. Darcy's Courtship" (like those in myth 2) indicated innate fitness for college study.

Thus nineteenth-century eugenic theories fueled interest in uniform ways to rank and select students. Still to come were tools for ranking that went beyond a single geographic area or institution.

3.1.2 *Intelligence* becomes innate and testable

As the nineteenth century turned, interest in evolution and evaluation grew. Charles Darwin's observations of his son excited interest in behavioral development, while studies by Darwin's cousin Francis Galton fueled interest in intelligence and individual variation. In 1905, psychologist Alfred Binet was commissioned by the French government to identify children needing an alternative to typical schooling. Based on their observations at a French boys' school, Binet and his student Theodore Simon created the Binet-Simon test.

As with intelligence tests that followed, the Binet-Simon test was based on the developers' definition of intelligence and how it could be measured. Binet and Simon saw attention, memory, and verbal skill as part of intelligence, and they selected thirty items to measure them, such as touching one's ear, drawing designs from memory, and defining concepts. Students took the test individually and received a score for those items they answered as expected. This score was then divided by the students' age and multiplied by 100, and the resulting number represented the student's "Intelligence Quotient," or IQ.

During the same period, England psychologist Charles Spearman and US psychologist Edward Thorndike were developing theories of testing and mental measurement. In 1904, Thorndike promoted tests for use on large populations, and Spearman promoted tests that "objectively measured general intelligence."

3.1.3 Writing Becomes Part of Ranking Intelligence

More interest in general intelligence testing meant more interest in going beyond institution-specific tests like the entrance exams we saw in the last myth. What could provide a single way to measure whether students were producing *correct writing*?

An answer came in 1912 in *A Scale for the Measurement of Quality in English Composition by Young People* by Milo Hillegas. Hillegas had worked with Thorndike to develop the scale, and he published it as a way to sort and rank *correct writing* across US secondary and college English courses.

In his introduction to the scale, Hillegas villified writing measurement that varied across classrooms. Instead, he promised, his uniform scale offered "proper" and "exact" standards for making comparisons across schools and school systems.

The scale included hundreds of short passages from several sources. Some were fabricated, some were by students, and others were by literary authors. For instance, "specimen 217" was by Nathaniel Hawthorne, while "specimen 221" was by a secondary-school student writer. "Specimen 519," with "the least merit of any of these," was also by a secondary-school student writer. The specimens were labeled by author (if by a published writer) or by level (if by a student), or by the label "artificial sample" (if fabricated). They were not labelled according to their writing task or genre (e.g., argumentative essay assignment; literary novel).

To use the scale, educators were told to compare their students' writing to the sample passages, which had been ranked by Hillegas and his team according to *correct writing* usage preferences, spelling, and punctuation, regardless of the task. A short artificial sample representing a value of 0, for instance, twice included the dialect-specific usage *ain't*, which was also used as an example of "inaccuracy" in nineteenth-century Harvard English exams.

Concerns about the scale arose at the time. Educators critiqued the accuracy of the samples, the methods used for the scale, and the insufficient detail about the results. They questioned whether any single scale could capture the complexity of writing, in terms of both discursive (style-based) and propositional (idea-based) content. One critique noted that the scale was of little practical value beyond supporting uniformity, then went on to question whether uniformity was desirable.

The supporters of the scale, however, said it represented writing "merit" and "superiority," regardless of writing task or classroom context. Similar scales followed that shared the goal of ranking writing according to a uniform instrument.

3.1.4 *Intelligence* Becomes a Tool for Ranking and Selecting

As the Hillegas scale was reaching writing classrooms, intelligence testing was gaining visibility in the UK with the help of British psychologist Cyril Burt. Burt was adapting the Binet-Simon test to measure character, learning, and intelligence, which was labeled "mental ability" and "mental defect." In 1914, Burt published a review of the Binet-Simon test that promoted three ideas about intelligence:

- Capability is innate and testable.
- Tests can rank individuals and groups according to uniform ability or "mental age."
- Tests and scales need ongoing work to increase uniformity.

In other words, for Burt, diverse test responses were a problem to be solved, rather than a sign of developmental diversity. For instance, the fact *normals* could define concepts before they could count thirteen pennies made *defectives* – who counted pennies before defining concepts – developmentally *backward*.[4] In addition to his ideas about intelligence, Burt promoted three ideas about tests:

- Tests should measure capability in units of their own (not age), according to how completely and quickly an individual performs a task.
- Tests should have separate, standardized schemes according to the race, sex, and social class of test takers.
- Tests should not leave room for diverse responses.

In the US, Lewis Terman at Stanford University promoted similar ideas. Terman adapted the Binet-Simon test to create the Stanford-Binet intelligence scale, which was a tool for measuring *innate capability* rather than capability at one point in time. In 1916, Terman published *The Measurement of Intelligence*, which promoted the Stanford-Binet intelligence scale as a quantifiable way to determine *idiocy, feeblemindedness,* and *genius* through a single, simple test.

Terman's own racist and misogynistic ideas – he believed that marriages of white Americans following traditional gender roles would promote eugenically fit children, for instance – informed his efforts. He aimed for an easy, scientifically accepted way to facilitate eugenic sorting. By 1920, the Stanford-Binet test, and its assumptions about innate and testable intelligence, were circulating in and beyond the US.

A prominent application of the Stanford-Binet test was US Army Alpha intelligence testing, which was used to rank soldiers for officer roles. The Army Alpha Test was timed, written in *correct English*, and included multiple choice questions with culturally specific answers. The three questions in Figure 3.1, for instance, were part of the test.

In 1923, Carl Brigham reported Army Alpha Test questions, results, and interpretations in his book *A Study of American Intelligence*. Brigham's main argument – supported, he said, by "the teeth of the

Christy Mathewson is famous as a	Carrie Nation is known as a	Crisco is a
• writer • artist • baseball player • comedian	• singer • temperance agitator • suffragist • nurse	• patent medicine • disinfectant • toothpaste • food product

Figure 3.1 Early IQ test questions, Army Alpha test

facts" – was that the Army Alpha test results showed "the superiority of the Nordic race." He further interpreted (surely based, again, on facts with teeth) that "In a very definite way," the results showed "pure Nordic peoples" were "rulers, organizers, and aristocrats," characterized by "a greater stability and steadiness than are mixed peoples." Furthermore, in light of test results showing that more time in the US led to better performance, Brigham blamed immigrants rather than the test, arguing that earlier immigrants were smarter. The absence of validity in the test questions is shown Figure 3.1. Knowledge of baseball players, suffragists, and food products is inextricably bound to cultures and places rather than innate ability.

Reviewers of *A Study of American Intelligence* questioned its scientific rigor at the time. Psychologist Edward Boring's review in *The New Republic* specifically argued that Brigham "discarded the effect of a knowledge of English in stating his differences." This matters singularly because, as Boring noted, "measurable intelligence is simply what the tests of intelligence test, until further scientific observation allows us to extend the definition." In this case, Boring noted, *intelligence* was knowledge of formal English.

Brigham did not agree. *A Study of American Intelligence* insisted that knowledge of English did not explain the Army Alpha Test results: the test measured "native or inborn intelligence," and the ability to use English was "a function of intelligence and education in its broadest sense." In other words, Brigham interpreted the test results in support of his idea of racial purity, and he paid no mind to the role of *correct English* or culturally specific knowledge.

Together, Burt's promotion of uniform tests of mental age, Terman's marketing of test efficiency, and Brigham's Alpha testing all sold the idea that testing innate ability could be simple and efficient. Plenty of support, in other words, for narrow tests, and narrow interpretations, of *intelligence*.

3.1.5 Intelligence Tests Appeal to Scared Racists

The myth that intelligence is innate and measurable had special allure for fearful racists in the early twentieth century, people concerned about growing immigration and diverse school enrollment. Robert Yerkes, an Army Alpha Test developer and Brigham's teacher, wrote the foreword to *A Study of American Intelligence*, basically characterizing the book as a primer for xenophobia:

[Brigham] presents not theories or opinions but facts. It behooves us to consider their reliability and their meaning, for no one of us as a citizen can afford to ignore the menace of race deterioration or the evident relations of immigration to national progress and welfare.

In these ideas, we can see the trend of *more access /more regulation* that characterizes several myths. Greater access to education and other national resources came with greater regulation of those resources. Intelligence tests could aid selection, and tests in *correct writing* could favor specific test-takers. Then, to use Eliot's logic, resources could be handed to those most deserving.

3.2 The Myth Emerges

From these origins, we can identify our third myth, in which *correct writing*, already narrowly defined, indicates *intelligence*, also narrowly defined. The characters in this story did not share identical motives, nor were their efforts identical. But phrenological thinking, error ranking, IQ tests, and writing scales came together in terribly complementary ways. The myth emerged, making ability innate and measurable in simple tests. In those tests, *correct writing* was either a clear indication of *intelligence*, or a neutral vehicle for reflecting it.

3.3 Consequences of the Myth

3.3.1 We Narrow *Intelligence*

The overall consequence of this myth is that we limit ideas about *intelligence*. Despite multiple learning domains, in this myth, only the *cognitive* (or discursive) domain, measured through *correct writing*, counts as *intelligence*. Left out are domains that emphasize collaboration, reflection, and well-being.[5] Figure 3.2 illustrates four domains of human ability, and here's how they apply to the Army Alpha test question about Crisco shown in Figure 3.1:

- The **cognitive** or *discursive* domain is related to reasoning and memory.
  Early tests and scales emphasized this domain. Test takers would, for instance, use the cognitive domain in the Alpha tests to recall how they had seen the word Crisco used, and what it was.
- The **interpersonal** domain is related to collaborating with others.
  Early tests and scales left out this domain. Had they included it, test taskers might have used the interpersonal domain to consider how to

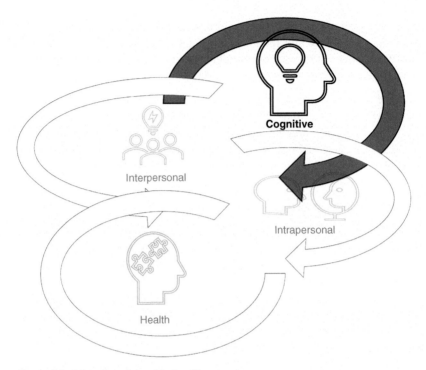

Figure 3.2 A four domain model of writing

ask others for information, or to brainstorm together to narrow down
their multiple-choice answers about Crisco.

- The **intrapersonal** domain is related to reflecting and self-moderating.
  Early tests and scales left out this domain. Had they included it, test
  taskers might have used the intrapersonal domain to consider what
  steps they had used in the past when they didn't know an answer, and
  to determine whether the same steps could be used to determine the
  meaning of Crisco.
- The **health** domain is related to well-being.
  Early tests and scales left out this domain. Had they included it, test takers might have used the health domain to ensure they were safe, rested,
  and fed enough to be able to focus on what they knew about Crisco.

This is the overall consequence of this myth: Instead of a complex,
dynamic understanding of knowledge and experience, we limit ideas
about *intelligence*. With that comes several more specific consequences
listed in Table 3.1.

Table 3.1 Consequences of myth 3

Once we believe	... Only some people are *intelligent*
correct writing **indicates natural intelligence,** then...	... Writing and ability are 2-D
	... Efficiency and ideal sameness become values
	... Trust shifts from teachers to tests
	... We trust tests without understanding tests
	... Extrapolation seems fine

3.3.2 Only Some People Are *Intelligent*

Early intelligence tests privileged the knowledge and experience of some people (including the test designers) and not others. In turn, they rendered only some groups and individuals *intelligent*. In obvious examples, early US IQ tests supported human ranking to the disadvantage of immigrants, women, and races considered mixed or not white.

This unfairness occurred on multiple levels: test design, test interpretation, and test use. Test design was unfair in that certain groups were much less likely to be familiar with *correct writing* or culturally specific details than others. Test interpretation and use were unfair because narrow test scores were used to label entire groups – like Brigham's "pure Nordics" – *capable* and *moral* or, alternatively, *feeble-minded and immoral*.

In cyclical fashion, ideas about *intelligence* were also used to bar people from even attempting to prove themselves through narrow tests. Eliot barred women from Harvard entrance exams because not enough was known (through exams) about their innate ability. It would be more than a century before undergraduate women were included at Harvard, despite the efforts of numerous women throughout that time.

In most of these examples, only the mythmakers told the stories. No one heard from the *nameless feebleminded girl* in the work of eugenicist Hendy Goddard. They heard from Goddard.

3.3.3 Writing and Ability Are 2-D

Writing and *writing in school* were already narrowed by myths 1 and 2, and with this myth, *intelligence* and *correct writing* are further limited. They become two-dimensional – treated as though writers and language can operate independent of context and purpose. IQ testing limited *intelligence* to something individual and testable, separated from other people and writing outside of test conditions. Writing scales similarly limited writing, suggesting published literature and student writing could all be ranked on the same scale.

When writing and ability are 2-D, *correct writing errors* do not depend on context and are an efficient focus for uniform tests. This explains why after 1915, errors, particularly in conventions like punctuation and spelling, became a central focus for large-scale writing evaluation.

3.3.4 Efficiency and Ideal Sameness Became Values

Three priorities fuel this myth:

- efficiency (a "simple test")
- uniformity (a single test or scale for everyone)
- ranking people (according to a single, simple test)

Through the myth glasses, anything that doesn't prioritize these values is suspect, and uniform tests are used even when they don't appear to serve all students, schools, and knowledge domains. Multiple ways to respond to the same task becomes too messy, for instance. Different assignments for different students becomes too time-consuming.

Even after overtly oppressive IQ testing was no longer permitted as a unitary judgement of intellect, many tests today maintain these priorities, valuing efficiency and uniformity over diverse domains and experiences.

3.3.5 Trust Shifts from Teachers to Tests

Valuing efficiency and uniformity inevitably shifts who, and what, has a say in education. More trust in externally designed tests and scales means less trust in specific schools and classrooms. More trust in timed writing means less trust in a teacher's observations of a student's work over a term or a year. And in the event of poor test results, more trust in tests means students and schools, rather than testing instruments, are to blame. Mann's publicized Boston school error rankings, for instance, placed Smith School, serving Black students in Boston's segregated common schools, in last place, based on Mann's interpretation of unanswered questions. But Smith and its students, rather than the uniform test and interpretation, took the blame.

In another example, Burt's 1914 description depicted test scores as the positive alternative to variation and teachers' input. Burt described the correlation between "teachers' estimates" on the one hand and "absolute mental age" on the other, arguing that internally graded tests that didn't align with uniform test scores were to be "rejected, as no tests of intelligence at all." Burt's wording illustrates a key consequence of this myth: A local teacher's evaluation is not only less absolute than that of intelligence tests, but it is also dismissible.

Some twentieth-century educators and leaders regretted this distrust in teachers. The 1943 Norwood Report described problems with uniform UK secondary examinations, saying that they neglected local teachers' knowledge. The report ultimately recommended that exams be set internally in schools by local teachers. But this did not come to pass.[6] With this myth came the message that teachers were more subjective and less reliable than tests, and that diverse assessment conclusions indicated a mistake rather than inevitable – or instructive – variation.

3.3.6 Learning Culture Shifts to Exam Culture

The shift away from teachers toward efficiency and uniformity was a shift toward exam culture. Exam culture means less emphasis on learning culture, because the needs of test designers are not the same as the needs of specific classrooms and students. If sometimes well intentioned, exam culture promotes consistency (or *reliability*) above all other concerns, no matter how narrow the tests or scale, and no matter what or who is left out. The same 1943 Norwood Report cautioned that students had begun viewing education only in terms of exams, but exams persisted.

3.3.7 We Trust Tests Without Understanding Tests

We've already seen that writing myths prioritize language regulation, even when that comes with language ignorance. The same thing happens in this myth: Limited ideas about intelligence, and limited knowledge of testing, flourish in tandem. In public campaigns for IQ testing, developers like Terman and Brigham emphasized accepting test results, not understanding test design.

A result is that tests and *correct writing* matter, even as they are not well understood. Early efforts to sort and rank immigrants, races, soldiers, students, and other groups didn't invite understanding of

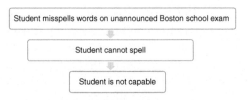

Figure 3.3 Extrapolating from a test to *intelligence*

tests or diverse language use. Early reports emphasized test results and didn't investigate the impact of test design on test taker performance. We will see this consequence persist throughout the coming myths, in headline stories that focus on exam results rather than exam details.

3.3.8 Extrapolation Seems Fine

When *intelligence* is limited and testable, extrapolating from test results seems fine. Extrapolation is a move from an instance (say, an IQ test) and a related instance (skills tested on the IQ test) to the widest possible inference (that a student is not capable). We go from "Jane can't write X" to "Jane can't write," and then from "Jane can't write" to "Jane is not *intelligent*." Figure 3.3 shows the logical failures that occur when causal logic in used without regard to the many factors that contribute to spelling ability, and the cruel leaps that occur when we consider *intelligence* as unitary.

We can illustrate this using the Boston school error rankings in Figure 3.3. Mann's reports moved from (1) a student misspelling on the Boston school examination, to (2) generalizing that the student couldn't spell, to (3) extrapolating that the student was lacking innate capability.

We can call this dynamic *limited test/general use*, because it means using limited test content to draw general conclusions about test takers. *Limited test/general use* implies that a score from a test can indicate abilities beyond that test. We saw this in the case of the Army Alpha intelligence tests. In content, the Army Alpha test emphasized cultural knowledge and *correct writing*. In use, the test results inferred innate capability and fitness for officer leadership.

In this myth, false extrapolation appears necessary and reasonable. In turn, the myth permits sweeping claims without sweeping information.

3.3.9 Uniform Tests Tell a 2-D Story about Writing

Early tools such as Mann's exams and Hillegas' scale offered a two-dimensional story about writing. They intended to do so: A 2-D story is most efficient and consistent. A 2-D story discusses writers, and writing, as though dimensions like context and multiple knowledge domains don't matter.

Still today, many tests imply that writers will write the same way no matter the circumstances: Students still sit down and take specific writing tests, after which people draw general inferences about their ability. In the case of many secondary leaving exams, for instance, examiners infer from individual, timed essay exams whether students can read and produce untimed writing, or whether the student is prepared for college study. In this 2-D story, it is easy to compare and rank writers against one another, and it is easy to extrapolate from *limited tests* to *general use.*

3.4 Closer to the Truth

3.4.1 Uniform Tests Are not Fair

It has been evident for decades that IQ tests are seriously biased and have other limitations. Documented most of all is the clear connection between IQ scores and socioeconomic status (SES), even for children as young as two years old. It is also clear that factors related to test conditions, such as test anxiety, test environment, and examiner effect, make IQ tests unreliable.

3.4.2 Writing Is 3-D

Closer to the truth is that writing is 3-D: it is not just a writer and written language, but writers and language and contexts in dynamic interaction. (Or, in a sentence more to the right of the continuum: Writing is socially constituted meaning-making.) A writing exam, for instance, occurs within an exam context, and it cannot represent a range of writing in non-exam contexts. Only a range of writing with different purposes and audiences illustrates writing for a range of purposes and audiences.

One reason writing is 3-D is that **writing is social**. It responds to audiences and identities across a continuum of writing. My practice at writing formal research articles doesn't get me far when I try to write an informal blog on the same topic, unless I realize what language patterns do and do not apply.

Relatedly, **writing is diverse**, across a continuum of different values and practices. It depends on diverse identities in diverse contexts. Even though Mann and Eliot wanted to believe that a single writing task measured fitness for college, in truth, engagement in and beyond college depends on diverse writing and ongoing practice.

In addition, as we know, **writing engages diverse knowledge domains**, which all interact in a given moment and context. Cognitive, interpersonal, intrapersonal, and health domains are all part of writing.

Finally, **writing is explicitly learned** and is, in this sense, **unnatural**. Unlike spoken language, which most speakers acquire naturally through interaction, writing must be explicitly taught. It is something we acquire with conscious effort. *Correct writing* can be especially unnatural, because it is less common and more full of dense noun phrases than informal writing.

Closer to the truth is that *correct writing* is no one's mother tongue. It is taught and learned through situation-specific practice, observation, and collaboration, and it responds to context, like all of the writing continuum. Closer to the truth is that no part of the writing continuum is innately *correct* or *incorrect*. No part can stand for the whole.

To illustrate what occurs when writing is naturally 3-D but tested as 2-D, we'll explore examples from from the Hillegas scale in Table 3.2.

3.4.3 Hillegas Scale Examples Are on a Narrow Writing Continuum

To add to the writing continuum in this chapter, we'll look at two samples from the Hillegas scale.

The samples are number 200, ranked as having moderate writing quality, and sample 571, ranked as having high writing quality. Neither sample is described in detail, but the high-value sample is described as written by "a boy in the Freshman class in college."

The mid-value sample is a letter, a bit like a formal email today, and the high-value sample is a description akin to a report or response paper. They represent different parts of the writing continuum, around the formal end of email and the informal end of college writing, respectively. In Table 3.2, each one is summarized in terms of cohesion, connection, focus, stance, and usage. Then, the two samples are represented in full and annotated for language patterns in each one. The patterns range from more interpersonal, personal, and informal in the letter to more informational, impersonal, and formal in the description.

Table 3.2 1912 Hillegas writing scale continuum

Texting Social

Email

Secondary

College

Published

1912 Hillegas Writing Scale Continuum Patterns

Continuum Purposes	Informal Interpersonal Personal Sample 200, Mid value	Formal Informational Impersonal Sample 571, High value
Cohesion	• **Hourglass organization** Clear moves from general greeting and orientation, to specific details, to coda and general closing	• **Hourglass organization** Clear moves from general topic (t*he statue, beauty*) to specific details (*the posture, the limbs*) back to general topic (*peerless beauty*)
Connection	• **Interpersonal connection** Direct address of audience (*dear*) Text external 1st person emphasizes feelings and experiences (*I hope I will*)	• **Informational connection** No direct address Use of 1st person (*we*) refers to shared experience of statue
Focus	• **Personal, interpersonal subjects** Simple nouns Active verbs	• **Informational subjects** Nouns and noun phrases focus on statue Passive verbs
Stance	• **Certain stance** Boosters (*prettiest, always*) show positive stance toward experiences	• **Certain stance** Boosters show positive stance toward statue (*no analysis, peerless*)
Usage	• *Correct writing* **conventions and usage preferences**	• *Correct writing* **conventions and usage preferences**
Opening	My dear Fred,--	In looking at this statue we think, not of wisdom, or power, or force, but just of beauty.

In the full samples below, marginal notes and annotations include transitional words **in bold**, connection markers [in brackets], *hedges* in italics, ***boosters*** and ***generalizations*** italicized and bolded, and passive verbs [[in double brackets]].

3.4.3.1 Mid-value 1912 Hillegas Scale Sample

[My] *dear* Fred,--

> **An interpersonal opening:**
> In the letter greeting and opening sentence, the writer addresses the reader directly

[I] will tell [you] of my journey to Delphi falls, N. Y. There is nice scenery along this route. The ***prettiest*** scene is in the gulf which is ***quite*** narrow, a small creek flows down it and the road follows along near its banks.

> **Interpersonal cohesion:**
> The writer directly orients the reader to what is to come in the letter

There are woods on either side, these trees look ***very*** pretty when they are white with snow.

In summer it is ***always*** shady and cool in them and the small fish may be seen darting back and forth in the water.

> **Interpersonal stance and personal focus:**
> The sentence subjects focus on personal experiences and boosted reactions, with no dense noun phrases

[I] hope [I] will have the pleasure of taking [you] over the route some time.

> **Interpersonal audience address:**
> the writer addresses the reader, expressing a hope to share the experience

[Yours] sincerely,

> **Interpersonal closing**

3.4.3.2 High-value 1912 Hillegas Scale Sample

In looking at this statue [we] think, not of wisdom, or power, or force, but *just* of beauty.

| **Informational focus:** Focuses on collective observation |

She stands resting the weight of her body on one foot, and advancing the other (left) with knee bent. The posture causes the figure to sway slightly to one side, describing a fine curved line. The lower limbs [are draped] but the upper part of the body is uncovered.

| **Informational, impersonal cohesion and focus:** The writer moves from the general opening statement to a more specific detail about the statue (posture), using passive verbs to emphasize the statue |

The unfortunate loss of the statue's arms prevents a positive knowledge of its original attitude.

| **Formal focus:** The writer uses a sentence with dense noun phrases to focus on the statue and show a regretful attitude toward the "unfortunate loss of the statue's arms" |

The eyes are partly closed, having something of a dreamy languor. The nose is *perfectly* cut, the mouth and chin [are moulded] in adorable curves.

| **Impersonal stance:** The writer begins to offer evaluation, while the focus of the sentences remains on the statue |

Yet to say that *every* feature is of *faultless* perfection is but cold praise. *No analysis* can convey the sense of her *peerless* beauty.

| **Hourglass cohesion and certain stance:** The writer moves from the specific details back to general statements to close. These statements offer a boosted, certain stance |

These samples show how writing across the continuum is both similar and different. Both examples fulfill the five continuum purposes, but each one has some distinct patterns.

The interpersonal letter moves from addressing the recipient, to sharing observations, to closing with a valediction. In so doing, the letter cohesively adds detail. It makes clear the focus of the letter, and it directly and politely addresses the letter reader.

The informational description moves from identifying the topic, to adding and explaining details, back to a general, summative statement. In so doing, the sample adds detail, makes clear the focus of the description and a (positive) stance toward it, and addresses the reader formally, in a shared observation (*we*) and in an evaluation expressed as a shared reaction (*the unfortunate loss…*).

Both the letter and paper share *correct writing* norms for spelling and punctuation. Neither includes flexible usage more common in informal writing, even as the letter is more interpersonal and personal than the description. Though they are ranked differently – with the writing on the left of the continuum receiving a lower rank – both are correct for their context and goals.

Closer to the truth, then, is that only within this myth does it make sense to put these different texts on one scale. Closer to the truth is that writing is not *correct* or *incorrect* on a single scale, but rather a 3-D practice that accounts for its task and context.

Nonetheless, we've inherited 2-D stories about writers and tests, and these continue in our next myth as tests become standardized.

CHAPTER FOUR

Myth 4 You Can't Write That on the Test

Or, Tests Must Regulate Writing

The following passages are from the early to the late twentieth century. See if you can put them in order.

1. An ideal test would be one in which practically everyone could obtain some score and which very few could finish. Then all people would be measured.
2. Experienced and conscientious examiners vary one from another, they cannot all have got the correct and absolute standard.
3. In assessing intelligence (i.e., innate general intellectual ability) teachers are decidedly less reliable than psychological tests.
4. In a climate of growing public interest in public examinations comparability of grading standards is a popular focus of attention.
5. [We] will expect to see far greater comparability in standards between similar examination syllabuses to avoid some papers being seen as "easy".

You guessed right if you thought the first passage was the oldest. Indeed, the passages are already ordered chronologically, and in this way they show a twentieth-century arc of interest in tests. Passages 1 and 2, from the 1920s, illustrate the continuation of myth 3 – the pursuit of a single way to measure and compare people. The first was written in 1923 by Carl Brigham, promoter of pure Nordic peoples and toothy facts. The second was written in 1928 by the Joint Matriculation Board of the universities of Manchester, Leeds, and Liverpool, as they sought an "absolute standard" for test examiners.

Passage 3 reflects where we get by the mid-twentieth century: less trust in teachers; greater trust in standardized exams for measuring ability. The statement appeared in Cyril Burt's 1945 "The Reliability of Teachers' Assessment of their Pupils," at the start of standardized UK exams we will see in the origin story below.

The final two passages reflect public expectations by the late twentieth century. Passage 4 was written in 1978 by the examining boards of the UK General Certificate of Education (GCE) as they faced pressure to publicize exam results. The final passage appeared in 1997, in a press release noting the consolidation of awarding boards in the UK Department for Education and Employment.

All five passages show enduring interest in measuring and comparing *intelligence* through tests, with added concern for standardized ways of doing so. The goal is uniform comparability. The villain is variance, whether in examiners, teachers, or standards.

We've seen similar passages already because this myth builds on all the myths so far. Once we have myths 1, 2, and 3 – and *correct writing* is regulated by schools and narrowly tested as an indication of innate ability – then it is easy to insist that uniform tests must regulate writing.

This myth's origin story begins at the start of written examinations, soon after the start of myth 3.

4.1 Context for the Myth

4.1.1 Exams Begin to Regulate Writing and Students

We know from the last myth that in the early nineteenth century primary and secondary learning was assessed in interactive community events, as was the case in Boston before 1845. Before Horace Mann's unannounced written tests that year, annual interactive events were open to family members, and they focused more on how schools were doing than on comparing individual students.

At universities, learning was also displayed in interactive public events in the eighteenth and early nineteenth centuries. It was uncommon to go to college at the time; essentially, only male, white students from privileged families went.[1] But if you were among them, you would prove your learning by speaking aloud in a classical language, during an interactive period of "verbal jousting." For instance, attending Cambridge University in 1820, you and a peer might debate an author's merits in a public, oral exam in Latin.

By the late nineteenth century, interactive university assessments in Latin were giving way to individual written examinations in English, and school-specific secondary assessments were being replaced by externally-designed written exams. This won't surprise us, given educational shifts we've already seen, away from classical languages in myth 2 and toward Mann's written testing in myth 3. But it entailed a significant change in how learning was evaluated.[2]

4.1.2 Higher Education Expands

Higher education options were expanding around this time. In the UK, Cambridge and Oxford were still socially exclusive and subject to religious tests, and Scottish universities and English dissenting academies began providing alternatives in the 18th and 19th centuries. By 1826, England gained the "godless college of Gower Street," or the University College London, and in the ensuing decades, more colleges were founded, more female students were accepted across social classes, and more leaders called for affordable, accessible institutions for working people.

The same nineteenth-century expansion happened in UK Commonwealth countries and in the US. In Australia, local legislation established the University of Sydney in 1850 and the University of Melbourne in 1853. In Canada, though its first university was established by colonial legislatures in 1789, McGill University and several others followed in the nineteenth century. In the US, the mid- and late-nineteenth-century federal Morrill Acts used Indigenous tribal land, usually obtained through violent seizure or forced cession, as locations and to provide seed money for new public institutions.[3] These new institutions were designed to offer practical training in areas such as agriculture and the mechanical trades. By 1890, private US institutions also began expanding enrollment.

4.1.3 College and Secondary English Writing Exams Begin

With more higher education came more written English exams. In the UK, a local examinations system was established in the 1850s for students leaving secondary school. If you were a male student finishing secondary school near Cambridge in 1858, for instance, you would write a timed essay in English about the queens and children of Henry VIII (in order, mind you) for your history exam. Your response would be evaluated by local examinations evaluators rather than your own teacher. In their evaluation, examiners would look for "correct punctuation, arrangement, spelling, precision, elegance, and completeness."

Students were wholly unused to written examinations like these, as examiner reports make clear. In response, Cambridge 1859 examiners proposed a solution that sounds a lot like today's idea of teaching to the test. "With the stimulus of open competition and the standard of regularly recognised examinations," examiners wrote, "carefulness and ability will receive clearer direction and more open reward."[4]

By the late nineteenth century, students were more accustomed to written English exams, though examiners were not necessarily more content with students' writing. The Cambridge Seniors English Composition Examination 1883 report was cutting:

The most usual faults were – statements of utter nonsense, general irrelevance, inexact and pretentious language, carelessness in punctuation and arrangement, and lastly the employment of Scripture texts when the candidate was at a loss for something to say.

Examiners found other written exams lacking as well. Cambridge history examiners lamented students' writing even though they found their historical knowledge satisfactory: "[students'] answers, even when accurate, showed a general uniformity of expression," the examiners reported.

In the US, we know from myth 3, the earliest English entrance exams appeared in 1853, under the direction of Horace Mann at Antioch College. These included an English grammar exam, a history exam, and a geography exam. All three were evaluated for *correct writing*: In a testament to myth 1, Mann saw the study of pure English grammar as a way to purify thoughts.

Harvard wasn't far behind, because by 1869 Charles Eliot was promoting *correct writing* as a way to rank and select students. Beginning in 1872, all of Harvard's student entrance exams were evaluated for "correct spelling, punctuation, and expression" in English. By 1874, Eliot hired one of his former Harvard peers, newspaperman Adams Sherman Hill, to design Harvard's English composition entrance exams. Applicants were furthermore advised that "writing on any entrance exam may be regarded as part of his examination in English."

Late nineteenth-century Harvard reports also documented the rise of English composition exams at other US colleges, including Princeton, the University of Michigan, and the University of Pennsylvania. English writing exams appeared at the US secondary level in the late nineteenth century, including the New York State Regents Examination for graduating secondary students in 1878.

4.1.4 College Exams Emphasize Timed Writing, Literature, and *Correct Writing*

Early English exams emphasized writing under time constraints. Oxford and Cambridge exams lasted around three hours; Harvard's lasted around one hour. Naturally, these exams measured whether students could write quickly, without substantial time for reading or revising.

Concerns about timed writing appeared at the time. In 1873, a Cambridge examination student named Amy wrote her parents that she ran out of time during her exams while "A fellow of the university, cap-a-pie, very severe looking, sat at the head of the room, or walked up and down, and frightened me."[5] In 1890, English composition examiner LeBaron Russel Briggs described similar conditions at Harvard. He bemoaned timed exams and rushed exam grading, and he described what today we would call test anxiety: "Again and again I have seen the untrained youth, however cultivated for his years, flinch before every searching test." Another early Harvard examiner, Byron Satterlee Hurlbut, argued in 1892 that students should practice timed writing in class, even though "The more elaborate advanced work must, of course, be done outside the class." This argument illustrates an enduring paradox of timed English writing exams: They are used in high-stakes evaluation, yet not viewed as students' best work.

In addition to being timed, we've seen that early writing exams often focused on literature. Harvard couched their early English entrance exams as responses to "standard authors"; early Oxford, Cambridge, and Harvard exams regularly focused on Shakespearean texts and characters. There were exceptions; an 1858 Cambridge English Composition exam, for instance, asked students to *Write a letter to a friend in Australia, announcing your intention to emigrate*.[6]

Writing knowledge is not the same thing as literary knowledge, and written responses to literature are different than literature itself. As imaginative writing, literature has different purposes and patterns than the writing continuum we are exploring throughout this book. Still, we know from myths 1 and 2 that literature, like *correct writing*, served nationalist goals of standardizing and celebrating English. Harvard president Charles Eliot put it this way: "It is enough to say of the English language that it is the language of English literature."

Finally, early exams were subject to *correct writing* expectations, even on exams in subjects other than English composition. We saw, for instance, that spelling, capitalization, and punctuation were checked across exams at Antioch and Harvard, and that "uniformity of expression" disappointed the Cambridge history examiners despite accurate historical information.

4.1.5 Standardized Exams Begin

The last myth and this one fueled confidence in uniform tests, and it was only a matter of time before local exams gave way to national, standardized exams. At the start of the twentieth century, for example, the US College Board tailored exams to individual colleges. By 1923, it commissioned Carl Brigham (of myth 4 Army Alpha Test fame) to develop a single Scholastic Aptitude Test (SAT). His charge was to create a single test for all US students, to determine which ones had "the power to think clearly."

The SAT was first administered for college entrance in 1926. Promoted as a test of innate ability, it was comprised of ten timed subtests, including definitions, arithmetical problems, classification, antonyms, analogies, and paragraph reading. Nine of the ten subtests included sentences or paragraphs in *correct writing*. For instance, a classification section included the following directions:

In each of the lines below, the first two words are related to each other in some way. You are to see what the relation is between the first two words, and find the one word in the parentheses that is related in the same way to the third word, writing the number of that word in the margin at the end of each line.

Some exam questions emphasized grammatical terms, such as, *An____is a word used to limit or qualify the application of a noun or a nominal phrase.* Other questions emphasized culturally specific information such as: *Three of the following words are related to each other in some definite way: Columbus, Socrates, Beethoven, Wagner, Verdi, Corneille. Which three words are most closely related?.*[7] As these examples show, to understand and respond to the 1926 SAT, the first requirement was to parse *correct writing*.

In the UK, secondary exams also became more centralized during the twentieth century. In 1918, the UK local examinations were consolidated in the British Board of Education's School Certificate Examinations. These were used across England and then the British colonies, based on the idea that uniform external examinations set an international standard. By the 1940s, UK standardized exams extended to primary schools. The 1944 Education Act, led by Cyril Burt, introduced the eleven-plus examination as a sorting tool. Only those students receiving high exam scores were selected for grammar schools, which emphasized university preparation.

The eleven-plus exam included sections on "general English," comprehension, and arithmetic. As in the SAT, students needed to comprehend *correct writing* throughout the exam, and in specific questions, they needed to know *correct writing* spelling and usage preferences, such as when to use *which* versus *whom*.

By the mid-twentieth century, standardized exams were common. By 1951, the UK had the General Certificate of Education (GCE) exam in England, Wales, and Northern Ireland, which expanded to secondary education certificates in the 1960s. By the 1960s, the US had the SAT, the American College Test (ACT), and several state exams for students graduating secondary school and applying to college. In these developments, we can again see *more access/more regulation*. As college access increased, so did entrance examinations, which emphasized *correct writing* within and beyond English exams.

4.2 The Myth Emerges

With standardized, high-stakes tests in the early and mid twentieth century, this myth emerged. Uniform, externally developed tests could now regulate writing. They could reward the right side of the continuum only, and select only *correct* writers for particular educational opportunities.

4.3 Consequences of the Myth

4.3.1 We Scale up Limited Definitions of *Writing* and *Intelligence*

In this myth, the writing and regulating valued in the first three myths becomes standardized in large-scale tests for secondary and college students. Regulating English was already *manifestly desirable*; in this myth, standardized tests become *manifestly desirable*, too.

Standardized tests depend on and propel all the myths so far. They scale up the limited mold of *correct writing* equated with ability, along with several related consequences noted in Table 4.1.

Table 4.1 Consequences of myth 4

Once we believe	... Every exam is an English exam
Tests must regulate writing, then...	... Exams emphasize exam writing
	... Exams emphasize English literature
	... Exams imply writing tasks don't matter
	... Exam culture overshadows learning culture
	... Efficiency and ideal sameness prevail
	... Exams become the only obvious option
	... Extrapolation seems fine

4.3.2 Every Exam Is an English Exam

Once exams were written in English, a history exam was no longer a history exam. It was a test of *correct writing*, too. Parsing *correct writing* was necessary to score well on the SAT, and *correct writing* errors could hurt your chances for college entrance whether they appeared on your English composition exam or not.[8]

4.3.3 Exams Emphasize Exam Writing

Today, we have a veritable alphabet soup for regulating *correct writing*. Well-known examples include the UK's General Certificate of Secondary English (GCSE) and Advanced Subsidiary and Advanced levels (AS and A Levels), the International Baccalaureate (IB) diploma exam; Australia's Special Tertiary Admissions Test (STAT) and National Assessment Program – Literacy and Numeracy (NAPLAN); and the US Collegiate Learning Assessment (CLA), Advanced Placement (AP), and Accuplacer exams. All of these standardized exams depend on producing and/or parsing *correct writing* under timed circumstances. All of them reinforce earlier myths, by conflating *correct writing* and *intelligence* and bolstering two-dimensional ideas about writing, in which circumstances and tasks don't influence what students write.

For one thing, standardized exams have scaled up timed writing, despite ongoing concerns about it. Research shows that writing quickly leaves no time for regressions, multiple knowledge domains, or complex processing. For another thing, by leaving no time for revision and by emphasizing *correct writing* errors, standardized exams have scaled up error-hunting and error-reporting, reinforcing what writing historians Robert Connors, Lisa Ede, and Andrea Lunsford call the "cult of correctness" dawning as tests began to regulate written English.

Contemporary exam support resources reinforce language regulation mode. I was able to take two practice tests online, the US ACT Writing Test and the College Board Accuplacer. The US ACT Writing Test is used for college admission, and the College Board Accuplacer is used for writing placement. Both exams include multiple choice sections focused on *correct writing* errors. Questions include distinguishing between *that* and *which, there* and *their,* and *whose* and *who's,* as well as identifying comma usage and subject-verb agreement prescribed on the right of the continuum. In their test tips, Accuplacer encourages students to use grammar and spell check apps, which suggests that test criteria especially concern conventions and usage preference errors.[9] This advice brings us full circle back to myth 1, because grammar-checkers are often informed by eighteenth- and nineteenth-century usage preferences.[10]

4.3.4 Exams and Courses Emphasize English Literature

Early English exams and courses emphasized literature more than language. There were exceptions: Some early university students received English language instruction in Scottish universities,[11] and before the 1970s, several US composition programs incorporated insights from linguistics. But it was not until a conference held at Dartmouth College in 1966 that educators began to challenge the exclusive emphasis on literature and lack of emphasis on written language instruction. By then, departments, courses, and exams had focused on literature for a century, and English composition courses were often taught by instructors trained in analyzing or producing literature.

Still today, many English instructors are trained in literary studies rather than (also) English linguistics, rhetoric, or composition. The university writing program I direct, for instance, is housed in an English department and largely follows this approach. In other words, many writing instructors are trained in literary studies, a discipline that favors particular genres (such as essays), evidence (e.g., literary forms), and other specific writing choices (e.g., emphasis on writers' interpretive reasoning versus empirical results). The instructors are rarely trained in language development or how writing in literary studies does and does not apply to other kinds of writing. In turn, many secondary and early college students end up practicing responses to literature, rather than studying a range of written English.

4.3.5 Exams Imply Writing Tasks Don't Matter

Early exams implied that exam writing tasks – what students were asked to do on a test or assignment – didn't matter. A good writer was a good writer no matter the task, a bad writer bad regardless, and so forth. In other words, if you were a good writer taking Oxford's 1884 English exam, you would write a good timed essay about "signs of the immaturity of Shakespeare's genius in Richard II," whether or not you had read and discussed *Richard II* in school before the exam. You would be the same *correct* or *incorrect* writer if you wrote a report on farming.

Fast forward seven decades, and Cyril Burt was promoting the same idea. After arguing that writing speed was an index of ability, Burt's eleven-plus exam offered writing tasks with no detail, such as the mid-twentieth-century exam task that was one word: School. Burt further specified that the exam topic "should not be stated until the last moment, when ... the test-period is about to commence."

It is still common to withhold exam topics until the start of exams, as was recommended by the UK Department of Education for the 2022 GCSEs:[12]

...for subjects in which a choice of topic or content is provided (English literature, history, ancient history and geography), advance information about the focus of exams should not also be given. We believe the combination of the two measures would have the effect of giving students taking those subjects an unfair advantage and making the qualifications less rigorous.

More generally, the implication persists that writing tasks don't influence writing performance. That is why the University of Cambridge Local Examinations Syndicate (UCLES) exam directions, for instance, state, "This examination paper tests how well you can read, write, and present information," rather than something like, *this examination paper tests how well you can read, write, and present information in a timed essay addressing literature on this exam.*

4.3.6 Exam Culture Overshadows Learning Culture

When we prioritize the values of exam culture, we overlook a century of documented problems with uniform tests, several of which are documented by assessment historian Andrew Watts. An early twentieth-century criticism of the UK's local examination system was that it was out of touch, "ruled and regulated by middle-aged and even elderly gentlemen, who now have little to do with the education of the young, and in many cases have never had to do with it." The local examinations were also described as inequitable: "The achievements of a few were purchased at the expense of many," because the curriculum was designed around the few deemed able to sit the exams.

A similar criticism was leveled in 1928 at the "distorting and harmful effects" of using external examinations in British Overseas Territories. The external exams, noted the UK parliamentary under-secretary, constrained local secondary education by emphasizing English language and culture, and they tended to "favor a small class of selected students." When the local examinations were further consolidated in the School Certificate Examinations, the UK Board of Education offered a "cardinal principle" for standardized exams: "The examination should follow the curriculum and not determine it." Later still, in the 1940s, UK school reports argued that standardized examinations should be stopped, because they threatened the independence of schools and teachers' freedom.

When exam culture overshadows learning culture, the priorities of test developers prevail despite these problems and cautionary tales. This is why timed writing and spelling errors persist – not because they relate to learning priorities, such as sustained inquiry, revision, and reflection on writing choices – but because they are efficient to administer and evaluate. This is also why the US Accuplacer exam uses commissioned writing for the passages that students read and correct during the exam. Authentic writing supports student learning, because it is what students will encounter and produce in the real world. But the commissioned writing, narrowly designed and efficient, fulfills the priorities of exam culture.

4.3.7 Efficiency and Ideal Sameness Prevail

In myth 3, we saw Cyril Burt argue that tests were more reliable than teachers, so we won't be surprised to hear that he promoted the eleven-plus exam along these lines. Burt described that two standardized exam scores tended to show close agreement, while those of two teachers often differed – and therefore could not both be correct. For Burt, variance meant inaccuracy. There was no room for diverse responses to student work.

A similar message appeared decades later, when league tables ranked schools according to students' performance on the UK GCSE and GCE A-level examinations. These 1990s rankings were based on exam scores without attention to 3-D details such as test conditions, and there were documented concerns about the rankings at the time. However, these concerns led to more, rather than less, uniformity, because the ranking reports ultimately called for a standard that would not change over time or tasks. As Rebecca Zwick wrote in *Who Gets In?* thirty years later, exam scores give the "an illusion of exactitude" even though scores can be affected by test takers' moods, testing conditions, writing tasks, and lucky guesses.

4.3.8 Exams Become the Only Obvious Option

It is no mystery that standardized tests offer extremely limited information about students. Teachers have reported this for decades – that standardized tests offer little to no useful information about students' writing or broader literacy. But once we believe the myth that *writing* and *intelligence* need to be regulated in efficient and uniform ways, standardized exams become the only obvious option. Today, school funding is regularly linked to test scores, and teachers often have to focus on standardized test writing at the expense of varied writing tasks. Schools are pressured to make reading and writing measurable and evaluative, meaning they have little choice but to focus instruction on exams.

4.3.9 Extrapolation Seems Fine

We saw false extrapolation in the last myth: Early intelligence tests went from "Jane can't write X" to "Jane is not capable." In this myth, we see similar moves here: going from "Jane can't write X exam" to "Jane can't write." This happens when we use specific tasks to draw general conclusions.

Standardized tests can affirm one another in cycles of generalization and extrapolation. This happens when similar standardized test results are seen as evidence of validity, rather than what they are: evidence of consistency across similar tests. This was the case in a much-cited study we will see in the next myth, in which students who did well on the Collegiate Learning Assessment (CLA) also had high SAT/ACT scores. The authors of the study argued that similar CLA and SAT scores proved their conclusions about student writing. A different interpretation is that students will perform similarly on similarly narrow testing instruments.

To label a student an *incorrect writer* because of spelling or usage on a timed exam generalizes and extrapolates beyond that timed exam, but this is how exam results are often used.

4.4 Closer to the Truth

4.4.1 Standardized Test Scores Measure Socioeconomic Status and Test Preparation

Closer to the truth is that – like IQ test scores – standardized exam scores (including SAT, ACT, and GCSE scores) correlate with socioeconomic status (SES). SES is also associated with choices in A-level subjects, which impacts college admission.

Also closer to the truth is that SES often determines whether students have money or time for test preparation, and test preparation impacts test scores. One-on-one test tutoring, for instance, has been shown to significantly improve standardized test scores. Because it is clear that test preparation makes a difference to make timed standardized writing exams more fair, all students would need regular practice with timed standardized exam writing. But this would mean even more exam culture.

4.4.2 Problems Are Well-documented, but Efficiency Rules

Standardized tests tend to be uniform and narrow, while writing and students are diverse and expansive. Anya Kamenetz, author of the book *The Test: Why Our Schools are Obsessed with Standardized Testing – But You Don't Have to Be*, puts it this way: "The way much of school is organized around these tests make little sense for young humans developmentally. Nor does it square with what the world needs."

Problems range from test design, to performance, to use. In terms of design, closer to the truth is that standardized tests leave out important knowledge we saw in the last myth, including interpersonal and intrapersonal knowledge related to leadership, collaboration, adaptation, and creativity. Another test deisgn concern is that when standardized tests emphasize culturally specific knowledge, they are not equally fair for all students. And when exams test language knowledge even when they are not language exams, they are not valid: There is a mismatch between what they are measuring and what they are claiming to measure.

In terms of test performance, closer to the truth is that students respond to test situations. Everything from misunderstandings to cognitive overload can influence students taking an exam on a given day. This is why for any test performance, there are myriad explanations aside from ability.

In terms of test use, standardized test scores are often used in college admissions, but closer to the truth is that test scores do not predict how most students will do in college. Standardized exams emphasize narrow tasks and narrow domain knowledge, while college learning is less narrow. The SAT Writing and Language Test, for instance, has a low correlation to students' first-year college grades, and an even lower correlation with their first-year course grades in English and writing. Perhaps the reason for this failure of concurrent and predictive value is the fact that the test requires no student writing whatsoever.

Closer to the truth is that standardized tests emerged after several writing myths had already emerged. Most of today's contemporary tests have been guided by past test instruments and have not been sufficiently tested for fairness. Educators have therefore called for alternatives, including portfolios and collaborative assignments. These alternatives are more like writing outside of test situations, meaning they are more varied and less efficient.

4.4.3 Tests Must Be Tested

Closer to the truth is that writing is complex, and testing tests is tricky. How can we tell a test is accurate? Test results can be compared with students' grade point average (GPA), but GPA is often partial and inconclusive. Secondary writing exams can be tested against how students do in their college GPA, but as we saw above, these measures have highlighted the poor predictive power of standardized test results.

Writing exam scores and GPA can be tested against student writing success throughout and after college, but such studies are challenging and rare. Even so, it is notable that rare research like this – following postsecondary writers for multiple years, based on how well they do on different kinds of writing – paints a rosier picture than standardized test results. Closer to the truth is that more diverse writing offers a more robust picture of how students write, and the robust picture is a more positive one. The bleakest picture we get is from narrow testing of narrow writing.

4.4.4 Tests Only Test What Is on the Tests

Closer to the truth is that no single writing test can test writing ability. Specific writing tasks directly shape writing, soliciting certain writing choices and not others, a phenomena that I've found fascinating to research over the past several years. I like the assessment term "constructed response tasks" for this reason. Reading and writing tasks construct the responses to them.

For one thing, as demonstrated in Table 4.2, students' familiarity with the **topic** matters. If students know something about a writing topic, they have more working memory for their writing choices, like cohesion and usage conventions. To use an earlier example, a student who had read and discussed *Richard II* before the Oxford 1884 exam would have more bandwidth for writing choices than a student who was less familiar with *Richard II*. This explains why students with relevant prior knowledge tend to produce what evaluators consider more fluent writing.

For another thing, **how** students are asked to write matters. Writing is influenced by whether it is timed or untimed, or takes the form of an essay or a report, and so on. When a test parameter changes, writing changes.

Let's start with the fact that students write differently if they have ample time to write. There are obvious reasons for this: Untimed writing means students have time to revise their spelling, punctuation, and other usage conventions. But there are less obvious reasons, too. Untimed writing means students engage more with other texts and perspectives, which is an expectation of most college writing.

Most subtle is that timed and untimed writing have different language patterns. When students write quickly, they tend to use language patterns on the left of the continuum, probably because they are the most

Table 4.2 Writing task details continuum

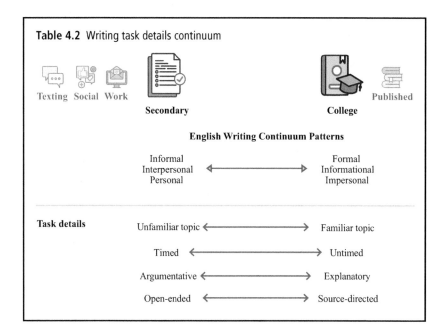

practiced and familiar. Timed writing includes significantly more personal and interpersonal language patterns, such as boosted statements and text-external first-person pronouns. This matters because *correct writing* tends to include impersonal, informational language patterns instead, as we've seen since myth 1.

Students also write differently based on genre – a personal narrative, an argumentative essay, and a summary report all have different language patterns, even by the same student. Personal narratives tend to include storytelling moves, interpersonal connection (*you won't believe what happened*), and personalized stance patterns (*I'm so excited*). Argumentative essays and other persuasive writing include significantly more generalizations (e.g., **everyone** *has cheated at some point*) and boosted claims (e.g., *cheating is **clearly** wrong*). Explanatory writing is less likely to include boosters and more likely to include noun phrases (e.g., *increasing reports of cheating are a concern for educators*). Here again, these patterns matter, because *correct writing* is usually informational and impersonal, or more toward the right of the continuum, meaning readers tend to expect few generalizations and more noun phrases.

Thus topic, timing, and genre all make a difference. But it doesn't stop there. Research shows that students responding to open-ended questions (e.g., *Why do students cheat?*) write differently than those responding to

Table 4.3 Writing task details continuum

Texting Social	Email	Secondary	College	Published

Continuum Purposes	**English Exam Writing Continuum Patterns**		

Informal Interpersonal Personal ← → Formal Informational Impersonal

	Email	Secondary	College
Cohesion	• Greetings and closings, **narrative** moves	• Explicit paragraphs	• Explicit **moves**, transition words, **paragraphs**
Connection	• 2nd person pronouns, text external 1st person	• 1st person references to collective needs or experiences (*we, our*)	• Rare 1st person, text internal 1st person
Focus	• Sentence subjects **emphasize people, experiences, events**	• Sentence subjects emphasize people, observations (***there is***)	• **Dense noun phrase subjects** emphasizing concepts, phenomena, research
Stance	• **Boosters and generalizations**, personal reactions including strong evaluations	• Boosters and generalizations, **some hedges**	• **Hedges, some boosters**, qualified generalizations
Usage	• *Correct writing conventions and usage preferences*	• *Correct writing conventions and usage preferences*	• *Correct writing conventions and usage preferences*

Example tasks:

The University of London Entrance Exam, 1838

Composition Exam

Give an analysis of the part of the first book of Thucydides, which relates the causes and occasions of the Peloponnesian War, with the substance of the arguments used in the speeches. How far did the character and actions of Pompey entitle him to the epithet of The Great?

Table 4.3 (cont.)

Cambridge Local Examination, 1858 English Composition Junior Exam	**Choice 3** Write a letter to a friend in Australia announcing your intention to emigrate, and asking for information	**Choice 4** Discuss the change produced in the habits of the people by Railways
Cambridge Examination for Women, 1870 English Composition Exam	**Choice 3** The question of compulsory emigration as a means of relief to national destitution	**Choice 1** The political position of Greece, with a review of its history from the beginning of the century.
	Choice 4 The question of opening to women professional careers, especially that of medicine.	**Choice 2** A comparison of French and English tragedy, illustrated by special comparison of Racine with Shakespeare.
Oxford University 1884 Women's English Examination	[Are there] any parts of *Macbeth* which seem so unworthy of Shakespeare as to justify a doubt as to their being genuine? [Are there] any signs of the immaturity of Shakespeare's genius in Richard II? [Are there] any traces of a failure of dramatic power in the *Tempest*?	
	Summarise Milton's arguments against the censorship of the press. Which do you consider the most convincing, which the most rhetorically effective?	Explain, by reference to this or any other of his prose writings, Milton's idea of Liberty.
Australia STAT 2009 Written English Part A	**Comment 1** Education helps individuals grow and has a civilising and **humanising influence on** society as a whole.	

Table 4.3 (cont.)

		Comment 2 Too much of current education is concerned with rote learning that has little relationship to real problems and real life.
Australia STAT 2009 Written English **Part B**		**Comment 6** Romances come and go, but it is friendship that remains. **Comment 7** It is important that we learn to be confident within ourselves rather than dependent on the good opinion of others.
Cambridge International A Level English Language 2016 Exam	Write a 150-250-word diary entry as though you are the author of the speech you read.	Comment on the style and language of a speech made by Australian Prime Minister Julia Gillard
New Zealand IELTS, 2022 Academic Writing Exam		Explain pie charts representing energy use across countries.

source-oriented questions (e.g., *Do you agree or disagree with what the author says about cheating?*). Specifically, students responding to open-ended questions use more informal, interpersonal, and personal patterns, including generalizations and references to personal experiences. By contrast, students responding to source-oriented questions use more formal, informational, impersonal patterns, including more references to source texts and fewer references to personal experiences. I've mapped all of these general writing task trends onto the continuum in Table 4.2.

Closer to the truth is that every writing task constructs *correct* and *incorrect* writing in specific ways, and only the writing done for a particular task is measured in its evaluation. Any writing exam score tells one story about a writer – based on the test conditions, topic, genre, and other test parameters – and not another.

This doesn't mean that all writing exams are bad. It means that what they can tell us is limited. Closer to the truth is that no writing exam can tell us whether a student can write. Each one tells us how a student writes on that exam.

4.4.5 Writing Exam Tasks Are on a Continuum

We can now use Table 4.3 to add secondary and college exam tasks to the writing continuum, according to the language patterns associated with them. More informal, interpersonal, personal exam writing such as diary and letter writing will tend toward the left end of the continuum, while summary and synthesis writing will tend more toward the formal, informational, impersonal end of secondary and college writing. Because it is both personal and informational, persuasive essay writing tends to fall in between.[13]

As you can see on this task continuum, several exams on this task continuum offered students a choice, as though the tasks were all the same. Closer to the truth is that the task matters, and there are writing patterns associated with particular tasks. Thus students choosing different options will have different chances of success, particularly if examiners expect only the formal, impersonal, and informational patterns of *correct writing*.

For all of these reasons, the design and use of most standardized exams keep the myth glasses firmly on. We'll see similar themes in the next myth, that most students can't write.

CHAPTER FIVE

Myth 5 Chances Are, You Can't Write

Or, Most Students Can't Write

5.1 Pick a Century

The following passages hail from fifty years ago, twenty years ago, and two years ago. Can you tell which is which?

1. University students express themselves clearly when they speak ... But when they sit down at a keyboard to put those thoughts on a page, they produce a confusing jumble of jargon, colloquialisms, and random punctuation.
2. Cambridge is admitting students who, bright as they are, cannot construct coherent essays or write grammatical English.
3. [M]any of the most intelligent freshmen, in some ways more articulate and sophisticated than ever before, are seriously deficient when it comes to organizing their thoughts on paper.

The message here is strikingly uniform, but you guessed right if you thought the first passage was the most recent. Passage 1 appeared in 2020 in the *Sydney Morning Herald*, the same year an opinion piece in *The Canberra Times* claimed, "The dire state of Australian students' writing is perhaps the worst-kept secret of our education system." Passage 2 appeared in London's *Telegraph* in 2002. Passage 3 comes from a 1975 *Newsweek* article called "Why Johnny Can't Write."

The passages paint a damning picture, and a contradictory one. Students are capable (*more articulate and sophisticated than ever*) but not able to write (*seriously deficient; cannot construct coherent essays*). A single London headline in 2006 put it this way: "University students: They can't write, spell, or present an argument. No, these aren't university rejects, but students at prestigious establishments." Even accounting for the best, so these messages say, most students can't write.

This myth rests on all the mythical thinking we've seen so far. Once *correct writing* is narrowly defined, regulated by schools, indicative of *intelligence*, and measured by narrow tests, we are left with very limited ideas about writing. When *correct writing* is then scaled up in standardized exams, we get this myth, that most students can't do it.

If this weren't a myth, we might question why we expect everyone to do something that most people – including successful students – can't do. But myths are untroubled by their contradictions, and multiple generations had been wearing myth glasses by the time these opening passages were written. Rather than expanding what *correct writing* is or how we are measuring it, we've done more regulating and more lamenting.

Our fifth origin story begins when examiners started complaining about students' written English exams, which is to say: As soon as students started writing English exams.

5.2 Context for the Myth

5.2.1 Early Exam Graders Say Most Students Can't Write

Summarizing the results of the first Harvard English exams, examiner Adams Sherman Hill described "almost exactly one half, failed to pass." (Spoiler alert: not so, as we will see later. But this claim has nonetheless been repeated over time.)[1] A decade later, Harvard's examiner lamented "unillumined incompetency" in three-quarters of the exam books. An even smaller percentage impressed Cambridge's 1883 Seniors English Composition examiner, who wrote that "seven and a half percent of the essays were extremely well done."

5.2.2 Early Exam Graders Sometimes Clarified What Students Were Doing Wrong

From early exam reports, we can tell that examiners lamented that student writing that didn't follow *correct writing* usage preferences. Harvard's examiners overwhelmingly emphasized conventions, including punctuation (using commas between words that "no rational being" would separate), capitalization, and spelling ("as if starting a spelling reform"). One condemned students' "second-rate diction" (confusion regarding *shall* versus *will*) and "inaccuracy" (the use of *ain't* and *like I do*) – "crimes," he complained, that were also committed by college professors and presidents.

Early Cambridge reports showed similar dissatisfaction with student usage in English writing exams, including misspelling, "carelessness in punctuation and arrangement," and "inelegant style" due to short, separate sentences. (Early Cambridge examiners were similarly unimpressed with English grammar exams: The exams "exhibited great want of thought and much blundering," and "much random guesswork and strange ignorance as to the meaning of some common English words.")

Volume also seemed to matter. Early Cambridge examiners were impressed by the few essays that were "9, 10, 12, and even 14 pages of closely-written matter, excellent in neatness as well as in quality." The examiners saw this as "a surprising achievement," given the age of the writers and the time constraints of the exam. More substantive feedback included "a painstaking and generous fairness of mind that was very striking," particularly in essays by female students, "many of whom summed up so conscientiously and sympathetically both for and against, that it was impossible to be sure on which side their adherence lay."

Other criteria were not so straightforward. Harvard grader Byron Satterlee Hurlbut wrote that students' "lack of the feeling of possession, of power over words" constituted a "very grave fault" in examination essays. Worst of all, according to Hurlbut, was a student who avoided "common expressions" to compose writing "stuffed with fine phrases." The ideal writer was instead "natural," able to "express his individuality" and "avoid all fine writing." 1880s Cambridge examiners similarly praised "simplicity and directness of style."

Harvard grader L. Briggs alluded to a "serious fault" in his 1888 report, the "fancied necessity of infusing morality somewhere ... usually the end." To illustrate this unhappy strategy, Briggs included the following ending from a student essay: "Many people can write a pretty frivolous story, but few is the number, of those, who can put into that story lessons that, if a reader learns them, he can follow all through life. This power has been given to Miss Austen."

Three kinds of criteria appeared in this early feedback: superficial and clear; substantive and clear; and decidedly vague. The first two categories favor patterns on the right side of the continuum rather than the left – *correct writing* usage preferences, and impersonal stance patterns. Criteria in the final category are difficult to connect to language patterns.

- **Superficial and clear**
  Correct writing usage preferences and conventions, neatness, length
- **Substantive and clear**
  "Fairness of mind," or impersonal treatment of multiple views
- **Decidedly vague**
  "Inelegant style," "feeling of possession, of power over words," "directness of style," "fancied necessity of infusing morality somewhere"

5.2.3 Mass Media Coverage Says Most Students Cannot Write

Nineteenth-century student writing, it's clear, was no rosy affair. Examiners were disappointed; criteria were narrow and confusing. Still, the myth that *most students can't write* didn't fully form until most students were required to take standardized writing exams. By the late twentieth century, thousands of students across thousands of schools were taking standardized tests, and media headlines were making claims based on the test results.

A potent example was the 1975 article "Why Johnny Can't Write" we saw in the opening, which is still among the most read *Newsweek* articles of all time. The article's claims were based on results from the National Assessment of Educational Progress (NAEP), the first standardized test taken by all US secondary students. In the article, senior *Newsweek* writer Meril Sheils argued that scores from the first six years of NAEP (1969 to 1975) were proof that most US students were "unable to write ordinary, expository English with any real degree of structure and lucidity." (For this, Sheils blamed "the simplistic spoken style of television," but more on that in myth 8.) Sheils reported that students showed "serious deficiencies in spelling vocabulary and sentence structure," which she illustrated in four one-sentence examples. The first-year college student example used *their* for *there*.

Bleak headlines didn't stop in the twentieth century, of course. Several twenty-first-century headlines complain that most students can't write, including several citing the 2011 book *Academically Adrift: Limited Learning on College Campuses*. The book, by Richard Arum and Josipa Roksa, argued that student writing was improving little during the first two years of college, and it was widely referenced in popular media, featured on ABC's *Nightly News* and reviewed in the *The New York Review of Books* for its "chilling portrait of what the university curriculum has become." Bill Gates was quoted as saying that before reading it, he "took it for granted that colleges were doing a very good job."

You probably saw this coming: Claims about student writing in *Academically Adrift* were based on standardized exam scores. Specifically, they were based on results from the Collegiate Learning Assessment (CLA), taken by 2,323 students at the time of college enrollment and then again in their second year. The book details only the CLA exam scores, not the CLA exam tasks or criteria, but based on past CLA exams, students might have had ninety minutes to read a set of documents and recommend a course of action to a company or a government official.[2]

These details led to critiques of *Academically Adrift*: the narrowness of the CLA, the lack of discussion about assessment challenges, and especially, the dearth of information about CLA tasks or criteria, which make the book's claims unverifiable. Furthermore, critics noted that in the book's study, 55 percent of students *did* make gains, which goes unemphasized in favor of claims about the other 45 percent. As happened with intelligence tests in myth 4, however, bleak prognoses – not critiques of test – drew the most attention. Among other sources, a 2017 *Study International* article cited the book and proclaimed, "Students can't write properly even after college."[3]

Other twenty-first-century headlines send a similar message. An *Independent* article in 2006 suggested that UK students couldn't write because they approached punctuation marks as "interchangeable" (a claim similar to nineteenth-century Harvard reports about commas between words that "no rational being" would separate). The same article argued that UK students lacked knowledge of the subject, verb, object parts of a sentence, unlike their US peers, though we have seen plenty of examples suggesting US pundits would not agree. (The contradictions abound.)

The article from *The Sydney Morning Herald* in the opening passages described student writing as a "confusing jumble," with "predominantly simple vocabulary" and a lack of "correct paragraphing."[4] These claims were based on results from Australia's forty-minute NAPLAN writing exam. Punctuation was the most specific detail noted: The article reported that punctuation scores declined from 80 to 62 percent between 2011 and 2020.

5.2.4 Contemporary Exam Tasks and Criteria Can Be Confusing

Like their nineteenth-century forerunners, today's exams often make more sense inside exam culture than outside of it. We'll look at the writing tasks and criteria of a recent Cambridge A-levels exam by way of illustration.

Each year, the first writing section on the A-level English Language exam includes two timed tasks, in which students (1) read and comment on the "style and language" of a passage, and (2) write a personalized text related to the first passage. In 2016, for example, students read a speech by Australian prime minister Julia Gillard about a colleague's sexism. The first task asked students to analyze the style of the speech, and the second task asked them to write a diary entry as though they were Gillard.

Both tasks show the conundrum of exam writing, because they are more suited to exam conditions than real-world writing. The first task requires focusing on the language of the speech rather than both ideas and language. The second task expects students to write something they never otherwise write – someone else's diary entry. This seems relevant context for what examiners viewed as common mistakes.

For the Cambridge evaluators, common mistakes in the first (analysis) task included:

- Focusing on the speech topic rather than the speech language ("responses listed the success and justice of the accusations without examining the rhetorical devices employed")
- Word choice ("awkward" and "uneven" expression)

In the second (diary) task, common mistakes included:

- Failure to "reflect a more personal mode of expression"
- Lack of "careful checking for accurate expression"

In these examples, we see continued reinforcement for this myth and myth 4, because the tasks are designed according to exam culture. Along similar lines, even if one could write with "even expression" in a timed exam without time for revision, criteria like "awkward" and "uneven expression" are decidedly vague. Another recent example of elusive criteria appears in the notoriously-vague *sophistication point* in the US Advanced Placement (AP) English exam. When I worked with the College Board on cut-off scores for this exam in 2021, even the most experienced evaluators felt this criterion was a "know it when you see it" category.[5]

5.3 The Myth Emerges

With standardized exam scores in mass media coverage, this myth emerged. It reinforces several earlier themes, including *correct writing* usage preferences, vague test criteria, and emphasis on test results instead of test details.

5.4 Consequences of the Myth

5.4.1 We Limit Media Messages about Writing

An overall consequence of this myth is that we limit media messages about writing. Not only do many media messages adopt the narrow mold for *correct writing* from myth 1, they reinforce trust in tests and 2-D ideas about writing. Table 5.1 notes this myth's more specific consequences, including several that scale up exam culture.

Table 5.1 Consequences of myth 5

Once we believe	... Test results define writing failure
Most students can't write, then...	... We accept vague criteria
	... We don't question whether tests are the problem
	... Writing means control versus practice
	... Limited standards are excellent standards, and failure is individual
	... We expect cycles of test results and alarm

5.4.2 Test Results Define Writing Failure

Prior myths made it commonplace to equate *correct writing* with *intelligence* and character. This myth makes it commonplace to write about test results without providing details about the tests themselves.

In turn, test results are cited as evidence that most students can't write, whether or not tests are well understood. Writing tasks can change over time, for instance, but coverage will report the results, not the changes. We need only accept test results – not understand them. Even if it means rewarding only "safe, dull essays without mistakes," as educational historian John Brereton put it, test results decide whether students can write.

5.4.3 We Accept Vague Criteria

This myth solidifies a tradition of accepting test-based criteria – which drive the test's design, scoring, and use of results – even when those criteria are confusing. Early examiners wanted students to write with "elegance" but "avoid fine phrases," and to avoid "all fine writing," but also avoid "general uniformity of expression." In an especially confusing example, eleven-plus exam founder Cyril Burt had the following expectations for student writing:

The one rule is to be "infinitely various"; to condense, to expand; to blurt, and then to amplify; to balance lengthy statements with a series of brief; and to set off the staccato emphasis of the short, sharp phrase against the complicated harmony, long-drawn and subtly suspended, of the periodic paragraph; to be ever altering, as it were, the dimensions of the block, yet still to preserve the effect of a neat and solid structure.

In the myth that most students cannot write, it is the students who are failing, not the expectations imposed on them. This consequence, in short, means test-trust and test-ignorance.

5.4.4 We Don't Question Whether Tests Are the Problem

Coverage claiming that most students can't write is more likely to blame students – or technology, or teachers – than to blame tests and evaluation criteria. As we've seen, this was true even before standardized exams: Examiners of the Cambridge 1858 exam lamented that "even when accurate," the students did not demonstrate "questionings or remarks of their own"; yet the exam task did not ask students to offer their own thinking. It asked students to describe historical details.

More recently, in response to standardized test scores, Australian officials called for more teaching of grammar in schools to improve low NAPLAN scores. Education professors responded with questions, arguing that officials "did not clarify what they saw as the problem or exactly how to resolve it."[6] This myth makes it hard to question whether tests are the problem, and we end up with claims about what students can and cannot do, without requisite interrogation of tests.

5.4.5 Writing Means *Control* versus Practice

A specific theme in large-scale tests and coverage is the theme of *control*, rather than experience or practice. Students who perform poorly on a writing exam lack control of *correct writing*, rather than practice at the writing on the exam. Table 5.2 illustrates a selection of significant examinations and the criteria upon which they are based. These criteria are grouped by their implications: that correct writing is universal; that correctness is superior to other writing considerations; and that context is important to writing.

The UK AS- and A-level English Language specifications, for instance, allude to "control" and "accurate expression," as part of achieving a "formal tone." For high marks, students are to "guide the reader structurally and linguistically, using controlled, accurate expression" and to "organise and sequence topics, using controlled, accurate expression." By contrast, low marks are associated with "occasional lapses in control."[7] From these, we can gather that a "formal tone" is the most *correct, accurate, controlled* kind of written English, the only kind with organized topics.

The GCSE English Language exam criteria specify the dialect of standardized English, associating the highest marks with writing that "Uses Standard English consistently and appropriately with secure control of complex grammatical structures."[8] Some GCSE criteria emphasize variation – e.g. variation in sentence types and vocabulary – but not variation from standardized English.

Australia's timed Tertiary Online Writing Assessment (TOWA) has two sets of criteria, "thought and ideas" and "language: structure and expression."

The "language" criteria are described as "effectiveness of structure and organization, clarity of expression, control of language conventions."[9] If these are understood according to writing myths, then *effectiveness, clarity,* and *control* specifically refer to *correct writing* usage preferences.

The American Association of Colleges and Universities has a written communication rubric referenced widely within and outside of the US. The rubric includes the category "control of syntax and mechanics," which implies errors and usage are always the same: The "capstone," or highest-scoring criteria (a score of 4) reads "Uses graceful language that skillfully communicates meaning to readers with clarity and fluency, and is virtually error-free."[10] In this rubric, then, *graceful language, clarity,* and *error* appear to be *controlled,* as well as self-evident and context-free.[11]

A final example, from the US Framework for Success in Postsecondary Writing, implies that correctness depends on context. The framework outcome for "knowledge of conventions" is described as knowledge of "the formal and informal guidelines that define what is considered to be correct and appropriate, or incorrect and inappropriate, in a piece of writing."[12]

These example guidelines fall into three types noted in Table 5.2: those implying that correct writing is always the same, those implying that *correct writing* is best regardless of context, and those implying that context matters. The most common guidelines imply that correct writing is always the same.

Table 5.2 Writing exam criteria

Implies correct writing is always the same		
Country	Source	Example terms associated with high marks
UK	AS and A-level English Language specifications	*guides the reader using controlled, accurate expression*
US	American Association of Colleges and Universities	*graceful language that skillfully communicates meaning to readers with clarity and fluency, and is virtually error-free*
Australia	Tertiary Online Writing Assessment (TOWA)	*effectiveness of structure and organization, clarity of expression, control of language conventions*

Implies *correct writing* is best		
Country	Source	Example terms associated with high marks
UK	GSCE English Language exam criteria	*uses Standard English consistently and appropriately with secure control of complex grammatical structures*

Implies context matters		
US	Framework for Success in Postsecondary Writing	*knowledge of the formal and informal guidelines that define what is considered to be correct and appropriate*

In a testament to language regulation mode, most of the examples emphasize *control* rather than practice. The most rewarded writers, the criteria suggest, regulate themselves according to *correct writing*. Other writing and writers are out of control and require more regulation.

5.4.6 Limited Standards Are Excellent Standards, and Failure Is Individual

When we accept the ideal sameness promoted by tests in myth 4, we downplay communal individual learning practices. In this myth, we get more of the same: If most students cannot write, then they are failing to meet excellent standards – not, instead, that the standards are limited or otherwise amiss. Accordingly, failure on standardized tests is due to an individual's lack of ability, while selective criteria are rigorous criteria. These values easily fuel competitive academic behavior, which connects *correct writing* to power in favor of certain kinds of language and language users.

Resistance to tests can in turn be framed as a resistance to high standards, as it was in a 1977 *Harpers* article by John Silber, president of the University of Boston at the time. Titled "The Need for Elite Education," the article called for what Silber called a "restoration of excellence" including the teaching of standardized English. Three earlier myths, and this one, all appear in Silber's article:

People are born with varying degrees of intelligence and talent ... Lowered expectations are a threat to all our students, since their ability to develop is very largely dependent upon the goals we establish for them.

The passage evokes myths about *correct writing*, innate *intelligence*, and school regulation of writing. It also suggests that Silber's narrow expectations are high expectations.

When we believe that narrow standards are high standards, college selectivity means high admissions standards, rather than specific or limited admissions standards. As such, low college acceptance rates are associated with prestige, even as research shows that selective college admissions practices favor certain kinds of students.

5.4.7 We Expect Cycles of Test Results and Alarm

The headlines we have seen so far contribute to a cycle of poorly understood tests and easily understood complaints. From myth 1, we have seen the public appetite for dire and authoritative claims about *correct writing,* and here we see it extend to claims about most student writing.

Even with scant or selective evidence, these claims appear to be terribly appealing. The aptly titled article "Why Johnny Can Never, Ever Read" by literacy researcher Bronwyn Williams puts it this way: "Fashion trends and politicians come and go, but one thing that never seems to go out of style is a good old-fashioned literacy crisis."

5.5 Closer to the Truth

5.5.1 Half of Harvard's Students Didn't Fail

We'll first get closer to the truth by correcting misinformation. Hill's oft-referenced account of Harvard's first English exam was not accurate. Half the students did not fail; around a quarter of them did. A follow up study by John Brereton showed that this passing rate was comparable to or better than those in Mathematics, Geography, Latin, and Greek. Thus Hill's account not only exaggerated English exam failure rates, but also neglected comparisons to other exams. (The Dean's report documenting the accurate passing rates does echo Hill's reasons for failure, as "spelling, punctuation, or both.")

5.5.2 Errors Are Not Increasing

Another claim to dispel is that errors are increasing. Even if we stand by a limited definition of *correct writing*, the empirical case is that errors change more than they increase. A study of US college writing across the twentieth century found that specific formal errors changed – as did teacher's interest in particular errors – but overall error frequency did not. More specifically, spelling and capitalization were the most frequent errors in 1917. By 1986, the *most frequent error* went to "no comma after introductory element."

Likewise, the claims in the famous article "Why Johnny Can't Write" were based on declining NAEP scores between 1969 and 1974, yet a series of NAEP reports revealed that writing, like reading, remained roughly stable in that period and after. Differences were small and could be explained by greater access by a wider population to the test. Later, a 2008 report commissioned by the US National Assessment Governing Board showed literacy "constancy" which "contradicted assertions about a major decline."

5.5.3 Tasks Change

In several ways, late secondary and early college writing exams today are similar to those 100 years ago. They are overwhelmingly timed, lasting from thirty minutes to a few hours. Many continue to emphasize argumentative essays, and many still emphasize literature.

But writing exams have also changed. Many exams today ask students to write on a general topic, rather than on literature. For US college writing placement, for instance, you might have one hour to "Write an essay for a classroom instructor in which you take a position on whether participation in organized school athletics should be required." For a Cambridge Certificate in Advanced English, you might have an hour and a half to write about whether museums, sports centers, or public gardens should receive money from local authorities. And for Australia's Written English section of the STAT, you might have an hour to write one essay on education and one on friendship ("Romances come and go, but it is friendship that remains."). Different writing tasks mean different writing, so it matters that writing exams change over time. Scores from different tasks cannot provide precise comparisons. Reports and headlines that compare scores over time without explaining changes depend on public trust in tests without test details.

For instance, we saw earlier that NAPLAN punctuation scores were used as evidence that university students couldn't write. The news reported that punctuation scores had declined from 80 percent to 62 percent between 2011 to 2020. What is not mentioned in the article is that within that time, the NAPLAN changed. In 2018, the test shifted from paper to online. Between 2011 and 2018, the test sometimes required narrative writing and sometimes required persuasive writing. Both are significant changes, in test conditions and writing tasks.

Indeed, based on a cautionary tale from US exams, the NAPLAN test change could significantly change student scores. Between 2011 and 2017, the US National Assessment of Educational Progress (NAEP) Grade 8 writing exam changed from laptops with one kind of software to tablet devices with a different software. The 2017 scores showed a pattern of lower performance, and so the National Center for Education Statistics conducted a comparability study. Ultimately, researchers were unable to determine whether the score differences were based on the device or based on students' writing abilities, so they could not tell if the test conditions disadvantaged students or not.[13]

5.5.4 Criteria Change

If you ask the question, "When was it that most students *could* write?," the answer appears to be: Never. Complaints about students writing are as old as assessments of student writing, so we don't have evidence of an earlier, better version of writing. This is true even as some expectations for *correct writing* have changed over the past century.

For instance, a student could disappoint Harvard's early composition examiners for using "second-rate diction," such as "the confusion of *shall* and *will*." Today, the distinction between *shall* and *will* matters little, and *shall* is rarely used (in point of fact, *shall* is now eclipsed by the phrasal verb *have to* in American and British English corpora, so Briggs must be turning over in his grave).

In another example, while "broad claims" were cited as a "serious fault" in early Harvard entrance exams, such claims are very common in incoming college writing today. They appear in exemplary writing and are common in responses to open-ended exam questions.[14] Similarly, a so-called error noted in "Why Johnny Can't Write" was used widely even when the article was published. The article closed with a "Writer's Guide: What Not to Do" focused on *correct writing* usage preferences. In it, students were advised to avoid "faulty agreement of noun and pronoun," with the following *incorrect* example: *Everyone should check their coat before going into the dance.* This use of plural *their* with singular *everyone* is grammatically possible and meaningful in English, and it is common across the writing continuum. Already in 1975, it was far more common than *everyone* used with *his or her* in books written in English. This trend is even more true today. Indeed, since 2010, *everyone* used with *their* has continued to increase, while *everyone* used with *his or her* has been declining since 2010.[15]

We also saw that while organization of ideas was not highlighted in nineteenth-century reports, it is emphasized in twentieth- and twenty-first-century coverage. In a final example, the Harvard graders' concern that a student failed to use "common expressions" in 1892 seems reversed in the 2020 *Sydney Morning Herald* complaint that university students use "colloquialisms."

In all of these cases, even as criteria change, the idea that *students can't write* persists, overshadowing changing expectations, and reinforcing test trust over test details.

5.5.5 Limited Does not Mean Excellent, and Standardized Does not Mean Complex

Closer to the truth is that limited criteria are not inherently excellent criteria. They aren't inherently bad criteria, either. They are narrow – limited to particular kinds of writing and writing expectations. There can be good reasons to narrow criteria according to what writing needs to do in a particular context. But limited does not make something *correct*, and student ability goes far beyond the domains and parameters conventionally privileged in standardized tests and other college selection metrics.

Along similar lines, standardized writing is not inherently complex writing. GCSE and other criteria imply that "writing with control of Standard English" is the same as writing with "complex grammatical structures." As the continuum shows, *correct writing* includes patterns, including dense noun phrases, just as more informal and interpersonal writing includes patterns, including shorter nouns and more verbs. That makes *correct writing* more grammatically compressed, but not necessarily more grammatically complex, than other writing on the continuum, a point documented in detail by applied linguists Douglas Biber and Bethany Gray.

A recent report from the US National Association for College Admission Counseling (NACAC) and the National Association of Student Financial Aid Administrators (NASFAA) states that beliefs about *selectivity* are harmful and pervasive, and college admissions selectivity has to date reinforced systemic racial and socioeconomic inequity. Closer to the truth is that selectivity remains elusive and ill-defined. In many cases, selectivity excludes even highly qualified students through what it includes and excludes. Selective admissions tend to emphasize uniform test scores, for instance, and we have seen the historic problems of such scores since IQ testing – sometimes operating as intentional barriers, and always operating as narrow measures.

5.5.6 Standardized Exam Writing Is on a Continuum

Closer to the truth is that like all writing, standardized exam writing is on a continuum. Student performance depends in large part on the exam writing task. Different exam tasks mean different writing, and most exams concern a very narrow part of the continuum.

To add to the writing continuum in this chapter, we will look at writing from two contemporary writing exams used for college admissions and hiring decisions: the UK Advanced-levels (A-levels) diary task we saw above,[16] and a New Zealand International English Language Testing System task that asks for an explanation based on a graph or other diagram.[17] In Table 5.3, we will specifically look at to two responses considered exemplary by test examiners.

Like all writing on the continuum, the two samples show cohesion, connection, focus, stance, and usage. But as responses to very different writing tasks, the linguistic patterns for fulfilling these purposes are different.

Table 5.3 Exam writing continuum

Texting   Published

                    Social   Email   Secondary   College

English Exam Writing Continuum Patterns

                        Informal   Formal
                      Interpersonal   ◄──────────►   Informational
                        Personal   Impersonal

Continuum Purposes	**Diary writing in UK A-levels exam** High candidate response to timed exam writing task	**Summary of graphs in New Zealand IELTS** Exemplar response to timed exam writing task
Cohesion	• **Movement from reaction to decision** Single paragraph, moves from reaction to a conclusion about what to do	• **Hourglass cohesion** Explicit paragraphs and cohesive words, moves from overall topic and statement to specific examples
Connection	• **Interpersonal connection** 2nd person pronouns, direct address 1st person pronouns and reactions	• **Informational connection** Reader not addressed
Focus	• **Interpersonal subjects** Sentence subjects are simple Some passive verbs	• **Informational subjects** Sentence subjects are noun phrases focused on graphs Some passive verbs
Stance	• **Personalized stance** Certain stance, boosters, generalization Adjectives, adverbs in strong evaluations (*absolutely baffling*)	• **Impersonal stance** Boosters and hedges (*only one fifth, quite similar*) focus on information No generalizations
Usage	• **Some informal conventions, some *correct writing* conventions and usage preferences**	• ***Correct writing* conventions and usage preferences**
Opening sentence	It is absolutely baffling to consider just how shameless some men can be. ...	The four pie charts compare the electricity generated between Germany and France during 2009, and it is measured in billions kWh. ...

The diary task writing leans more toward the informal, interpersonal, personal end of the continuum, while the summary task lands more at the formal, informational, impersonal end of secondary and college writing.

Below the examples appear in full and are annotated. Marginal notes and annotations include transitional words **in bold**, connection markers [in brackets], *hedges* in italics, ***boosters*** and ***generalizations*** italicized and bolded, and passive verbs [[in double brackets]].

5.5.6.1 Exemplary A-levels Diary Entry

It is ***absolutely baffling*** to consider *just how shameless* some men can be.

> **Certain stance and hourglass cohesion:**
> Writer opens with a general and boosted statement

To go about [your] way being ***a living insult*** to the rights of women, ***blatantly*** labelling them as less of people and ***suddenly*** become pure and innocent one morning and rebuke a smaller version of [yourself] for being just like [you].

> **Certain and interpersonal stance:**
> The writer moves to more specific details (about what is "shameless"), using the second person and several boosters and attitude markers to show a strong reaction.
> This detail appears in a long infinitive phrase rather than a "complete sentence" with subject and verb in an independent clause

The evidence of what that ***rogue*** Abbott had to say to ***vilify*** women, even [myself], the "witch" is ***considerable***.

> **Personal, certain stance:**
> The writer moves to mention evidence, including using the first person and mentioning Abbott called her a "witch," with continued use of boosters and attitude markers

How *anyone* can overlook all this and *even* entertain the thought of dismissing Slipper, however sexist he is, is *beyond me*. I *will not stand for* such disrespect. Abbot [has been tolerated] for long enough. I *must* abase him and leave him in his place.

> **Generalized, personal stance:**
> The writer closes by generalizing and personalizing a response to the evidence and a call to personal action

5.5.6.2 Exemplary IELTS Graph Summary

The four pie charts compare the electricity generated between Germany and France during 2009, and it is measured in billions kWh. **Overall**, it [can be seen] that conventional thermal was the main source of electricity **in Germany, whereas** nuclear was the main source **in France**.

> **Informational focus and hourglass cohesion:**
> The writer opens with overall informational statements focused on the charts and electricity that will be summarized. The transitional word "overall" signals explicitly that these are general opening statements

The bulk of electricity in Germany, whose total output was 560 billion kWh, came from conventional thermal, at 59.6 percent. **In France**, the total output was lower, at 510 billion kWh, and **in contrast to** Germany, conventional thermal accounted for just 10.3 percent, with most electricity coming from nuclear power (76 percent). **In Germany**, the proportion of nuclear power generated electricity was *only* one fifth of the total.

> **Informational, impersonal stance:**
> The writer moves to more specific details, focused on the electricity sources and leading the reader with cohesive phrases that indicate the movement from discussing France to Germany

Moving on to renewables, this accounted for *quite* similar proportions for both countries, ranging from around 14 percent to 17 percent of the total electricity generated. **In detail, in Germany**, *most of*

> **Explicit cohesion, informational focus, balanced to certain stance:**

the renewables consisted of wind and biomass, totaling around 75 percent, which was *far higher* than for hydroelectric (17.7 percent) and solar (6.1 percent). The situation was *very* different **in France**, where hydroelectric made up 80.5 percent of renewable electricity, with biomass, wind and solar making up the remaining 20 percent. Neither country used geothermal energy.

> The writer signals that they will move on to discuss renewables, with boosted and hedged ("most of") statements about quantity and proportions. The writing continues to have an informational focus, offering specific details about renewables. In these final sentences, the writer uses boosted statements and explicit transitions, which emphasize the contrast between energy in Germany and France

These continuum examples help illustrate different tasks and different writing. The A-levels task and response is more interpersonal and personal, while the IELTS task and response is more informational and impersonal. These patterns illustrate what is closer to the truth: Tests only test what is on the tests, and the claim that *most students can't write* is highly dependent on how *writing* and *can't write* are conceived by tests. Test results offer information about how students write according to the conditions, tasks, and criteria of that test.

5.5.7 Most Students Write

Closer to the truth is that most students write, whether or not their test scores relate to the broad range of writing they do. Simultaneously, many headlines consider *correct writing* patterns to be the reference patterns for discussing student writing.

Writing exams give us some information, but they are not comprehensive ways to tell if students can write. Still, it is hard to escape the persistent myth that *most students can't write*, which disposes people to believe there is a problem whether or not they understand how the problem is being tested. It can even mean – as in the case of the book *Academically Adrift* – that in the presence of data that affirms student writing, people focus on the bleaker, more attention-grabbing conclusion that students can't write.

It seems fair to assume that most students today write with varying proficiency, depending on what they are writing and in what circumstances. But unless we explore a range of writing, we will not know if most students can write. Exploring diverse writing patterns can give us more insight than hand-wringing and regulating has done.

But more hand-wringing, alas, is still to come. Like this one, our next myth is also bolstered by standardized tests.

CHAPTER SIX

Myth 6 You Can't Write if You Didn't Write Well in High School

Or, Writing Should Be Mastered in Secondary School

6.1 Pick a Century

See if you can identify which of the following comes from the twentieth century, and which from the twenty-first.

1. Students continue to arrive on college campuses needing remediation in basic writing skills.
2. What's happening in the United States is that the universities have, in effect, given up on the [secondary] schools.
3. Many high school teachers have simply stopped correcting poor grammar and sloppy construction.

If you guessed a reverse order, you are correct. The first passage appeared in *The New York Times* in 2017, while passage two, also from the twenty-first century, appeared in Australia's *The Age* in 2007. Passage three appeared in 1975 in the famous *Newsweek* article you read about in myth 5.

Across fifty years, the passages repeat a twofold lament: Student writers are showing up to college unprepared, and secondary schooling is to blame. If secondary schools did their job, college students would not need any help with *correct writing* in college. Writing instruction, it follows, is a burden that colleges should not have to bear.

In these complaints, we can see earlier myths at work. The first five myths give us a limited version of *correct writing*, regulated by schools and tests, which most students can't do. This myth further suggests that secondary schools are to blame. If only secondary teachers would teach *correct writing*, so this myth goes, it would be mastered before students go to college.

One of two presumptions underpins this myth. Either secondary and postsecondary writing are sufficiently **similar** that students who learn secondary writing will meet college requirements easily. Or, if secondary and college writing are **different**, then *intelligent writers* will easily adapt to meet new college demands after secondary writing. Either way, the message is: Writing development is linear and finite, basically intact by students' late teens.

In a way, *writing should be mastered in secondary* school is not a separate myth, but a different, mythical way that previous details come together. We've seen much of this myth's origin story already, in other words, because we've seen how written English exams, designed and interpreted by university educators, shaped early ideas about secondary writing. We also know from earlier myths that different tasks lead to different writing choices, so we know we have to consider typical secondary and college writing tasks to consider this myth. We will bring these threads together to fill out this myth's context.

6.2 Context for the Myth

6.2.1 Early university educators and tests define secondary writing ability

Several myths so far show how university leaders and tests influenced early ideas about secondary learning. Horace Mann's tests in the 1840s and 50s suggested secondary student ability should be measured through individual, timed writing and *correct writing* errors, then used in public rankings and college admissions. England's local examinations in the 1850s meant that university educators defined secondary student writing achievement, even for those students not pursuing university education. Harvard examiners, beginning in the 1870s, designed written English exams and wrote about the results in persuasive reports. Those Harvard reports fueled the establishment of mandatory general English composition courses designed to remediate secondary writing, first at Harvard and later at hundreds of other institutions.

Both England's local examination reports and the Harvard reports directly addressed secondary student writing. Regarding the first local examinations in 1858, Cambridge examiners remarked that "little attempt had been made by [secondary] instructors to excite the interest of their pupils." The examiners' solution, as we saw in myth 4, included "regularly recognised examinations." In the Harvard examiner report of 1892, B. S. Hurlbut expressed alarm at "the number of persons who are sent out annually from our high schools unable to express their thoughts with a fair degree of clearness, unable to write passably good English," which led him to "but one conclusion…: there is something fundamentally wrong in the method of teaching English in the secondary schools." In 1896, Harvard's three earliest English examiners (Hill, Briggs, and Hurlbut) underscored their conclusion, also the conclusion of the

Committee of the Board of Overseers, "that the Secondary Schools need to pay more attention to English."

Reports like these communicated several assumptions at a time when education and written English literacy were expanding, and before the time that secondary examinations became standardized in the twentieth century. These assumptions overlap and follow from one another (picture a Russian assumption doll), but we can identify them one at a time. One assumption was that university educators knew what it meant for secondary students "to write passably good English," and another was that timed, externally-designed tests could measure it. A third assumption was that the end of secondary school was a definitive time for measuring said English.

We've seen these assumptions reflected in exams in earlier myths: any college entrance exam task, on Thucydides, Mr. Darcy's Courtship, or otherwise, implies that a timed writing task at the end of secondary learning can represent the student's past secondary writing, and the student's future writing ability. Exam tasks like these, particularly with high stakes such as secondary graduation or college admission, also make it so that brief writing tasks are essential for secondary student success. We will see related ideas about writing tasks and exams persist in this myth's contemporary context, where we turn next.

6.2.2 Secondary Writing Tasks Tend to Be Brief, Persuasive, and Rigidly Organized

6.2.2.1 Secondary Writing Is Brief

Educational research across the US, UK, and Australia shows that many secondary students write brief responses in school. Genrally, they do not regularly write more than a paragraph at a time or regularly practice substantial analysis or interpretation.

Secondary English courses sometimes serve as the exception, offering more extended writing and instruction than other courses, though this trend places pressure on secondary English teachers and can limit writing instruction across the curriculum. Secondary students report that they write most in English classes, even though they would benefit from writing guidance across all of their courses.

6.2.2.2 Secondary Writing Includes Few Genres

When they write more than a few sentences, secondary students often write in a handful of genres only. In English courses, brief tasks include timed, on-demand writing, especially in the past decade, while in other subjects, brief writing tends to appear in worksheets or one-sentence questions. Particularly in standardized writing exam tasks like those in myth 4, secondary students tend to write timed argumentative, analysis, or narrative essays (sometimes emphasizing literature) more often than summaries, case studies, or reports. We'll look at a few contemporary examples.

For the UK GCSE, two recent tasks required argumentative writing: Students wrote a persuasive letter to a newspaper about their view of whether the UK drinking age should be increased to 21, and students wrote a "lively review" of a film, TV programme, or book. Less overtly persuasive tasks include the Cambridge A Levels English examples in myths 4 and 5 (analyzing a speech, and writing a diary entry).[1] Those tasks required reading argumentative writing but responding with analysis and narrative, which are less argumentative – and further right on the continuum – than open letters.

In the US, standardized exams regularly emphasize persuasive arguments. For the ACT in 2018, students needed to write "a unified, coherent essay about the increasing presence of intelligent machines" and were told to "clearly state your own perspective on the issue and analyze the relationship between your perspective and at least one other perspective." Similarly, the 2008 California High School Proficiency Examination (CAHSPE) included this task: "Some people believe that high school classes should not begin before 9:00 a.m. Do you agree or disagree? Write an essay clearly explaining your opinion." A similar example, the 2016 Common Core State Standards (CCSS) Argument/Opinion task, asked students to write an essay in response to the question, "Should your school participate in the national 'Shut Down Your Screen Week'?". Although the CCSS includes both "persuasive writing" and "informative/explanatory writing," both emphasize the writer's argument in the task and the evaluation criteria.

Australia's STAT tasks, as we saw in myth 4, also emphasize persuasive argumentative essays;, for instance, about a public issue (the role of education) or personal sense (romance versus friendship). Finally, for earlier secondary students, Australia's NAPLAN exams include persuasive tasks, such as "Some people think the country is the best place to live. Others think it is better to live in a city. What do you think? ... Write to convince a reader of your opinions."[2] As we saw in myth 5, there can be good reasons to narrow criteria according to what writing needs to do in a particular context. Along these lines, there can be good reason to limit genres. But, as we also saw in myth 5, limited does not make something correct, and student practice with different genres goes beyond the domains and parameters of standardized tests.

6.2.2.3 Secondary Writing Follows Template Organization

Secondary students are often introduced to template formulas to organize their writing. For example, a template in the UK is "PEEL," or point, evidence, evaluation, link. A common template in the US is the five-paragraph essay, with an introductory paragraph ending in a thesis, three main idea paragraphs addressing one example each, and a concluding paragraph that restates the thesis. These templates are often used in standardized exam preparation, because they can be used quickly in timed essay writing.

6.2.3 Exams Impact Secondary Teaching Conditions

The long reach of standardized exams extends beyond writing tasks and templates, to secondary curricula and teaching as well. Frustrated teachers report that teaching is devalued because of "heightened pressure to perform on standardized testing" and that officials have placed more importance on data and results than on students' needs and learning.[3] Teachers face pressure to make time for exam practice and to tailor their teaching to templates used in standardized writing exams.

Indeed, even secondary teachers who love their students are often driven away from the profession by standardized tests. In the UK and Australia, around 30 percent of schoolteachers leave within five years.[4] In the US, more than 50 percent of teachers quit teaching before retirement.[5] Meanwhile, education jurisdictions such as Finland, which place less emphasis on standardized tests, report teacher attrition rates below 5 percent.

In a negative cycle, standardized tests and teacher attrition fuel one another. Standardized tests and the use of test results in top-down school policies are common reasons that secondary teachers leave teaching. In turn, this makes working conditions worse, because high teacher dropout and low student achievement often fuel one another.

6.2.4 Secondary and Postsecondary Writing Are Different

New college students encounter several important differences between secondary and postsecondary writing. While secondary writing often emphasizes timed and argumentative essays, postsecondary writing often requires sustained inquiry and substantial revision over days or weeks. Rather than overt arguments, postsecondary writing is usually expected to be open-minded, written for a reader looking for information rather than opinions. And rather than only persuasive or narrative essays, postsecondary writing regularly requires explanatory genres such as reports and research reviews. Indeed, the farther along they are in college, the less likely students are to write argumentative essays.

This brings us, again, to the fact that different tasks mean different writing. Secondary and postsecondary tasks are different, so their writing patterns are different. Secondary writing, often in response to persuasive argumentative tasks, includes significantly more boosted, generalized, interpersonal language patterns. Postsecondary writing, often in response to explanatory tasks, includes more hedged, informational language patterns. Developmental maturity may contribute to more hedges and fewer generalizations in college writing, since postsecondary students have more education and life experiences than secondary students. Still, the differences go far beyond maturity, as evidenced by divergent patterns in different writing tasks even at the same level. Secondary writing is different enough from postsecondary writing that it is no simple feat to transition between the two, even as this myth suggests otherwise.

6.3 The Myth Emerges

Bolstered by earlier myths, and without clear attention to differences between secondary and postsecondary writing, this myth emerges. With it comes a limited view of *writing development*.

6.4 Consequences of the Myth

6.4.1 We Limit *Writing Development*

The myth that writing should be mastered in secondary school suggests that writing development is linear and finite. Visualized in Figure 6.1, this view of *writing development* implies a line with an end point at the end of secondary school, as though writing is learned once and for all by then (see Figure 6.1).

This larger consequence entails more specific consequences listed in Table 6.1.

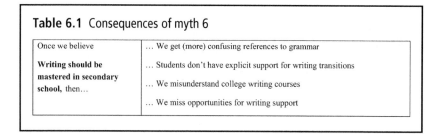

Table 6.1 Consequences of myth 6

Once we believe	... We get (more) confusing references to grammar
Writing should be mastered in secondary school, then...	... Students don't have explicit support for writing transitions
	... We misunderstand college writing courses
	... We miss opportunities for writing support

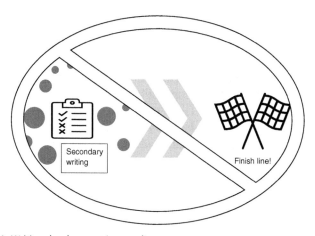

Figure 6.1 Writing development is not a line

6.4.2 We Get (More) Confusing References to Grammar

As in earlier myths, several headlines related to this myth use terms such as *spelling, grammar,* and *writing* interchangeably. Some statements specifically blame secondary teachers for students' spelling, punctuation, and capitalization, but they refer to these choices as *grammar* or *writing*. Rarely are these terms explained or separated.

For instance, spelling is a headline problem in the 2007 news article noted in the opening passages. Titled "Can't write can't spell...," the article argues that Australian students and teachers "fail to grasp the English language." This leads to "the big question," the article says, which is really a series of questions:

[W]ho is ultimately responsible for those teachers and students who fail to grasp English language somewhere along the way? Is it the education system for not teaching the teachers; the teachers' approach to teaching; an evolving English curriculum that never quite attains perfection; students' own lack of aptitude; or their need for tailored teaching?

The article speculates that "there has been less emphasis placed on grammar and language structure over the past 10, 15 years in teacher training."[6] The article does not aim to explain or illustrate what is missing, or what *grasping English language* means. It does not, for instance, offer examples for "grammar, punctuation, and spelling," beyond stating they are related to the ability "to write sentences."

In another example, *Maclean's* coverage of Canadian university language entrance exams is summarized in a 2010 article titled "University students can't spell," with the subheading "Profs say high schools aren't teaching grammar." Yet the "writing horrors being handed in" appear to be related to conventions, especially spelling, rather than grammar: "emoticons, happy faces, sad faces, cuz [rather than because]" as well as *a lot* written as one word and *definitely* spelled with an *a* (defanitely).[7] Since emoticons are perceptually salient but proportionally rare, we might well wonder how often these errors are taking place. But we'll get to that in myth 8.

In one more example, "Cult of Pedagogy" blog author Jennifer Gonzalez titles a 2017 post "How to Deal with Student Grammar Errors" and notes that in using the term *grammar*, she is "broadly referring to all the conventions that make writing correct: spelling, punctuation, usage, capitalization, and so on."[8] As we've seen in other myth chapters, this use of *grammar* to refer to conventions or usage preferences – rather than what is grammatically possible and meaningful in English – is common. In this myth, sources furthermore imply that secondary students can learn *grammar* once and for all, before college courses.

6.4.3 Students Don't Have Explicit Support for Writing Transitions

Because different tasks require different writing, it is not easy to transition from one task to another. It is, specifically, difficult to transition between secondary and college writing, each of which entails its own contexts and tasks. Students who have practiced argumentative secondary essays, for instance, will not automatically adapt (or disregard) relevant writing patterns in college writing. Indeed, that is why linguists who study academic writing variation say that students should write a range of writing assignments, not just argumentative essays, in high school and early college.

This myth makes the transition between secondary and postsecondary writing harder, because it assumes secondary students should be able to move from one part of the continuum to another without support. The myth glasses justify paying little explicit attention to similarities and differences between secondary and college writing.

Without attention to similarities and differences between secondary and college writing, secondary writing templates can inhibit rather than help students. Templates such as the five-paragraph essay, for instance, are valued in exam culture because they are efficient to evaluate. They may also provide useful scaffolding and help reduce anxiety for secondary students when they are new to writing multi-paragraph essays. But unless those students explore what makes cohesion in a five-paragraph essay different than cohesion in a college paper, the template can thwart rather than help them when they get to college.

6.4.4 We Misunderstand College Writing Courses

This myth makes us misperceive college writing as remediation, instead of ongoing writing development. If we believe that writing can be mastered in secondary courses, we can believe college writing courses are catch-up classes, or classes for only some students, rather than classes that help all students transition to new writing practices.

College composition courses are often misperceived along these lines. As we saw in this myth's context, composition courses are especially prevalent in the US, where they are required for most college students based on the influence of Harvard's late nineteenth century composition exams and courses.

The use of secondary courses and standardized exams to *exempt* students from college composition courses similarly suggests secondary writing can stand in for postsecondary writing. One example is the common practice of using secondary advanced placement (AP) English exam results in this way. Another example is the use of standardized exams taken before college, such as the SAT or Accuplacer, to exempt students from college writing courses.[9]

Assigning English for Academic Purposes (EAP) courses only to non-native English writers reinforces these misconceptions. EAP writing courses provide explicit support in postsecondary writing. But they are commonly required only for international or additional-language students. This practice sustains the false idea that native English students do not need explicit writing instruction as they take on new postsecondary tasks.

6.4.5 We Miss Opportunities for Writing Support

When we view writing as linear and finite, we make struggles with post-secondary writing the fault of students and their prior schooling. We miss the point that postsecondary writing tasks are new for new college students, and we miss opportunities to draw explicit attention to similarities and differences between one part of the writing continuum and another. We miss the possibility of EAP or other explicit writing instruction for all kinds of students. Likewise, in cases where some students "test out" of college writing courses, we miss chances for more writing practice and feedback as students encounter new writing tasks.

The related myth that writing should be developed in English courses places undue pressure on English departments and instructors. It often overlooks the fact that disciplinary training in literature is not the same as training in English language. In turn, we miss opportunities to raise students' conscious awareness of how writers in different disciplines use language similarly and differently.

6.5 Closer to the Truth

6.5.1 Spelling Memorization Is Different from Writing Development

To get closer to the truth, we can first circle back to spelling, in this case, secondary spelling. As we saw in myth 1, conventional English spelling is an awesome mess dating back to the fifteenth century, and it requires memorization and practice. Memorizing spelling rules is not the same thing as practicing and developing writing, so references to *grammar* and *writing* that really mean *spelling* and *punctuation* are misleading. Spelling can also be strongly influenced by timed writing in standardized exams.

6.5.2 Writing Development Is a Spiral, not a Line

As long as writers keep writing, their writing development continues. In the process, some writing choices are harder or easier depending on the context and task. For both children and adults, choices that seem simple in a familiar writing task are harder in an unfamiliar or high-stakes task. Put another way, students writing their first few college research papers will not be able to focus equally on all their writing choices, because they need a lot of bandwidth for any topic and genre details that are especially unfamiliar.

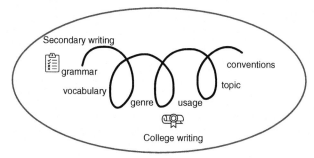

Figure 6.2 Writing development is a spiral

In sum, writing development is a spiral (as in Figure 6.2) rather than a line (recall Figure 6.1). And in the spiral of writing development, the different elements – topic ideas, organizational choices, vocabulary, and so on – do not come together at once. As we develop as writers, they come together at different times, on a spiral like the one in Figure 6.2. New writing tasks and contexts require practice, again and again, to bring everything together.

Thus headlines misrepresent writing development when they suggest that secondary students who struggle with college writing have missed something. Closer to the truth is that writing development is a continual spiral, across the full lifespan. Even successful writers, at all levels, must write repeatedly in new contexts and tasks to fulfill new writing expectations.

6.5.3 College Courses Demand new Writing

Painting college writing courses as remedial doesn't help, because it suggests that writing development can be, and should be, intact at the end of secondary school. The 2007 news article in the opening passages, for instance, suggests US composition courses exist because universities have "given up" on secondary education. Claims like these place responsibility on secondary schools and students rather than on ongoing writing resources in all schools and workplaces.

Closer to the truth is that college writing is different than secondary writing. This isn't to say that all college composition courses are effective. As you can already tell, I'm of the mind that such courses should spend more time exploring language patterns on a wider writing continuum. But it is to say that labeling college writing as remedial is not accurate, nor useful for students or instructors, because college writing is new for new college students.

To help students, college writing instruction can support language exploration that draws explicit attention to similarities and differences between secondary and postsecondary writing. Along similar lines, because college EAP courses support writing transitions through explicit instruction, they can help support students from all language backgrounds transition between secondary and college writing. We should not assume that such transitions are neutral nor equally valuable for different students. But we can offer more bridges between different kinds of writing to make the transitions better supported and more transparent.

6.5.4 We Need to Build Metacognitive Bridges

Better alignment across secondary and postsecondary writing would make the transition easier between them. But bridges between the two can help regardless. Even with their current differences, explicit attention to their similarities and differences can help students transfer their writing knowledge from secondary to postsecondary writing.

Writing metacognition, which we can think of as writing analysis and self-awareness, specifically helps writing transitions. In particular, writing research shows two kinds of metacognition support writing transitions:

- Analysis of relevant writing strategies
- Awareness of some relevant steps and prior experiences

This would mean, for instance, that a college student writing a college Biology lab report for the first time would need:

- Attention to strategies typically used in Biology lab reports
- Attention to experiences they can draw on, and what they need, to make choices regarding strategies typically used in Biology lab reports

We can continue this example by using the writing continuum. Writing metacognition would be helped by attention to typical strategies in Biology lab reports – typical **cohesion** strategies (e.g., formatted sections and rhetorical moves), typical **connection** and **focus** strategies (e.g., directions to tables or calculations; sentence subjects emphasizing experiment steps), and **usage** norms (e.g., *correct writing* spelling and usage preferences, and subject-verb-object order used across the continuum). It would also be helped by attention to how these strategies are similar or different than ones the writer had used before. Transitioning between old and new writing tasks is helped by this kind of attention to similarities

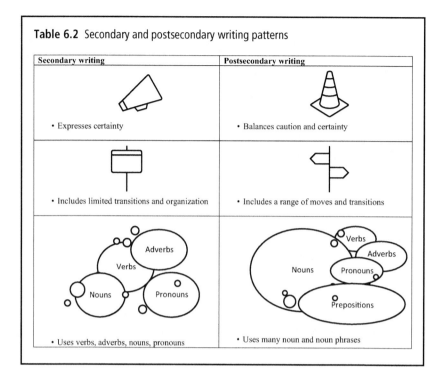

Table 6.2 Secondary and postsecondary writing patterns

Secondary writing	Postsecondary writing
• Expresses certainty	• Balances caution and certainty
• Includes limited transitions and organization	• Includes a range of moves and transitions
• Uses verbs, adverbs, nouns, pronouns	• Uses many noun and noun phrases

and distinctions, both in individual student reflections and in students' discussions with other students.

Because most writers have to write across the continuum, metacognition across different writing is more useful than mastery of one kind of writing. Students can analyze strategies across the continuum, in all kinds of writing they do, in order to metacognitively reflect on what makes distinct writing tasks different and similar.

6.5.5 Language Patterns Provide Bridges

We'll build metacognitive bridges here by noting differences between secondary and postsecondary writing. This is especially fun for me (nerd alert), because I've spent the past decade analyzing language patterns in secondary and postsecondary writing using large databases of student writing.[10]

In particular, I've found three language patterns, shown in Table 6.2, that distinguish college writing (and published academic writing, too) from secondary writing:

- **Civility** versus certainty: Secondary writing favors certainty and counters, while college writing balances caution and certainty and concessions and counters.
- **Cohesion** versus few transitions: Secondary writing includes few transitions, while college writing shows a range of transition words and moves for leading readers.
- **Compression** versus few noun phrases: Secondary writing includes few noun phrases and a mix of nouns, verbs, adverbs, and pronouns, while college writing favors dense noun phrases.

These patterns appear in Table 6.2, and we'll address them one at a time, with example passages before adding them to the writing continuum.

6.5.5.1 Secondary Writing Expresses Certainty, while Postsecondary Writing Balances Caution and Certainty

Postsecondary writing includes regular cautious choices such as hedges (*perhaps* or *might*) and concessions (*Author X is correct that...*), along with choices that show certainty, such as boosters (*definitely* or *demonstrates*) and counters (*nonetheless, Author X does not account for...*).

By contrast, secondary writing tends to include more boosters and counters, and fewer hedges and concessions. A college instructor used to postsecondary writing can find secondary writing overstated or aggressive as a result. A balance of caution and certainty can be what instructors mean when they say *correct writing* is "impartial" or "objective." A secondary student accustomed to using boosters in persuasive secondary writing or interpersonal social media writing may perceive these as part of emphasizing their ideas regardless of what they are writing.

When secondary students express a lot of certainty, this doesn't mean they can't write. It means they have less practice writing farther to the right on the continuum, with a balance of caution and certainty. We'll add this information to our language continuum below, as part of stance and connection patterns.

6.5.5.2 Secondary Writing Uses a Few Cohesive Strategies, while Postsecondary Writing Includes Diverse Cohesion[11]

Cohesion indicates a piece of language is a unified whole, instead of a collection of unrelated words or sentences. Postsecondary writing includes many forms of cohesion, from cohesive words (*in other words, however*) to cohesive moves (introductory moves, *known-new* moves).

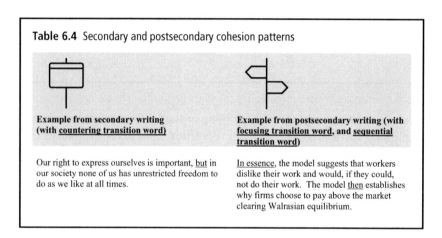

Table 6.3 Secondary and postsecondary stance patterns

Example from secondary writing (with counter and *generalizations*)	Example from postsecondary writing (with *hedge* and *booster*)
Our right to express ourselves is important, but in our society *none of us* has unrestricted freedom to do as we like at *all* times.	In essence, the model *suggests* that workers dislike their work and would, if they could, not do their work. The model then *establishes* why firms choose to pay above the market clearing Walrasian equilibrium.

Table 6.4 Secondary and postsecondary cohesion patterns

Example from secondary writing (with countering transition word)	Example from postsecondary writing (with focusing transition word, and sequential transition word)
Our right to express ourselves is important, but in our society none of us has unrestricted freedom to do as we like at all times.	In essence, the model suggests that workers dislike their work and would, if they could, not do their work. The model then establishes why firms choose to pay above the market clearing Walrasian equilibrium.

By contrast, secondary writing uses a narrower set of cohesive strategies. Secondary writers especially use counters such as *but* and *however*, and more rigid, template moves, such as PEEL (point, evidence, evaluation, link) or paragraphs in five-paragraph essays.

A range of cohesive ties and moves is often what college instructors mean when they say *correct writing* is "well organized."

6.5.5.3 Secondary Writing Uses Verbs, Nouns, Pronouns, and Adverbs, while Postsecondary Favors Noun Phrases

Most of the writing on the continuum, including secondary writing, favors a balance of parts of speech (or lexical categories). Alternatively,

Table 6.5 Secondary and postsecondary noun patterns

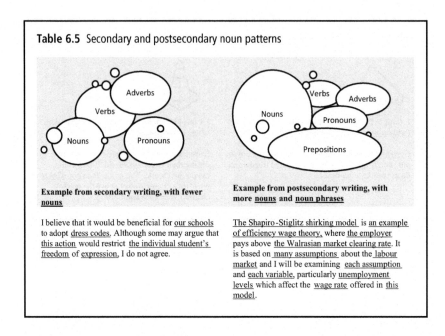

Example from secondary writing, with fewer nouns	**Example from postsecondary writing, with more nouns and noun phrases**
I believe that it would be beneficial for our schools to adopt dress codes. Although some may argue that this action would restrict the individual student's freedom of expression, I do not agree.	The Shapiro-Stiglitz shirking model is an example of efficiency wage theory, where the employer pays above the Walrasian market clearing rate. It is based on many assumptions about the labour market and I will be examining each assumption and each variable, particularly unemployment levels which affect the wage rate offered in this model.

as we know from myth 1, the far right of the continuum favors nouns, in phrases that include additional prepositions and nouns. Linguists call this compression, because it compresses information into phrases, rather than spelling it out in longer clauses.[12] Here's an underlined example of a dense noun phrase: *College writing expected in postsecondary courses and characterized by compressed phrases can be challenging for new students.*

Like other writing on the right of the continuum, postsecondary writing uses a lot of dense noun phrases and independent clauses. Secondary writing includes simpler nouns, as well as more verbs and dependent clauses beginning with words like *when* and *because*. These contrasting noun patterns are shown in Table 6.5.

Compression can be what instructors mean when they say that *correct writing* is "concise" and "formal."

6.5.6 Secondary and Postsecondary Writing Are on a Continuum

To bring these together, we'll add discussion of cohesion, civility, and compression patterns to secondary and postsecondary writing on the continuum shown in Table 6.6.

In this case, we can see that both secondary and postsecondary writers fulfill the continuum purposes of cohesion, connection, focus, stance,

Table 6.6 Secondary and postsecondary writing continuum

Texting Social Email   Published

Secondary   **College**

Secondary and Postsecondary Writing Continuum Patterns

	Informal Interpersonal Personal ⟷	Formal Informational Impersonal
	Secondary writing sample	**Postsecondary writing sample**
Continuum Purposes	Exemplar 12th grade argumentative essay, Common Core college placement exam	Level 2 student critique paper, Macroeconomics course, BAWE document number 681
Cohesion	• **Hourglass organization and 5-paragraph essay organization** 5-paragraph structure Transition words *(likewise, lastly, in conclusion)*	• **Hourglass organization and rhetorical moves** Introductory moves, end of paper moves back to overall topic Transition words (*also, for example*)
Connection	• **Interpersonal connection** Broad, collective audience addressed *(we)* 1st person is text-external	• **Informational connection** No direct address of audience 1st person is text-internal (*I will be examining*)
Focus	• **Personal and informational subjects** Sentence subjects are mostly simple pronouns and nouns (*students*) Some passive verbs	• **Informational subjects** Sentence subjects include nouns and noun phrases focused on models, researcher, and research Passive verbs
Stance	• **Certain stance** Boosters and generalizations (*must all, at all times*) and few hedges create tone of certainty	• **Impersonal stance** Text does not contain regular boosters or hedges No generalizations
Usage	• *Correct writing* **conventions and usage preferences**	• *Correct writing* **conventions and usage preferences**
Opening sentence	I believe that it would be beneficial for our schools to adopt dress codes. …	The Shapiro-Stiglitz shirking model is an example of efficiency wage theory, where the employer pays above the Walrasian market clearing rate. …

and norms. But they do so in different language patterns, in response to different tasks and contexts. Thus secondary writing tends to be more informal, personal, and interpersonal, while postsecondary writing tends to be more formal, impersonal, and informational. These are overall patterns, which may vary (or slide along the continuum) depending on the writers, tasks, and contexts, but they allow us to draw explicit attention to similarities and differences.

More paragraphs of these secondary and postsecondary examples appear below. As in earlier chapters, marginal notes and annotations draw attention to cohesive moves and **transition words** (in bold), connection markers [in brackets], passive verbs [[in double brackets]], *hedges* in italics, and **boosters** and **generalizations** in bold and italics.

6.5.6.1 Secondary Writing Example

[I] believe that it would be beneficial for our schools to adopt dress codes. Although some *may argue* that this action would restrict the individual student's freedom of expression, [I] *do not agree*. [Our right to express ourselves] is *important*, but in [our *society none* of us] has unrestricted freedom to do as [we] like *at all times*. [We] *must all* learn discipline, respect the feelings of others, and learn how to operate in *the real world* in order to be successful. Dress codes would **not only** create a better learning environment, **but** would **also** help prepare students for their futures.

> **Five-paragraph hourglass essay cohesion, personalized connection, certain stance:**
> The writer opens with an introductory paragraph with a thesis, using the first person to offer a personalized reaction and boosted, generalized claims

Perhaps the most important benefit of adopting dress codes would be creating a better learning environment. Inappropriate clothing can be distracting to fellow students who are trying to concentrate. Short skirts, skimpy tops, and low pants are fine for after school, but not for the classroom. T-shirts with risky images or profanity *may be* offensive to certain groups. Students *should* express themselves through art or creative writing, not clothing. With fewer distractions, students can concentrate on getting a good education which can help them later on.

> **Informational focus, balanced stance:**
> The writer moves to body paragraph and idea 1, which is focused on learning distractions and includes hedged and boosted claims

Another benefit of having a dress code is that it will prepare students to dress properly for different places. When [you] go to a party [you] do not wear the same clothes [you] wear to church. **Likewise**, when [you] dress for work [you] do not wear the same clothes [you] wear at the beach. Many professions even require uniforms. Having a dress code in high school *will help* students adjust to *the real world*.

> **Explicit cohesion and interpersonal connection:**
> The writer moves to body paragraph and idea two, with explicit transitions and several uses of the second person

Lastly, with all the peer pressure in school, many students worry about fitting in. If a dress code (or even uniforms) were required, there would be less emphasis on how [you] look, and more emphasis on learning.

> **Explicit cohesion and interpersonal connection:**
> The writer moves to body paragraph and idea three, with an explicit transition and more use of second-person pronouns

In conclusion, there are *many important* reasons our schools *should* adopt dress codes. Getting an education is hard enough without being distracted by inappropriate t-shirts or tight pants. Learning to dress for particular occasions prepares us for the real world. And teens have enough pressure already without having to worry about what they are wearing.

> **Explicit cohesion and certain stance:**
> The writer explicitly moves to the conclusion and closes with boosted claims

6.5.6.2 Postsecondary Writing Example

The Shapiro-Stiglitz shirking model is an example of efficiency wage theory, where the employer pays above the Walrasian market clearing rate. It [[is based on]] many assumptions about the labour market and [I will be] examining each assumption and each variable, particularly unemployment levels which affect the wage rate offered in this model. [I will show] how the model establishes an equilibrium and **also** what empirical evidence there is to support to support it.

> **Explicit cohesion, informational stance:**
> The writer uses introductory moves (territory, niche, writer contribution to the niche) to open the paper, and the paragraph includes text-internal first-person and noun phrases that focus on information

The Early Classical economists believed that in market equilibrium, unemployment did not exist and that the markets cleared. If unemployment did exist, it was *purely* voluntary and caused by wage rigidities. **Another theory** of unemployment suggested is one of efficiency wages which offers an explanation of involuntary unemployment, even at equilibrium. The ShapiroStiglitz shirking model is one such an example. **In essence**, it *suggests* that workers dislike their work and would, *if they could*, not do their work. The model then *establishes* why firms choose to pay above the market clearing Walrasian equilibrium.

> **Explicit cohesion, informational connection, impersonal, balanced stance:** This paragraph includes development moves (topic, example, analysis), focuses on information, and uses boosters and hedges

The shirking model [[is founded upon]] many assumptions, of which the first one is that workers dislike their work and if the firm was *completely* unable to monitor their work, they would choose not to do it. The second assumption is that workers either shirk, or they work at effort level e (i.e., it is a discrete variable); there is *only* one level of effort and this *cannot be* higher or lower. If they do shirk, the model assumes that they [[are dismissed]].

> **Explicit cohesion, impersonal, boosted stance:** The writer uses transitions to signal new assumptions and several boosters to convey a certain stance focused on information

The other main assumptions are that *all* workers and firms are identical; the probability of being dismissed due to reasons other than disciplinary ones, b, is 1 in the long term; and the level of unemployment benefits given out, w, is treated as an exogenous variable.

It has *always* been difficult to observe each individual's effort to ensure that they do not shirk, but in more recent times it *has proved increasingly so*. Teamwork, use of initiative and flexibility have become more important skills in the workplace, but the quantity of effort [[put into these]] is *very difficult* to measure in comparison to, **for example**, the speed of a production line. ...

Judging from exemplary student writing such as these two examples, shifting from secondary to postsecondary writing entails moving from more interpersonal, informal, personal writing to more informational, formal, impersonal writing. Students accustomed to focus, cohesion, connection, stance, and usage in secondary writing or in any writing farther to the left on the continuum will not necessarily have practice or familiarity with reading and writing postsecondary writing. These are reasons why secondary standardized writing exams cannot represent how secondary students will do in their postsecondary writing.

Closer to the truth is that *correct writing* reinforced by myths 1 through 5 is not learned once, in secondary school, and then finished. Secondary writing is different than postsecondary writing. Each one requires practice, and moving between them requires transitioning between the patterns in each one.

Closer to the truth is also that many educators who work with student writers – designing writing assignments, evaluating writing, and offering feedback – have not explicitly studied differences between secondary and postsecondary writing. They may not have studied connections between the writing their students know and the writing they expect from them, making it harder for them to build metacognitive bridges for students.

Closer to the truth is that writing development is not linear or finite. It is an ongoing spiral, in which different writing knowledge comes together at different times when writers encounter new tasks. Closer to the truth is that we can create metacognitive bridges through explicit attention to similarities and differences across the writing continuum. These bridges can help support transitions between parts of the continuum.

We can start by not assuming that writers will easily transition from one writing context or task to another. And we can continue by exploring language patterns within and across contexts.

The next chapter addresses our penultimate myth, that college writing ensures professional success. That myth shares a similar premise with this one: that writing used on one part of the continuum will easily translate to another part of the continuum. We are more ready to recognize that myth after this one. We can see how the assumption that writing development is linear and finite fuels both myths, and we can recall that transitioning from one writing context to another is challenging, particularly without bridges.

CHAPTER SEVEN

Myth 7 You Can't Get a Job if You Didn't Write Well in College

Or, College Writing Ensures Professional Success

The following passages are all recent. Their advice is clear: You won't get a good job if you don't write well in college.[1]

- In a technologically driven world, many students no longer see writing as a relevant skill to their career path. This mistaken view, unfortunately, leaves students who fail to take writing seriously in college at a disadvantage after graduation. *Pennsylvania State University website*
- As expert graduate recruiters, we have witnessed first-hand, time and time again employers choosing to hire one graduate over another because of their writing skills. *Give a grad a go website and blog*
- [Written] responses riddled with typos or confusing and improper grammar may cause co-workers or superiors to question your professionalism or attention to detail. *Tulane University website*
- Having excellent writing skills can make you an indispensable member of your team or company. And it's one of the best ways to remain consistently employable – no matter your profession. *Forbes Magazine*
- Writing well is one of those skills that can help you rise above in your career, no matter what you do. When done well, strong writing almost falls into the background as your information is seamlessly delivered to your audience. On the flip side, poor writing is immediately recognized and can damage your standing. *Oregon State University website*

From university and professional sources alike, the passages imply that *correct writing* will ensure professional opportunity. They say students who ignore their writing will be less employable, and those who make *correct writing* errors will be judged and will "damage their standing."

Like myth 6, this myth makes assumptions about writing transitions. It assumes one of two things. College and workplace writing are similar enough that college writers will transition to workplace writing easily. Or, college and workplace writing are different, but *correct writers* will easily adapt to workplace writing. In either case, this myth makes *correct writing* even more manifestly desirable – necessary for school, and also for what comes afterward.

As with other kinds of writing we've explored, workplace writing is not all the same. It varies according to fields, places, roles, and relationships. But relative to college writing, workplace writing has broad similarities, if we define it as written communication used in professional industries including medical, governmental, and corporate workplaces, such as emails, memos, and reports. We can likewise see broad similarities in college writing, defined as written communication used in college courses, in genres including term papers and essays, response papers, written examinations, lab reports, and case studies. We'll explore both in this myth, by way of addressing the myth that one guarantees the other.

Our origin story starts when college writing and employability first became linked in public conversation.

7.1 Context for the Myth

7.1.1 College Writing and Employment Were Purposefully Linked

Claims linking college and employment, such as those in the opening passages, were not always common. They grew within a more general literacy myth taking root in the nineteenth century.

Discussed in depth by historian Harvey Graff, the general literacy myth suggested that school-based reading and writing and would guarantee economic development and upward mobility. It was reinforced through British and US culture and institutions. This myth sends similar messages, specifically about college literacy.

For the myth to start, college writing and professional success had to be linked, and universities had good reason to promote this connection. As they expanded enrollment and shifted from classical languages to English, early dissenting academy leaders framed English study "as a means of economic advancement and political reform." This means the earliest English composition courses connected *correct writing* and employability.

Popular periodicals included pointed messages about college literacy during the same years. Readers of London's *Lady's Magazine* in 1779, for instance, would encounter the fictional Tom, "ashamed of his father's illiteracy and vulgarity" and headed to university to build a different life.[2]

Still, universities did not have a large audience in the eighteenth and nineteenth centuries. Even those with access to education usually stopped after secondary school.[3] There was a growing UK and US middle class with written literacy, but many were skeptical of college study, which came at the expense of work experience and wages.

Many thought college came at the expense of practical sense, too. University students, wrote London journal editor William Chambers in 1876, were "so devoid of pliability and common-sense, as to be less useful members of society than young men who have received the barest elements of education." The same editor concluded that "it is not profound learning which carries on the business of the world."

The same message appeared in the US and Scotland. "The great thinkers of today are outside of the Universities," quoted The *Normal Teacher* in 1879, and "practical businessmen" even thought college graduates needed to *unlearn* their education to succeed in business. A speech printed in 1900 in the *Edinburgh Review* stated, "History is full of the lives of men who have left behind them deep 'footprints on the sands of time' and yet who never had a university education."

To counter such skepticism, university presidents welded (and wielded) college study and economic mobility. They did so in what literacy researcher Tom Reynolds called a "tacit partnership" between magazines and universities. In twentieth-century articles, fiction, and advertisements, mass-readership magazines sold college literacy just as surely as they advertised hats and cleaning products.

Consider the case for a college degree promoted by Princeton president Francis Patton in a 1900 issue of *The Saturday Evening Post*. Patton started by acknowledging skepticism: Those who go from "school to office," he conceded, do gain "certain advantages." Still, he went on, they will lack something "essential" that can be gained only in college. Plus, Patton argued, there would soon be no choice. In the future, the "most coveted places in the business and the social world" would only be accessible with a college education.

In other examples, magazines helped promote and explain the college experience by sharing details about campus life and curricula. They specifically provided writing advice and reading material used in English composition classrooms.

By 1915, Patton's prophesy seemed to have been fulfilled. In the education journal *School and Society*, Harvard president Charles Eliot (there he is again...!) wrote in 1915 that secondary learning was no longer sufficient: "The situation is completely changed to-day. For the earning of a good livelihood to-day the workman needs much more than the bare elements of reading, writing, and arithmetic."

In the same year, University of Maine President Robert Aley wrote:

Higher education is no longer the luxury of a few. Neither is it secured merely as a matter of culture. To the great majority of people higher education is simply more education and is sought because it is believed that its possession will make the individual a more efficient member of the social world and will enable him more readily to meet the fierce competition of modern life.

The assured relationship between college literacy and economic mobility meant *correct writing* became an even more powerful gatekeeping tool in the twentieth century. Any number of secondary or college writing assignments and exams could exclude students from postsecondary learning and professional opportunities.

Today, there is no need to engineer an association between college education and employment. Any amount of college means more exposure to the far right of the writing continuum. Having some college education or a college degree almost always means higher earnings and less unemployment.[4] College study even follows generations, as having parents with some college education means statistically higher chances for economic stability College writing exams and courses continue to be lucrative enterprises for schools and testing organizations, who benefit from the association between college writing and economic success.

7.1.2 College and Workplace Writing Are "Worlds Apart"

Less clear, however, is the link between the actual writing done in college and in workplaces. For many instructors and students, college writing only happens at college, while workplace writing happens in the "real world." Indeed, many university faculty members are trained in academic writing and lack deep knowledge of workplace writing and how it differs from academic writing. By virtue of different experiences and goals, some postsecondary students know more than their instructors about writing beyond the far right of the continuum.

What happens, then, as students move from colleges to workplaces? In the twentieth century, writing researchers Chris Anson and Lee Forsberg observed a remarkably consistent pattern. Students went from "expectation" to "frustration" and finally to "accommodation." One new business intern described feeling "back at square one" in the process. He struggled with workplace writing, finding himself "too formal" at first and then "too touchy-feely" after that.

Similar observations left a group of faculty members dissatisfied with how universities were preparing graduates for workplace writing. They designed a large study to compare twenty-first-century college writing with that of workplaces. Ultimately, they found the differences between them so "radical" and "essential" that they titled their study *Worlds Apart*.

In 2020, a research team followed up the *Worlds Apart* study because they, too, saw students struggling to transition from college to workplace writing. In their study, they found good news and bad news. The good news was that students' struggles led to new collaboration with coworkers. The bad news was that the responsibility to bridge college and workplace writing was falling to students, who were "left to find ways to transition between what might as well be different planets."

7.1.3 College and Workplace Writing Have Different Expectations

The metaphor of different worlds or planets is apt because college and workplace writing have different goals, cultures, and norms. These differences, manifest in everything from writing processes, to language patterns, to what it means to author a piece of writing.

College writing, for its part, is driven by epistemic goals such as taking a stance and showing knowledge, and it is common to hear people characterize academic writing as "objective" and "skeptical." Regardless of academic discipline, showed a study by Chris Thaiss and Terry Zawacki, university faculty expect writing characterized by "the dominance of reason over emotion or sensual perception."

We can identify how these characteristics connect to continuum patterns we've already seen. College writing tends toward the formal, impersonal, and informational end of the writing continuum. It tends to avoid broad generalizations, and to emphasize informational processes rather than personalized experiences and reactions.

These patterns do not mean college writing is "neutral." It conveys stance in patterns we've seen, such as hedges (*perhaps*) and boosters (*clearly*), as well as adjectives to show novelty and significance. But it does mean that readers of college writing expect relatively little interpersonal and personal language.

The specific institutional role of college writing matters, as well: It is often used to evaluate student learning and to sort and rank students. As it is conventionally carried out, graded student writing emphasizes obvious beginnings and endings (the start and end of a term) and single authors and readers (a single writer, and an instructor-reader). There are alternatives, such as collaborative writing assignments and writing in courses paired with community or professional organizations, but these are exceptions rather than the rule.

By contrast, workplace writing has transactional aims, such as securing clients or selling a service or product. The writing is rarely an end in itself (like the culmination of coursework), but rather supports a network of events, pieces of writing, relationships, and readers. It is regularly collaboratively authored, and its timelines change as needs and collaborations change.

Workplace writing	College writing
• Informational and interpersonal • Fluid beginnings and endings • Collaborative authors and readers • Emails, memos, reports • Workplace email example: between interpersonal text message and informational college paper	• Informational and epistemic • Obvious beginnings and endings • Single authors and readers • Term papers, essays, lab reports • College term paper example: informational end of continuum

Figure 7.1 Workplace writing and college writing worlds

The most common workplace writing genre, email, prioritizes both informational and interpersonal goals and language patterns. It might share information such as specifications and directives, with attention to selective data reporting and arrangement. It might simultaneously fulfill interpersonal goals, including concern for others (what linguists called *positive politeness*) and attention to the need not to impose on others (*negative politeness*); generally, for example, workplace email includes explicit greetings and closings. At the same time, workplace email must attend to status relationships like boss to employee and vice versa, and so it is different than most informal digital writing.

In sum, while college writing prioritizes goals and patterns on the right side of the continuum, workplace writing often prioritizes patterns around the middle of the continuum. And while college writing tends to have finite deadlines and individual writers, workplace writing has more fluid timelines and collaborative authorship.

7.1.4 College and Workplace Writing Have Different Genres

With different goals and language patterns, college and workplace writing favor different genres (see Figure 7.1). Workplace and school survey responses show that essay writing is almost exclusively done in schools, for instance: While 65 percent of college respondents completed essay writing tasks, only 7 percent of workplace respondents had to write essays in their job.

In fact, only a fraction of the seventy-four different genres in the survey overlapped between college and workplace writing. Twenty genres were required more often in college writing than workplace writing. Fifteen were required more often in workplaces than colleges. And in that study and others, the most common workplace writing by a large margin was email, which was not reported as a college writing assignment genre.[5]

In her book *Because Internet: Understanding the New Rules of Language,* linguist Gretchen McCulloch describes four quadrants of contemporary English: informal speaking (e.g., conversations with friends), formal speaking (e.g., academic or professional presentations), informal writing (e.g., informal text messages or social media posts), and formal writing (e.g., academic papers). McCulloch places internet writing in the informal writing quadrant, due to its accessibility and focus on efficiency and spontaneity.

These quadrants highlight the productive diversity of English, but they also suggest that workplace email occupies a hybrid spot, more in between informal and formal writing than one or the other. Workplace email may not be fully accessible or spontaneous, but it is more accessible and spontaneous than formal academic writing. It fulfills informational as well as interpersonal goals, and it blends formal and informal language patterns. It dwells around the middle of the writing continuum, between text messaging and college writing. It might include formal interpersonal patterns such as conventional greetings and closings, informal interpersonal patterns such as emojis, and informational requests and directions.

The world of workplace writing presents new demands for writers transitioning to it. They might have practiced informational choices in college term papers, but they will need to use informational and interpersonal patterns in workplace email, which will vary according to workplace relationship and rank. Meanwhile, students may have only received feedback on their school writing, and they may not have received explicit instruction on what makes college writing different from workplace writing. Technical or professional college writing courses may offer that kind of explicit instruction, and they are growing in number. But to date these courses are rarely required, and not always available, in university curricula.

Whether or not students receive explicit instruction in email writing, university faculty do have strong feelings about it. Online advice – and complaints – suggest lecturers and professors much prefer formal, informational writing norms in their emails from students, including *correct writing* conventions and usage preferences.[6]

7.1.5 Learning Is Linked to Some Writing Tasks

The fact that college and workplace writing are different doesn't mean college writing is not valuable. It means college writing does not explicitly prepare students for workplace writing, even as it may contribute to their learning overall.

How exactly college writing contributes to learning is not easy to determine, because we can't isolate writing from other parts of learning. Mixed observations may also be inevitable: They all depend on what counts as *writing* and *learning* at a given time and place; and they are influenced by tasks, peers, teachers, disciplines, and extracurricular interests. Still, research offers a few observations.

Some studies show that more college writing means more student satisfaction, but not necessarily higher student achievement. Other research suggests that across their years of college, students develop as writers, in two ways. First, students develop in a nonlinear fashion. This won't surprise us, as we know from myth 6 that writing development is a spiral, not a line. And second, students develop toward more knowledge domains, which won't surprise us because we know from myth 3 that writing entails cognitive, interpersonal, intrapersonal, and health domains.

Other research shows a correlational relationship between some kinds of writing and learning, meaning we can picture the two – select college writing, and student learning – like two seats on a tandem bicycle. Some college writing appears to help students develop understanding, because students have to conceptualize and connect ideas to write about them. And learning appears to help students develop some of their writing, because as they learn, students develop more vocabulary, details, and connections they can use in their writing.

A large study of US college writing led by Paul Anderson specifically showed that learning was connected to three kinds of writing practice:

* Writing tasks with clear expectations
* Interactive writing processes (with collaborative feedback, discussion, and revision)
* Meaning-making projects (or working with new or original ideas)

In other words, all writing tasks are not created equal, but some writing tasks do contribute to student learning. That means mixed results in writing research may be related to the type of writing in question. Standardized writing tasks with no interaction, for instance, do not appear to enhance student learning, even if they do impact student access and therefore employment.

7.2 The Myth Emerges

Beginning with messages deliberately linking college education and economic opportunity, this myth emerged. Today, it is bolstered by the connection between college education and economic outcomes, and the tandem relationship between student learning and some college writing. But the mythical idea that college writing ensures professional success obscures important truths: College and workplace writing are different, and writers need explicit support to transition between them.

7.3 Consequences of the Myth

7.3.1 We Limit Bridges between Writing Worlds

An overall consequence of this myth is that we limit bridges between writing worlds. With limited bridges come other consequences noted in Table 7.1.

7.3.2 Workplace Writing Is a Sink or Swim Scenario

Without bridging experience between academic and workplace writing, students face the transition between these writing worlds without explicit support. The authors of *Worlds Apart* call this "jumping into the rhetorical pool and swimming."

Rhetorical sinking or swimming means means trial and error is the only way to learn what makes college and workplace writing similar and different. Even more important, sink or swim chances are not equitable. They depend upon individual resources in moments of need. Those most likely to swim are those with life preservers and swimming communities, who may feel sufficiently entitled to support to ask for it. Those likely to sink are those without resources or communities already oriented toward swimming. To belabor the metaphor: Those with the most swimming

Table 7.1 Consequences of myth 7

Once we believe	
College writing ensures professional success, then…	… Workplace writing is a sink or swim scenario
	… College curricula and tests are limited
	… Students struggle to transition between worlds
	… Students who do not attend college are at a disadvantage
	… We believe college education is worth any cost

resources are most likely to swim, no matter how capable everyone is of swimming *with* instruction. Sinking opportunity for people who would swim if supported to do so, in other words, is a serious consequence.

Lest I keep us treading water forever (ha, ha), let's illustrate this point in terms of writing. Research shows significant differences between student writers who are first in their families to attend college (first-generation students), and students whose parents attended college (continuing-generation students). These differences don't relate to college performance or ability, as measured in student GPA and course grades. Instead, the differences have to do with what students believe about themselves and how much support and time they have. First-generation students report a higher level of self-doubt in their college reading and writing. They are less likely to have disposable time and resources; they are more likely to have responsibilities such as work and family obligations; and they are more likely to leave college before finishing their degree. Even with college performance beginning similarly, students' self-perceptions and their time and other school-related resources directly influence the writing they are able to do.

When there is no clear bridge between college and workplace writing, then opportunity is not equally available. It will most likely go to those with more time, more practice with relevant kinds of writing, or more practice asking for help with writing. Unequal opportunity is a dire consequence, in other words, of assuming that writers will adapt to new writing tasks without explicit support.

7.3.3 College Curricula and Tests Are Limited

Isolated from workplace and other "real world" writing, college writing commonly takes the form of individual writing, in academic genres, with informational, formal, impersonal language patterns. That is the kind of writing most college faculty members are trained to assign and to write themselves. Even if students need to write around the middle of the continuum after college, college instructors know the most about the right side of the continuum.

The emphasis on individual assignments in college courses, based on how we've evaluated ability since the emergence of myths 3 and 4, particularly contrasts the collaborative expectations of workplace writing. Students may write collaborative digital texts out of school, but in school they rarely gain practice in or feedback on collaborative authorship.

This common version of *correct college writing* is limiting. The Penn State University website passage that opens the chapter, for instance, begins thus: "In a technologically driven world, many students no longer see writing as a relevant skill to their career path." Implicit in this either/ or framing – either technology *or* writing – is that digital writing on the left of the continuum is not part of the "relevant skill" of writing.

7.3.4 Students Struggle to Transition between Worlds

This myth implies that the transition between postsecondary and workplace writing will happen without bridges between them. But as we saw in myth 6, transitioning between writing situations is not easy. It is hard to move from one writing context to another, particularly without explicit attention to their similarities and differences.

7.3.5 Students Who Do not Attend College Are at a Disadvantage

The correlation between postsecondary education and employment today is real. Whether or not students practice the three kinds of writing related to learning and development (clear expectations, interactive processes, and working with original ideas), they are still likely to hear that college writing will help them professionally. And even with college and workplace writing worlds being apart, people are likely to face this myth when they try to get jobs.

Consider this 2021 BBC news story, "Improving my literacy helped me get a different job."[7] The article tells the story of James Sykes, who describes how in secondary school he viewed writing only in terms of boring and irrelevant exams. At the age of forty, he took his GCSE English exam and was awarded a B, which the article suggests will help him at the Territorial Army. Sykes explains why this will help him: "It's a tick in the box that you've got to have to allow you to progress," he notes, "so it will potentially help me in the future with my military career." Sykes' reasoning is sincere, but it doesn't concern learning or writing development.

This myth lasts so long as workplace employees are judged according to *correct writing*. Consider this response from a contemporary employer asked about *correct writing errors* in job applications: "I tend to think that the person who writes poorly is both poorly educated and not interested in improving their skills. I also think that the person is perhaps not the most qualified person for the job."

The upshot here is that the disadvantage for students without college writing is real, because of how people *think* about college writing – not necessarily because college writing will prepare them for workplace writing.

7.3.6 We Believe College Is "Worth it at any Cost"

Today, there is evidence of skepticism about the value of a college education. In 2022, for example, a coalition of US public universities began a campaign to "prove college is worth it." To *Inside Higher Education*, the campaign indicated that "the belief in a college degree as a stepping-stone to social mobility, once nearly universal, is fading."[8]

So long as this myth persists, however, it easily fuels the idea that college is worth it at any cost. Meanwhile, college education presents extreme financial and other challenges for many families, particularly in the US where college debt is notoriously high. A US economist recently put it this way: "Much of the student debt weighing down millions of Americans can be attributed to false promises."

7.4 Closer to the Truth

7.4.1 Postsecondary Writing Is not Workplace Writing

For more than a century, this myth has linked college writing and employability. Closer to the truth is that certain kinds of college writing help student learning, but this doesn't mean postsecondary writing will be the same as workplace writing, or that students have learned strategies for transitioning between them.

7.4.2 Workplace Writing and Speaking Matter

Employer surveys reported in *Education Weekly* show that many employers emphasize both oral and written communication skills. A representative example appears in the American Management Association's 2010 Critical Skills Survey, which identified "effective communication," or "the ability to synthesize and transmit your ideas both in written and oral formats," as one of the four central skills employers value. There is good reason to help college students see where college writing is on the continuum, and understand how it is similar to and different from communication they will need to do later.

7.4.3 Writing Is Context-specific

As we've seen several times already, different writing tasks entail different writing choices. It is for this reason that the authors of *Worlds Apart* describe "the tremendous power of context" in shaping college and workplace writing.

This means that students need practice in workplaces to develop work-place writing. Full practice in workplace writing only happens over time, in workplace contexts, with the help of feedback and guidance. Just as there is no way to teach college writing in secondary school, there is no way to teach workplace writing in college classrooms, because class-rooms and workplaces are not the same contexts. What we can do is consider changes and bridges.

7.4.4 Higher Education Can Change

The fact that writing is context-specific does not mean that college and workplace writing have to stay worlds apart. One way instructors have brought them closer together is by tailoring college writing courses to students' workplace needs. In "needs-driven" writing courses, instruc-tors determine students' workplace requirements and design courses accordingly, using examples and assignments specific to the genres and fields students are pursuing. Needs-driven instruction is not always pos-sible, because it depends on the student make-up and what students and instructors know when the course begins.

More generally, college writing courses can incorporate a wider range of college writing assignments. More college writing tasks could include collaborative as well as individual authorship, and interper-sonal as well as informational goals, to give students practice with a range of writing choices. This would allow students to practice writing choices valued in workplace as well as academic tasks, and it could help build greater awareness across the two. Furthermore, writing research shows that even aside from future writing demands, there are bene-fits to collaborative writing, including enhancing students' learning and understanding.

Higher education representatives could also do a better job of accu-rately portraying what college does and does not offer, for the sake of informed choices about college attendance. New economic mobil-ity index rankings, for instance, already add nuance to the message that college is worth it at any cost.[9] This index ranks schools according to how long it typically takes students after graduation to recoup the costs of college. In addition, administrators and instructors can pro-vide more details about differences between college and workplace writing, and how college writers fare when they enter workplaces. Writing courses can provide more bridge-building in instruction and assignments.

7.4.5 We Can Build Metacognitive Bridges

Building metacognitive bridges by analyzing different kinds of writing seems the most flexible solution. In the last myth, we saw that explicit instruction and reflection can build metacognitive bridges between secondary and college writing. The same idea applies here, between college and workplace writing.

Closer to the truth is that those students who can recognize differences between college and workplace writing have an easier time moving from one to the other. In the *Worlds Apart* follow-up study, for instance, a student who successfully moved from college writing to internship writing described how she first learned how to conduct concise analysis in an Environmental Ethics course in college. Then, with the help of reflecting on how the writing was similar and different, she applied some of the same choices in her internship at the Environmental Protections Agency.

In this example, the student reflected on her own writing to build a metacognitive bridge between two kinds of writing. Both required focus and cohesion choices related to picking and prioritizing information, but each one also had some unique language patterns. College courses can support this kind of analysis, building bridges across different parts of the writing continuum.

Recalling that we know writing development occurs in a spiral across a lifespan, we can see repeated analysis opportunities as ongoing bridge building. With ongoing opportunities, writers can reflect on language patterns in college and workplace writing such as those in Table 7.2 to help them discern what to apply and leave behind in each one.

7.4.6 Workplace and College Writing Are on a Writing Continuum

We'll build metacognitive bridges here by comparing a workplace email and a student executive summary from an undergraduate business program. Both are exemplar texts offered online to support writers: One was a 2022 example for successful workplace emailing,[10] and one was a 2022 exemplar model used at the University of Technology Sydney.[11] Together, they allow us to explore different parts of the continuum: workplace email around the middle left of the continuum, with interpersonal and informational patterns, and college writing toward the formal, informational, impersonal side of the continuum.

Table 7.2 Workplace email to postsecondary writing continuum

Texting Social

Email

Secondary

College

Published

Postsecondary and Workplace Writing Continuum Patterns

	Informal Interpersonal Personal	Formal Informational Impersonal
Continuum Purposes	**Exemplar email:** **Top Google example for workplace email**	**Exemplar paper:** **Model executive summary of management decisions**
Cohesion	• **Hourglass organization** Clear moves from opening greeting, to sharing information and requesting meeting, to closing	• **Hourglass organization and rhetorical moves** Clear introductory moves and paragraphs detailing the report's purpose, methods, conclusions, and recommended actions
Connection	• **Interpersonal connection** Collective 1st person *(our)* and direct 2nd person address	• **Informational connection** No 1st or 2nd person pronouns
Focus	• **Informational and interpersonal subjects** Sentence subjects include 1st person pronouns and simple, general nouns Active and passive verbs	• **Informational subjects** Subjects include nouns and dense noun phrases focused on organizations, systems, and processes More passive verbs
Stance	• **Certain stance** Boosters and generalizations emphasize collective and positive tone *(very good, all of us)*, and hedging anticipates possible problems *(in general)*	• **Neutral stance** Boosters and hedges balance assertion with caution *(readily, might, could)* No generalizations
Usage	• *Correct writing* conventions and usage preferences	• *Correct writing* conventions and usage preferences
Opening	Dear Team:	This report provides an analysis and evaluation of dysfunctional performance measurement.

The examples appear in full below, annotated according to continuum purposes and patterns. Marginal notes and annotations include transitional words **in bold**, connection markers [in brackets], *hedges* in italics, ***boosters*** and ***generalizations*** italicized and bolded, and passive verbs [[in double brackets]].

7.4.6.1 Workplace Email Example

Subject Line: Departmental Changes
  Dear Team:
  Good morning. There are some *exciting* changes coming to our department that I wish to alert [you] to.

> **Formal, interpersonal connection, hourglass cohesion:** This email formally but directly greets readers and signals what is to come

Due to ABC Inc.'s recent acquisition of XYZ Company, [our] executive management has decided that some restructuring of [our department] is in order so that [our transition] through this merger can be as seamless *as possible*.

> **Interpersonal connection, informational focus:** The writer evokes a collective experience without focusing on the writer's reaction

This is, ***in general***, ***very good*** news for ***all*** [of us], for [we] will be onboarding ten new sales representatives – which will both relieve [our] current understaffing situation and prepare [us] for the heightened sales operations this merger is anticipated to trigger.

> **Generalized, certain stance:** The writer offers a generalized, positive evaluation of the collective experience

[I] am scheduling a staff meeting for tomorrow from 12 pm to 1 pm where [I] will outline the steps of this important transition; lunch [[will be provided]].

> **Informational, interpersonal invitation:** The writer uses first person and passive verbs to extend an invitation while remaining impersonal

(You) Please feel free to reach out to [me] at *any* time during the next few weeks with *any* questions or concerns.

> **Interpersonal connection, hourglass cohesion, certain stance:** The writer closes with a direct, polite invitation and boosted emphasis on availability

Best regards,
Julie Adams
Email: email@ABCinc.com
Phone: 555–555–1234

7.4.6.2 Postsecondary Writing Example

This report provides an analysis and evaluation of dysfunctional performance measurement. The issue of a lack of controllability breaches the controllability principle, and this report examines the accountability of factors and fairness of their responsibility. Performance measurement is defined as a quantifiable indicator used to assess how well an organisation or business is achieving its desired objectives. *Many* business managers *routinely* review various performance measure types to assess such factors as results, production, demand and operating efficiency in order to acquire a more objective sense of how their business is operating and whether improvement is required.

> **Explicit cohesion, informational, impersonal focus, certain stance:** The opening follows introductory moves (contribution, territory, gap), and includes two boosters that emphasize the importance of the contribution

By analysing the cause of the problem, the report discusses four categories of uncontrollable factors: (1) external environmental; (2) decisions taken by others within the same company; (3) decisions taken by superiors and (4) inability to change the decision. The report then examines the consequences of dysfunctional performance management for both individuals and organisations. The Department of Veteran Affairs (VA) scandal in the USA is

> **Explicit cohesion, informational focus, balanced stance:** These paragraphs move from topics (factors discussed) to examples to analysis (goals and

discussed as an example of organisational practice. The aim is to apply theory to the case and explore *possible solutions* to the problems. Due to a multitude of factors responsible for the VA *scandal*, this report focuses on the problem of uncontrollability and management systems issues in the organisation.

findings). Dense noun phrases focus on information, and sentences include hedges and boosters

The report finds that, although there is *no single solution* to overcoming issues such as lack of controllability in performance measurement, this phenomenon *can actually* render positive effects on management. The conclusion is that organisations *should* determine the level of uncontrollability that is permissible for achieving their objectives.

The recommendations in this report detail the importance of selecting appropriate indicators to accomplish the organisation's objectives together with establishing properly designed management control systems (MCS).

Informational focus:
The summary closes with impersonal, dense noun phrases focused on information

Both examples build cohesion through paragraphs and moves, even as the specific moves are different. Likewise, both texts connect with their audience, but differently: The workplace email uses direct, personalized address to emphasize shared work experiences (*for all of us*), and the report summary uses formal, impersonal patterns to emphasize what the text offers to readers (*this report provides*). Along similar lines, the sentence subjects are simple and text-external in the workplace email (*our executive management; This*). In the report summary, as in other writing toward the right of the continuum, the sentence subjects and objects are more compressed and informational (*the issue of a lack of controllability; the accountability of factors and fairness of their responsibility*).

Both texts also convey author stance, with the email offering a clearly positive description of workplace developments, and the report offering a balanced stance that anticipates reader doubts (*although there is no single solution …, this phenomenon can actually*). Both texts follow *correct writing* conventions and usage preferences, though the email is more informal and interpersonal than the report summary. Overall, the language patterns make for a workplace email that is personalized, interpersonal, and informational, and a college report summary that is impersonal and informational.

Closer to the truth is that while this myth implies a direct connection between college and workplace writing, we have seen a more mixed picture:

- College education leads more often to employment than secondary education alone
- Some postsecondary writing assignments contribute to student learning
- Some people expect *correct writing* conventions and usage preferences in workplace applications
- College and workplace writing are different in their goals, genres, and language patterns
- It is challenging to transition between college and workplace writing, especially without explicit attention to similarities and differences between them

Closer to the truth is that without bridging the worlds of college and workplace writing, students are thrown into rhetorical pools without equitable support. Alternatively, diverse assignments and explicit attention to similarities and differences can support metacognitive bridges.

Our final myth will give us more opportunity to explore the writing continuum, and a chance to address the myth I hear most of all: New technology, especially the internet, threatens writing.

CHAPTER EIGHT

Myth 8 You Can't Write That Because Internet

Or, New Technology Threatens Writing

The following headlines span about fifty years: earlier claims about television, and later claims about texting and the internet.

- The High Linguistic Crimes Committed by Television's Newscasters Have Impoverished the Richest Language in the World. *The New York Times*, US, 1974
- [After] Television Turned our Minds into Cucumbers, the Written Word Has Been in Decline. *The Washington Star*, US, 1975
- Television [leads to] Aborted Literacy. The *Guardian*, UK, 1978
- Watching TV Harms Kids' Academic Success. *New Scientist*, US, 2005
- Text Message Slang Invading GCSEs and A-levels as Teenagers Abandon Basic Grammar and Punctuation. *Daily Mail*, UK, 2012
- The Internet Is Making Writing Worse. *The Atlantic*, US, 2013

In these headlines, the culprit changes, but the myth remains: New technology threatens writing – luring people away from *correct writing* until there's no saving it.

Versions of this myth are a bit of an occupational hazard for me. People hear "professor of English" and immediately want to talk about whether anyone cares about writing any more (yes), or whether people will soon communicate using only emojis (no). And so on.[1]

Interestingly, these conversations tend to be about *other* people, because the people who voice the myth have not suffered its fate. My undergraduate students don't worry for themselves, but they worry for their younger siblings. My friends write formal reports and send informal texts, but they fear their children won't be able to do both.

There are some headlines that tell people not to worry. A 2014 study showed that British and Australian students kept informal texting and formal papers separate, and it was featured in *Vox* under the headline "OMG! Texting doesn't actually hurt kids' grammar or spelling skills," and in *The Conversation* with the title "Text-messaging isn't, like, ruining young people's grammar." These articles aren't free of myths – they imply informal language is *incorrect* and lacking *grammar*. But they do not say that new technology ruins writing, and they employ a range of language patterns in their titles, besides.

Most headlines about new technologies, however, are myth bonanzas. They go something like this: *Correct writing*, which is one thing only, should be regulated by schools and tests, and when most students cannot write *correctly* according to schools and tests, it is because they are using new technologies. In the opening passages, for instance, the 1975 article blames low SAT scores on TV, and the 2012 article says text messages are lowering GCSE and A-level scores.

Like other writing we've explored, digital writing, the contemporary focus of this myth, is not all the same. It varies according to platforms, writers, purposes, and relationships. But relative to *correct writing* on the right end of the continuum, informal digital writing has some broad similarities, if we define it as writing commonly used in informal social media and text messaging.

Recent as these technologies are, our tale begins with an age-old story: New technology scares people.

8.1 Context for the myth

8.1.1 New Technology Comes with Old Concerns

In the eighteenth century, people feared that the printing press would lower writing standards. In the nineteenth century, people argued the telegraph and telephone would harm literacy. In the twentieth century, people worried about television, then instant messaging and chat rooms. Today, people are concerned about texting and the internet. These claims are part of a long tradition: When a new communicative technology emerges, people express concerns about literacy. (They often proceed to use the new technologies to air those concerns, but I digress.)

Like other myths we've seen, this one follows the trend of *more access/ more regulation*. The printing press made reading and writing more widely accessible, which worried government and church leaders who had hitherto controlled what was written, printed, and read. Coverage in the 1970s connected a literacy crisis to television and increased college access, particularly for people of color and women. Coverage today implies that the internet, which widens access to writing and information, undermines *correct writing*.

This isn't to say there are no legitimate concerns about new technologies, but rather that it is hard to parse them from fear of change and increased access. Headlines commonly express what Christian Thurlow describes as "moral panic" about "the communicative ineptitude of young people." Many imply that democratizing writing weakens or taints it.

There are more positive views, from linguists who praise the innovative creativity of online language, and from writing educators who describe the internet's role in a supporting literacy. Both positive and negative coverage show interest in language. Still, the most common response is language regulation mode – specifically, alarm over perceived writing decline.

8.1.2 *Correct writing* Is Kept Separate from Informal Writing

The 2012 *Atlantic* article "The Internet Is Making Writing Worse" reports a common fear: Digital writing makes students more likely to perform "academic atrocities" like "using informal language." The article is based on an online survey of about 2,500 secondary teachers in the US, Puerto Rico, and the US Virgin Islands. In the survey, most teachers agreed that digital writing fostered creativity and expression, but they also worried about the boundary between informal and formal language.[2] Many responses used invasion or takeover metaphors, as though digital language were a slang-slinging militia out to get formal writing.

A key premise is that *correct writing* is formal, and digital writing is informal, and never the two should meet. As we saw in myth 1, this division dominates university writing advice for students. The University of Sydney, for instance, describes, "Academic writing is generally quite formal, objective (impersonal) and technical. It is formal by avoiding casual or conversational language, such as contractions or informal vocabulary."[3] Academic usage guides show similar consensus about formality. They say writers should avoid a "casual" or "conversational" style, including unattended pronouns (*this means* versus *this rule means*), split infinitives, sentence-initial conjunctions, sentence-ending prepositions, and contractions. The total effect of advice about English academic writing, wrote K. Bennet after studying academic style guides, implies it is a "massive impersonal machine" that is "by nature formal." In turn, *Time* magazine writer Kim Bubello cautions, "The formal, unemotional writing we were all taught in the classroom simply won't do in places designed for virtual mingling."[4]

8.2 The Myth Emerges

Reinforcing other myths, this myth emerges. Myth 8 continues to limit *correct writing* to one kind of writing, regulated by schools and tests. It furthermore puts *correct writing* at odds with new technologies, especially today's digital writing technologies.

8.3 Consequences of the Myth

8.3.1 We Keep Limiting *Writing*

When we pit new technologies against *correct writing*, we continue to lose opportunities for language exploration, bringing us full circle back to myth 1. We continue to judge more, and learn less, about writing. We get a host of specific consequences listed in Table 8.1 as a result.

8.3.2 We Make Enemies of Informal and *Correct* Writing

This myth keeps the left and right side of the writing continuum disconnected and opposed to one another. From limited preferences in usage guides, to limited tasks and criteria in schools and tests, *correct writing* appears in a hierarchy, at the top, instead of on a connected continuum.

In turn, we keep more common, familiar writing at odds with *correct writing*. And we expect students to perform their learning only in the least familiar, most inflexible writing on the continuum, no matter how meaningful the rest of the continuum.

A dichotomy between "personal" and "academic" writing sometimes reinforces the same divide, for example, in school curricula that moves from "creative and personal narrative" in the beginning to "formal argument" at the end. This order and terminology can imply that personal narrative is a step in a linear process of informal to formal writing development, rather than important for its own purposes and part of a connected set of language choices.

Table 8.1 Consequences of myth 8

Once we believe	... We make enemies of informal and *correct* writing
New technology threatens writing, then...	... We believe only *correct writing* is *controlled* writing
	... We view language diversity as bad
	... We tolerate (even more) confusing references to grammar
	... We limit our responses to artificial intelligence
	... We limit audiences and learning

8.3.3 We Believe Only *Correct Writing* Is *Controlled* Writing

This myth puts a new spin on the *control* metaphors we saw in myth 5, by implying that people lose control of *correct writing* after being lured by new technologies. The 1978 *Guardian* article warned that literacy was "aborted" due to television. The 2012 *Daily Mail* article suggested that "basic grammar and punctuation" were "abandoned" by teenagers writing text messages. These messages imply that *correct writing* is both entirely separate from, and left behind by, the use of new technologies.

8.3.4 We View Language Change and Diversity as Bad, rather than Inevitable and Positive

By the logic of this myth, *correct writing* must not be influenced by the language variety or change that comes with new technologies. Thus language adaptation becomes a bad thing, instead of inevitable and productive. Instead of exploring what makes informal digital writing what it is, we view informal digital writing as a threat.

8.3.5 We Tolerate (even more) Confusing References to Grammar

References to informal digital writing as having *no grammar* are examples of how language regulation mode can reinforce language ignorance. First, as with other examples we've seen, many said references actually refer to conventions – spelling or punctuation – rather than grammar. Second, many examples of informal digital usage, such as emojis, exaggerations, and the use of phrases rather than clauses (or complete sentences), are all grammatically possible and meaningful choices in English. Like formal writing patterns, they show cohesion, connection, focus, stance, and usage, but differently.

8.3.6 We Limit our Responses to Artificial Intelligence

Artificial intelligence tools have alarmed educators for years, but perhaps none more than the ChatGPT AI tool that emerged at the end of 2022.[5] ChatGPT is an open access tool that uses scores of linguistic data to produce writing eerily like human writing. In the months after its appearance, secondary and postsecondary educators expressed the concern that students would cheat without detection, and even that the tool would replace educators.

These responses are understandable, but some are also limited, more focused on language regulation than exploration. Without taking away from important discussions about AI, ethics, and authorship, we can also choose language exploration as one approach to AI-generated writing. In support of metacognitive bridge building, students can critically analyze patterns in AI writing, and where they fall on the continuum, just as they do with human writing.

For instance, AI writing relies on formulaic templates like the ones in myth 6, because templates are easy to identify at scale. If you ask ChatGPT to "write a paper on linguistic features of internet English," for example, you will get a five-paragraph essay, with an introduction stating a thesis, three body paragraphs describing one example each, and a conclusion restating the thesis and making a generalization about the internet or English. As part of understanding cohesion, students can analyze these moves, compare them to human writing, consider how the writing could be more flexibly organized, and so on. Likewise, analyzing AI writing for how it builds (or fails to build) connection can highlight the limitations of AI, which does not possesss human interpersonal or intrapersonal awareness. Because AI tools can parse information into segments but not process information like humans, its connection patterns can be blunted, creating opportunities for recognizing and revising according to purpose.

The upshot is: The more writers analyze writing across the continuum (whether it be their own, AI writing, or writing they hope to do one day), the more chances they have to build metacognitive bridges. Meanwhile, AI will only keep developing. The better we become at exploring it, the better prepared we will be to recognize and use it for learning.

8.3.7 We Limit Audiences and Learning

Keeping *correct writing* and informal digital writing at odds ultimately limits writing audiences and writing knowledge. It means formal writing will remain inaccessible to many audiences. And it means fewer bridges, and less explicit learning, across the full writing continuum.

8.4 Closer to the Truth

8.4.1 Writing Is a Scapegoat (or, It's Complicated)

Before directly responding to this myth, we should note that some responses to new technologies are not necessarily about writing. Some are rooted in understandable but distinct social concerns, and some are about many worries at once. *Correct writing* is often a repository for a range of concerns.

For instance, some fears about student internet writing relate to social behaviors. Studies show that excessive use of digital technology can make students less motivated and more anxious, and can replace interactive communication. Important though they are, these observations pertain more to relational behaviors than to language use within them.[6] On the flip side, digital technologies sometimes facilitate positive social behaviors. At one university, more than half the students felt university social media helped them to feel part of their academic community. But again, that finding appeared more related to social behavior than to specific language use.

In another example, the spread of misinformation is a pressing issue of our time. But misinformation is not specifically about writing, insofar as *correct* and *incorrect writing* can both spread misinformation.

Other concerns relate to contemporary encounters with writing, if not writing itself. Nicholas Carr's well-known claim that "Google is making us stupid," for instance, is based on his decreasing attention span when reading online. Recent research does suggest that collective attention is decreasing, with popular content accelerating and diminishing in shortening intervals. And research on media multitasking (using two or more media at once) shows that such multitasking interferes with attention and working memory.

An additional view of encounters with writing is that the internet creates a more flexible view of language. In *Because Internet,* McCulloch argues that before the internet, language was seen as fixed, slow to change, and controlled by distant authorities. Now, she argues, language is seen as fluid and collectively negotiated.

As for writing itself, closer to the truth is that *how* people use digital technologies seems to matter more than *whether* they do. A study of undergraduates showed that students who used their phones to shift their attention away from class lectures – to receive or send an unrelated text message, for example – remembered little. But those students who used their phones to write lecture notes recalled about as much as students who turned off their phones. Research on language learning classrooms likewise shows that what makes the difference is how, not whether, new technologies are used.

8.4.2 More Claims Are Proffered than Proven

Also closer to the truth is that it is easier to say new technologies threaten writing than it is to prove it. Multiple forces affect new technologies and writing, making them hard to disentangle, and many generalizations cannot be proven one way or the other. Many headlines based on standardized test scores, for example, go from "students use informal punctuation" to "students cannot write," and then they say that digital writing is the culprit. Likewise, many accounts evoking this myth use anecdotal or selective evidence, which might all be true but is not generalizable.

Also closer to the truth is that writing is not changing substantially due to digital writing. Academic writing does not include significantly more abbreviations or slang than in the past, for instance, and no research shows changes in fundamental grammatical structures such as the subject-verb-object construction that we read about in myth 1. Only a very small (but much-discussed) percentage of student writing contains abbreviations and other digitally mediated language patterns. A national US study of college writing in 2008 directly contradicted "hard-core worriers who see a precipitous decline in student writing ability" based on digital writing. Instead, the study suggested college students are capable of keeping parts of the continuum separate when they write. Other research, in 2015 and since, argues that students make a conscious effort to avoid informal internet language in academic writing.

8.4.3 If it Surprises You, You Notice it More

One reason people think writing is dramatically changing is because new usage is noticeable, even when it accounts for a small proportion of language use. This is akin to what scientists call perceptual salience. Surprising language use will call our attention more than unsurprising language patterns, and that can make this myth can seem true.

By way of example, a reader concerned about texting language – perhaps after reading media headlines about it – is much more likely to dwell on two uses of *idkw* (*I don't know why*) in a student paper than on the 798 other words (for instance) that have been around for decades, arranged in a grammatical order of subject-verb-object that has been around for centuries.

Closer to the truth is that even proportionally small choices can feel frequent, and it is common to overstate the extent of language change and difference. Steeped in a 150-year history of writing myths, we may particularly notice what doesn't conform to *correct writing*. We end up, again, with language regulation mode focused on error, rather than language exploration of diverse writing patterns.

8.4.4 *Correct Writing* Is Expected to Be Formal and Is Disliked for Being Formal

Even as students regularly hear that *correct writing* should be formal and detached, it is criticized for the same – for being "impersonal," "dry," and "stodgy." Helen Sword's *Stylish Academic Writing* describes most

academic writing as "bland." Steven Pinker's *Sense of Style* advises writers to avoid writing too academically. Here we can see resonances with
the Plain English movements discussed in myth 1, which strive to make
writing more accessible but sometimes can't escape language regulation
mode. Still, Sword's project began by exploring patterns in several pieces
of formal writing, and she recommends considering occasional informal
patterns, such as second-person pronouns.

8.4.5 Informal Is not the Same as Careless

Iterations of this myth imply that digital writing is careless. For instance,
"The Internet is Making Writing Worse" reported that 68 percent of
teachers said that digital tools made students "more likely to take short-
cuts and not put effort into their writing," while 46 percent said that digital tools made students more likely to "write too fast and be careless."

A couple of considerations get us closer to the truth. One is that the
survey presumed a direct relationship between digital writing and fast,
careless writing – rather than, for instance, between timed standardized
exams and careless writing. In the same survey, more than half the teachers said digital technologies increase the likelihood that students would
revise and edit their work. Teens said the same thing in their own survey.[7] A majority of the teachers furthermore responded that digital technologies made students more creative and collaborative in their writing.

Another consideration is that some research reports thoughtful attention in digital writing, particularly for certain audiences. My own students echo this: Every term, I poll them about whether they sometimes
revise their text messages, and all of them say they do.

Closer to the truth is that writing across the continuum can be done
quickly and without thought, or with time and thoughtful revision.
Furthermore, the informal writing on the continuum is not separate from
the formal writing: All writing on the continuum shares some purposes
and norms, and includes sliding degrees of interpersonal to informational, informal to formal, and personal to impersonal language patterns.

Also closer to the truth is that informal English has long been important for language users, providing unique opportunities for meaning,
connection, and innovation. In 1883, Walt Whitman called slang "the
accretion and growth of every dialect, race, and range of time." One
hundred and thirty years later, researchers called text messages creative
approximations of conversations, full of innovative idioms, puns, and
other word play.

Indeed, one distinguishing characteristic of informal digital writing is
that it allows for more flexible and innovative usage. For example, the

use of *because* as a preposition, as I've used it in this myth title, is relatively new and informal – and rather a breakthrough innovation, since
prepositions belong to a closed lexical category that doesn't get new
members very often. The same myth title on the right of the continuum
would be something like *you cannot write that because of the nature of the
internet, which is informal,* in which the use of *because of* is more traditional and less innovative.

8.4.6 The Ends of the Writing Continuum Are Fundamentally Similar

When we believe that new technology threatens writing, it is easy to
overlook norms used across the writing continuum, from informal digital
writing on the left to formal published writing on the right. One shared
grammatical norm discussed in myth 1 is subject-verb-object order. Our
earlier example of *idkw* might be used in informal digital writing, while
a similar statement in formal academic writing might be *Contemporary
research is unclear regarding why*. Both use the subject-verb-object structure of English, even as the digital example uses interpersonal, informal first person and abbreviations, and the academic writing includes an
informational focus and *correct writing* conventions.

Likewise, while slang is more likely on the left side of the continuum,
new words, including slang, follow morphological processes used across
the continuum. *Okayest* was one informal example we saw in myth 1, and
we'll add another here: *hangry. Hangry (hungry +angry)* is more likely
in writing on the left of the continuum. But it follows the morphological
process of blending (combining two words by clipping one or both), just
like the words *malware (malicious + software)* and *Brexit (Britain + exit)*
that we find on the right side of the continuum.

8.4.7 The Ends of the Writing Continuum Use Similar Features, Differently

Rules like "don't use *I* in academic writing" imply that language features
used on one end of the continuum are not used on the other end. Yet as
we saw in the introduction and myth 1, first-person pronouns are used
across the continuum, just differently.

Like first-person pronouns, punctuation and capitalization regularly
appear in usage guides and they, too, are used across the writing continuum, but differently. In informal digital writing, punctuation, capitalization, and emojis are regularly used to show stance and build connection

and cohesion.[8] In formal academic writing, punctuation and capitalization are also used to build cohesion, and to follow usage norms for breaking up information into grammatical units.

For instance, if I'm writing on the left of the continuum, following informal digital writing norms on social media, I could write: *Writing patterns are SO FASCINATING!!!* ☺. In that sentence, the informal, interpersonal uses of capitalization, punctuation, and an emoji prioritize sharing my enthusiasm with others. Those choices are complemented by the balance of lexical categories: one simple noun phrase (*writing patterns*), a verb, an adjective, and an adverb.

In this book, though, you expect a more informational sentence, such as: *Writing patterns highlight intriguing similarities and differences across shared language use.* In that sentence, my capitalization, punctuation, and dense noun phrases prioritize formal, impersonal information sharing, rather than sharing my enthusiasm. As you know already, formal academic writing hearts nouns, so all the nouns won't surprise you. But here again, both examples use the subject-verb-object construction.

8.4.8 Informal Digital Writing and Formal Academic Writing Are on a Continuum

Closer to the truth is that writing across the continuum has some shared purposes and patterns, and some different patterns. With exploration and practice, writers can learn to consciously notice different writing patterns across the continuum. For our final additions to the continuum, we will look at seven brief examples in Table 8.2. Two come from social media, two are from online news sources, two are from marketing emails, and one is from an academic research article. Each one reached wide audiences, as you'll see in the details below.

The examples land on different parts of the continuum. The social media posts on the same platform alone vary, with the Twitter.com (now X.com) company post more informal and interpersonal than the post by US President Joe Biden. The marketing emails use patterns around the middle of the continuum: punctuation to convey an excited stance, an emoticon to transition to a new topic. The academic writing example is the most informational, impersonal, and formal. It includes dense noun phrases that prioritize research, along with punctuation to break up compressed sentences. Every one of the seven examples is grammatically possible and meaningful in English, and all seven examples also follow distinct norms based on their locations on the continuum.

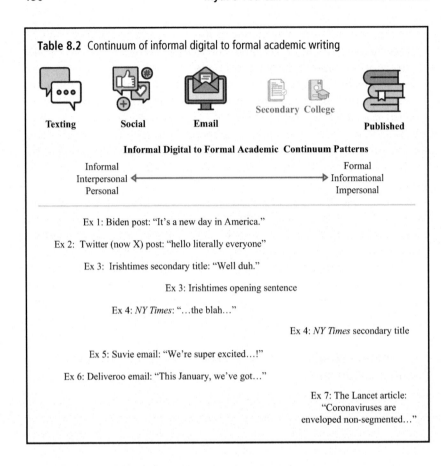

Table 8.2 Continuum of informal digital to formal academic writing

Texting   Social   Email   Secondary College   Published

Informal Digital to Formal Academic Continuum Patterns

Informal		Formal
Interpersonal ◄──────────────────────►		Informational
Personal		Impersonal

Ex 1: Biden post: "It's a new day in America."

Ex 2: Twitter (now X) post: "hello literally everyone"

Ex 3: Irishtimes secondary title: "Well duh."

Ex 3: Irishtimes opening sentence

Ex 4: *NY Times*: "…the blah…"

Ex 4: *NY Times* secondary title

Ex 5: Suvie email: "We're super excited…!"

Ex 6: Deliveroo email: "This January, we've got…"

Ex 7: The Lancet article:
"Coronaviruses are
enveloped non-segmented…"

Of course, any seven examples are only a limited sampling. In this case, they capture published rather than private examples, and several are dominated by US events and culture. Even so, they show some of the rich diversity of writing that characterizes contemporary life. And even their brief exploration below makes it clear that *correct writing* is neither isolated nor singularly correct.

8.4.8.1 Social Media Writing: Examples 1 and 2

Example 1: It's a new day in America.

Example 1, by US President Joe Biden, was the most liked Twitter (now X) post of 2021, with more than 4 million likes. The post includes writing patterns between the most formal and informal ends of the continuum. Toward the formal, impersonal side, the example follows *correct writing* conventions and usage preferences: It includes a full independent clause and norms for spelling, capitalization, and punctuation dating back to myth 1. Toward the informal, interpersonal side, the post includes a contraction (*it's*) and avoids the dense phrases characteristic of formal and informational writing. The post follows English norms of subject-verb-object sentence construction, as well as social media norms of brief length.

Example 2: hello literally everyone

Example 2, posted by Twitter (now X), was the second most-liked post of 2021, with more than 3.3 million likes.

This post follows informal digital writing norms by avoiding capitalization and punctuation. It uses *literally* to add humor and emphasis (rather than to mean "by the letter"), by drawing attention to the global outage on the social media site Facebook that drove even more users to the site. This use of *literally* is not new but is usually informal. These choices prioritize informal, interpersonal connection and follow social media norms for brevity and conventions.[9]

8.4.8.2 Online News Articles: Examples 3 and 4

Example 3: "Harry and Meghan: The Union of Two Great Houses, the Windsors and the Celebrities, Is Complete."[10]

Example 3 is the most-read story in 2021 on irishtimes.com (surpassing even the COVID-19 vaccine tracker), by Patrick Freyne. This article, which analyzes the Royals' 2021 interview with Oprah, moves fluidly around the middle of the writing continuum. It blends informal and formal, interpersonal and informational, and personal and impersonal language patterns.

For instance, the article's secondary title starts with formal written patterns, and ends with informal ones: "After Harry and Meghan, the monarchy looks archaic and racist. Well duh." Then, the opening sentence uses formal syntax and mechanics, with some informal wording: "Having a monarchy next door is a little like having a neighbour who's really into clowns and has daubed their house with clown murals, displays clown dolls in each window and has an insatiable desire to hear about and discuss clown-related news stories."

In its compressed noun phrases, this sentence uses formal, informational patterns along with informal phrasing (e.g., "really into"). The article continues this blend throughout, using mostly *correct writing* conventions and usage preferences while also using informal phrasing, all of which is grammatically possible and meaningful in English. The patterns work together to make the writing both informational and interpersonal. For example, the author uses the informal phrase "hysterical batshittery," which is innovative but understandable because it follows morphological processes we use to create nouns in English: compounding two nouns (*bat* + *shit*), then adding the noun suffix *-ery* (think *bakery*), to convey, in this case, a set of inexplicable behaviors.

Example 4: "There's a Name for the Blah You're Feeling: It's Called Languishing."[11]

Example 4 is the most-read article of 2021 in *The New York Times*, by Adam Grant. This *New York Times* title uses some informal wording while following formal syntax and conventions, as well as English morphological norms. Like "well duh" in example 3, the use of "blah" approximates speech. At the same time, the writer uses subject-verb-object construction and the determiner *the* to help readers understand that "the blah" refers to a state of being and functions grammatically as a noun.

The secondary title of example 4 is somewhere between interpersonal and informational writing, but it is more formal: "The neglected middle child of mental health can dull your motivation and focus – and it may be the dominant emotion of 2021." This sentence follows *correct writing* usage preferences and favors noun phrases over verbs; it also hedges with the use of *may* to avoid a generalization. Simultaneously, the passage connects directly with the reader with the use of *your*.

8.4.8.3 Marketing Emails: Examples 5 and 6

Example 5: "We're super excited to let you know that your new Suvie 2.0 has shipped!"

Examples 5 and 6 are online exemplars for marketing emails.[12] Example 5, by Suvie, is a personalized shipping confirmation email that addresses the recipient by name and opens with a blend of informal and formal patterns: "We're super excited to let you know that your new Suvie 2.0 has shipped!". The sentence follows *correct writing* conventions and usage preferences, and it also uses second person address and a balance of nouns, pronouns, verbs, and adverbs to emphasize personalized reaction, interpersonal connection, and interpersonal focus.

In and after this opening sentence, the email continues its blend of informal, interpersonal, and formal patterns, including formal capitalization and informal, interpersonal punctuation, emojis, and boosters.

Example 6: This January, we've got more plant-powered deliciousness
than you can shake a celery stick at.
Another featured email campaign is from Deliveroo, from their 2021
Veganuary email campaign (here again, we get innovative language
following old morphological processes, with the blending of *vegan* +
January to make *Veganuary*).

The Deliveroo email follows *correct writing* conventions and usage
preferences, with full clauses and *correct writing* punctuation and spelling. It also includes informal, interpersonal patterns like second-person
address and contractions, as well as more examples of innovative words
that follow established morphological processes of English: *Deliciousness*
turns *delicious* into a noun with the suffix *-ness* (like *closeness*). Like
example 5, the email follows subject-verb-object construction throughout its sentences.

8.4.8.4 Academic Research Article: Example 7

Finally, the most cited academic paper in 2021 was "Clinical Features of
Patients Infected with 2019 Novel Coronavirus in Wuhan, China" in *The
Lancet*.[13]

The article opens with the following noun-heavy sentence:
"Coronaviruses are enveloped non-segmented positive-sense RNA
viruses belonging to the family Coronaviridae and the order Nidovirales
and broadly distributed in humans and other mammals.[1]"

This opening sentence contains a noun subject (*Coronaviruses*) and a
single, simple verb (*are*). The remaining 22 words of the sentence appear
in two dense noun phrases coordinated by *and*. These noun phrases
emphasize research phenomena and are followed by a citation. In other
words, this sentence follows formal, impersonal, informational language
patterns characteristic of the far right side of the continuum. The article
continues in the same way, with additional patterns such as passive verbs
(e.g., *patients were admitted*) and text-internal use of first-person pronouns (e.g., *we collected and analyzed*).

Closer to the truth is that most contemporary adults need to read and
write across the writing continuum. Informal digital writing is widespread, practiced by diverse language users following what is grammatically possible and meaningful in English, and characterized by
informal, interpersonal, personal language patterns. Formal academic
writing is prioritized in universities, practiced by some language users
following what is grammatically possible and meaningful in English,
and characterized by formal, informational, impersonal language

patterns. Contemporary writing spans the full continuum, and the full continuum is connected, but schools and tests rarely focus on exploring patterns across it.

Related questions get us closer to the truth. What if diverse writing was explored in school, according to a range of purposes and patterns? What if it was equally important for students to recognize how to represent their biology experiment in a tweet as in a lab report? What if students could use their ability to tell what is grammatically possible and meaningful in a social media post to help them recognize what is grammatically possible and meaningful in a school paper? What if students had ongoing chances to recognize and describe language differences, without a hierarchy suggesting only one kind of writing is *correct* and *intelligent*? This approach would take advantage of, rather than miss, a wide range of writing already used.

To support that kind of language knowledge and exploration, we need to recognize old myths and metaphors but conceive of writing anew. That's what we'll do in the concluding chapter.

CHAPTER NINE

Conclusion: Writing Continuum, Language Exploration

Acknowledging the Myth Glasses

In the past eight chapters, we've seen the myths and metaphors we are up against. We've seen the ideas in Table 9.1 appear subtly and explicitly, in the past and today. Before considering what it means to take off the myth glasses, we'll recount what shutters the view in Table 9.1.

Table 9.1 *Correct writing* myths and metaphors

Correct writing is...	Anything other than *correct writing* is...
... a sign of a good person	... a sign of a bad person
... a national bond	... a threat to national unity
... superior	... inferior
... a standard for excellence	... a threat to standards
... controlled	... careless
... proof of *intelligence*	... proof of lack of ability
... testable in narrow tasks	... not important enough to test
... learned by college	... disregarded by college
... rarely used by students	... commonly used by students
... the key to college	... unwelcome in college
... a path to a good job	... a path to unemployment
... under threat	... on the rise

9.1 Looking Through the Myth Glasses

9.1.1 Myths Are What We Are up Against

Bolstered by tests, headlines, and schools, the myth glasses make *correct writing* the only writing that counts. This mythical view is real. It is not a figment of our imagination, but a reality we have constructed for ourselves. Within that reality, language regulation mode is the only viable way to approach English.

9.1.2 But We've Seen Alternatives

We've seen that English spelling is an awesome mess that must be memorized, and that writing and spelling knowledge are not the same thing. We've seen that *correct writing* is explicitly taught and gets easier with practice: It is not natural, and it is no one's mother tongue. We've seen that many tests are based on timed, limited writing tasks that do not represent untimed, varied writing tasks.

We've seen that tests and criteria change over time, even though claims about *correct writing* and student writing remain similar. We've seen that standardized exam scores do not predict how students will write in other circumstances. We've seen that secondary and postsecondary writing are different, and postsecondary and workplace writing are different.

We've seen that written English is not changing terribly fast, even though it can feel like it is: Writing choices that stand out to us can overshadow unchanging patterns shared across the continuum – especially if we are seeing them through the myth glasses. We've seen that many students make a conscious effort to avoid informal patterns in formal writing, and we've seen that informal language entails language knowledge and creativity.

We've seen that writing is 3-D: It depends on contexts and tasks. We've seen multiple reasons that people don't use *correct writing* – to connect with others, prioritize personal reactions, attract readers or clients. We've seen that writing across a continuum shares purposes related to cohesion, connection, focus, stance, and usage, and we've seen diverse language patterns for fulfilling those purposes. Different patterns in informal digital writing, workplace email, secondary and postsecondary student writing, and published formal writing create a continuum of informal to formal, interpersonal to informational, and personal to impersonal writing.

We've seen that even though we have inherited language regulation mode, it is possible to approach writing as a continuum for exploration. We have seen that explicit attention to similarities and differences creates bridges to new kinds of writing.

9.1.3 We Don't Have to Regulate First, and Explore Second

We've therefore seen why we don't need language regulation first, and language exploration second. We don't need to use *correct writing* rules before breaking them. Three reasons include:

- **Writing is already diverse**
  Even in the basic writing continuum we have been using, we can see a range of writing familiar to most grown students and other adults. In the world outside schools and tests, writing diversity is a boon rather than a bane. It allows us to fulfill diverse writing purposes with a range of available language patterns.
- *Correct writing* **rules are often confusing and vague**
  Correct writing rules can be vague and can also change. Undefined expectations like *elegant* (early Harvard and Cambridge examiner reports), *lucid* ("Why Johnny can't write"), and *careless* ("The Internet is Making Writing Worse") are common, as are references to *grammar* that mean spelling and capitalization. By exploring language patterns, we can learn more about writing, and be more precise when we describe it.
- **Language exploration means more writing knowledge**
  Analyzing diverse writing means more writing knowledge, and more metacognitive bridges across the writing continuum.

9.1.4 All Grammatically Possible and Meaningful Writing Is Correct

Exploring a writing continuum means thinking about correctness in terms of what is possible and meaningful in a language, according to a range of contexts, tasks, purposes, patterns, and norms.

All the writing on the continuum is linguistically equal: It all follows norms and responds to purposes and contexts. We've seen, for instance, how informational, impersonal patterns fulfill college writing goals, while interpersonal and informational patterns fulfill workplace email goals.

This doesn't mean that everyone values different kinds of writing equally. After a century of myths, *correct writing* is attached to educational and socioeconomic opportunity: It influences college admission and employment decisions as well as assumptions about character. This means that even though a continuum of writing is possible and meaningful, only a small part of that continuum is conventionally valued in schools and job applications. It follows that only a fraction of *writers* are valued in schools and job applications, even though existing their writing knowledge and other abilities may never have been rewarded in schools or tests.

To shift to language exploration, we have to recognize myths and their power, as well as treat diverse writing in terms of what is possible and meaningful. If we can understand differences across the writing continuum and know they do not mean differences in capability, we are closer to the truth. If we can use more accurate terms in our talk about writing, we are closer to the truth.

For instance, we can clarify what labels such as *concise* and *informal* mean according to language patterns – that *concise* often means "uses dense noun phrases," while *informal* often means "uses interpersonal punctuation conventions." We can clarify several common writing terms by using *grammar* to refer to what is grammatically possible and meaningful in English; *conventions* to refer to norms of spelling and punctuation; and *usage preferences* to refer to grammatical and conventional choices that might be preferred in a task but are not inherently *correct*.

9.2 Taking Off the Myth Glasses

9.2.1 We Can Use a Continuum Metaphor for Writing

A writing continuum reflects different possibilities, rather than *incorrect* and *correct* options. It emphasizes the inevitability of writing similarities and differences, and the value of metacognitive bridges across them. The writing continuum in Table 9.2 consolidates details of the continuum we have seen throughout the book in order to illustrate how all parts of the continuum illuminate the others. This consolidated continuum is representative of what is already true of written English in the world – it has the shared purposes of cohesion, connection, focus, stance, and usage as well as informal to formal, interpersonal to informational, and personal to impersonal patterns. But this is an aspirational writing continuum for education, because it accounts for all parts of the continuum.

9.2.2 We Can Shift to Language Exploration Mode

With a change from language regulation to exploration, we focus more on learning and less on judging. We gain explicit, conscious knowledge of similarities and differences across the writing continuum. We see how writing diversity and change are meaningful, and we see that writing across the continuum still follows many of the same fundamental rules. We avoid false separations between informal and formal writing, which are connected on the continuum, even as they have some useful distinctions.

In schools, this means making English writing classes what they sound like: courses that explore writing in English, including students' own diverse writing, on a continuum like Table 9.2. Then, we make writing about more than *correct writing* errors. Then, a range of writing and language knowledge such as the details becomes fodder for learning. Then,

Table 9.2 Writing continuum language patterns

	Informal Interpersonal Personal ←	**Continuum Patterns**	→ Formal Informational Impersonal	
Continuum Purposes				
Cohesion	Pragmatic markers, emojis, hashtags, reactions, new posts and messages	New paragraphs or bullet points, transition words, moves such as greetings and closings	Transition words, introductory moves such as opening "hook" and closing generalization, templates such as 5-paragraph essay	Diverse transition words, introductory and development moves, sections such as intro, research review, methods, discussion
Connection	Retweets, text external 1st person 2nd person direct address	Greetings and farewells, questions, 2nd person and text external 1st person	References to general experiences and common knowledge, sometimes sources, text-external 1st person	Directives, citations and references to other sources, text internal 1st person
Focus	Simple sentence or phrase subjects, emphasizing people, events, experiences, active verbs	Simple sentence subjects, may emphasize people and events, active or passive verbs	Simple sentence subjects, emphasizing broad phenomena, experience, active and passive verbs	Dense noun phrase sentence subjects, emphasizing ideas and processes, active and passive verbs
Stance	Boosters, generalizations, punctuation, vowels and capital letters, emojis	Hedges, boosters, punctuation marks, capital letters	Boosters, generalizations, hedges	Regular hedges, some boosters, rare generalizations
Usage	Flexible, adaptable spelling, punctuation	Usually *correct writing* conventions and usage preferences, with some **flexibility in** punctuation and spelling	*Correct writing* conventions and usage preferences and spelling	*Correct writing* conventions and usage preferences and spelling
Full continuum		subject-verb-object construction open and closed lexical categories morphological rules of English		

Table 9.3 Language exploration don't's and do's

Language exploration don't's and do's	
Don't	**Do**
Don't acknowledge only part of the writing continuum in school	Do address and analyze multiple kinds of writing
Don't imply that studying literature in English is the same thing as studying English language	Do address different genres explicitly
Don't use hierarchical metaphors	Do use continuum metaphors
Don't interpret standardized test results as general indications of ability	Do recognize that writing responds to tasks, and a test only tests what is on the test
Don't treat writing development as linear or finite	Do treat writing development as ongoing
Don't imply only one kind of writing is *controlled* or *intelligent*	Do emphasize that diverse writing is possible and meaningful and acquired with practice
Don't imply *grammar* and conventions are the same	Do refer to conventions as spelling, punctuation, and capitalization norms on a continuum
Don't imply that norms for grammar and conventions are always the same	Do refer to grammar according to what is grammatically possible and meaningful in a language

we support more of the writing experiences and resources people already have, and we support informed choices in students' writing.

Language exploration shifts what we do, and how we talk about, writing, toward the right column of Table 9.3.

With language exploration mode, we expect and study a continuum of writing. We recognize writing myths and look for answers closer to the truth. We support the human rights of language diversity and language knowledge, using a continuum metaphor and language exploration, to move ahead differently.

9.3 Concluding

We have good reason to hope that we can, in fact, change common approaches to writing. We have language patterns and subconscious language knowledge to help us. We have plenty of possible and meaningful writing for exploration. Even the persistence of language regulation is a reminder that language diversity persists, too.

But hoping is not our task. So said the scientist David George Haskell when asked about whether he was hopeful about the future of nature.[1] It is up to future generations, Haskell said, to decide if there was reason to hope. Our job in the present is to get to work.

Let us get to work exploring. Later, let us say we had grounds for hope for a more open, knowledgeable approach to writing.

Afterword

I wrote a lot of this book on the islands that are home to me, where much of my family lives. My favorite writing haven is the smallest island, a place of frigate birds, a single store, and a population of 150 souls, none faint of heart. One morning, as the sun rose over the sea grape trees and I sat down to write, I got a call from my 85-year-old second mom, Suzy.

The wind! She breathed into the phone. *It's a beautiful wind. Can you come over for a sail?*

There is no saying no to Suzy, not really, and I hopped on a bicycle to ride down the quiet road toward her house, startling a night heron on the way.

When I arrived, Suzy was standing outside in a hot pink bathing suit and yellow latex kitchen gloves. *Do you like my sailing gloves?*, she laughed, and we made our way slowly over the pocky sand to the dock. Tied to the dock and floating several feet beneath it was the sunfish boat we would take. I looked for a way Suzy could get in without bending her knees and heard a thump. She had dropped herself down on the dock and was scooting on her behind toward the boat.

Once on our way, Suzy wrapped the mast line around her kitchen glove, stared in peaceful concentration at the sail, and caught the wind. With a low chuckle, she told me she hoped I wasn't concerned when she scooted on her behind: She had had to do a lot of scooting when she had polio at 12, and she was good at it. Then, as we sailed, Suzy alternately prayed, cooed, and cursed the sail, keeping it a shallow bowl of light and air. At one point, I made a mistake, and Suzy and I laughed, real belly laughing, before we moved on.

When we finished, we walked up the sand to my bicycle, so that I could get back to writing. Suzy asked a passing question about the book, and I said: *I'm writing about how schools and tests don't capture what writing is … they tell people they are dumb, or not good writers, when writing, and writers, are a lot more than that.*

Suzy became very still then, her expression serious. *Those tests told me I was an idiot,* she said, her tone quiet and bitter.

After a long moment, she went on. *I was so afraid my kids would inherit something from me, that they wouldn't be smart. I wasn't good at tests. Said I was an idiot.* I never knew this about Suzy, only that she is a force on the islands, known for successfully running businesses, editing books that document island history and cuisine, and generally getting her way.

Shame on those tests, for never capturing a fraction of Suzy's ability. Shame on us, if we don't learn something different.

Notes

Introduction: When Writing Means *Correct Writing*

1 See some recent examples below: The 11 extremely common grammar mistakes that make people cringe—and make you look less smart: Word experts, by Kathy and Ross Petras, March 2021: https://www.cnbc.com/2021/03/24/common-grammar-mistakes-that-make-people-cringe-and-make-you-look-less-smart-word-experts.html 22 grammar mistakes that make you look really stupid, by Steve Adcock, December 2020: https://www.theladders.com/career-advice/22-common-grammar-mistakes-that-make-you-look-really-stupid Why are students coming into college poorly prepared to write? https://www.cmu.edu/teaching/designteach/teach/instructionalstrategies/writing/poorlyprepared.html Our students can't write very well—It's no mystery why: https://www.edweek.org/teaching-learning/opinion-our-students-cant-write-very-well-its-no-mystery-why/2017/01

2 Thank you to my students in English linguistics courses in the fall of 2022 for sharing their ideas and consenting to my sharing them. The first three notes where offered by students who wished to share their work anonymously, while one note about family and friends was shared by Mary Hoskins.

3 For the full blog entry, see: www.essayhell.com/2015/06/how-to-write-a-college-application-essay-even-if-you-cant-write/

4 In these ways, the writing myths in this book can be thought of as contributors to the broader literacy myth characterized by Harvey Graff; like the broader literacy myth, *correct writing* myths are commonplace, articulated through institutions, and capable of imbuing *correct writing* with immeasurable, ineffable grandeur.

5 The pronouns *it*, *I*, and *you*, and negation words, commonly collocate, or hang out with, *ain't* in the 1.9-billion word corpus of Global Web-based English (GloWbe) developed by M. Davies. See more here: www.english-corpora.org/glowbe/.

6 Because *correct writing* has been used to keep so many people outside the proverbial gates, some writing researchers argue we should write differently in higher education, avoiding academic writing and standardized English. This book takes a different tack. It assumes we need to explore the history and nature of *correct writing*, and it focuses as much on language itself – patterns across different kinds of writing – as it does on language beliefs. It assumes that exploring a continuum of writing (including *correct writing*) gives us the best chance of learning more and mythologizing less.

Myth 1 You Can't Write That

[1] As happened, for instance, with the spelling of Biowulf and Beowulf in the tenth century; see the British Library images and descriptions here: https://blogs.bl.uk/digitisedmanuscripts/2013/05/you-say-beowulf-i-say-biowulf.html.

[2] Before efforts to make spelling more uniform were attempts to make handwriting, style, and form more uniform in thirteenth-century land deeds and other legal documents; see Flanders, J., *A Place for Everything: The Curious History of Alphabetical Order*. London, Picador: 2020. Likewise, earlier than the sixteenth century were smaller efforts toward standardization; see: C. Upward, and G. Davidson, *The History of English Spelling*, vol. 26. Hoboken, NJ: John Wiley & Sons, 2011.

[3] Bishop Lowth wrote his popular *Short Introduction to English Grammar* in 1763 in the hope of supporting his son's future Latin studies. Although Lowth does not seem to have intended this, his book is credited with bringing about the rise of prescriptive grammar and dialect-specific rules for rewarding certain writers and shaming others. See I.T.-B. van Ostade (2010), *The Bishop's Grammar: Robert Lowth and the Rise of Prescriptivism*. Oxford, Oxford University Press. Some sources indicate that Murray plagiarized Lowth as a principal source for his own usage guide. See E. Vorlat (1959), *The Sources of Lindley Murray's "The English Grammar"*, Leuvense Bijdragen, 48, 108–25.

[4] A classic example is the great vowel shift, which moved vowel sounds from being produced (through air propulsion) higher to lower in the mouth, and from front to back in the mouth, through several shifts in the fourteenth to the seventeenth century (e.g., here are some examples transcribed into the International Phonetic Alphabet (IPA): /knaɪt/ → /naɪt/; /gnæt/ → /næt/; /nemə/ → /nem/). Standardized spelling didn't keep up with this shift, and vowels continue to change in this direction without changes in standardized spelling.

[5] English has six vowel letters: *a, e, i, o, u* and sometimes *y*, but it has at least 15 vowel sounds in the International Phonetic Alphabet (IPA).

[6] Resources that separate informal and formal writing, for instance, include: the BBC (www.bbc.co.uk/bitesize/guides/z996hyc/revision/1); Cambridge Assessment (www.cambridgeenglish.org/learning-english/activities-for-learners/c1w001-formal-and-informal-writing), and resources from various universities: Massey University (https://owll.massey.ac.nz/academic-writing/writing-objectively.php), the University of Southern California (https://libguides.usc.edu/writingguide/academicwriting), University Technology Sydney (www.uts.edu.au/current-students/support/helps/self-help-resources/grammar/formal-and-informal-language), Lund University (https://awelu.srv.lu.se/grammar-and-words/register-and-style/formal-vs-informal/), the

University of Melbourne (https://students.unimelb.edu.au/academic-skills/
explore-our-resources/developing-an-academic-writing-style/key-
features-of-academic-style).

7   Calls for formal English to be "direct" and "plain" appear over several centuries. Generally, these calls tend to evoke a single, moralized standard of
correct writing – with less jargon and shorter sentences. Linguist Deborah
Cameron charts the Plain English debates throughout the past 500 years,
identifying times when "Latin eloquence" won over "plainness," as well
as times when "plainness" won: the Enlightenment period emphasized
the need for plain English; in the mid-twentieth century Sir Ernest Gower
published *Plain Words* for British civil servants; and the late twentieth
century *The Times* style guide espoused plainness (D. Cameron, *Verbal
Hygiene*. Abingdon, Oxfordshire: Routledge, 2012). In these debates,
Cameron writes, "using a certain style of language becomes a *moral* matter" (p. 67; emphasis hers). Ultimately, discussions about plain English do
not clearly agree on what makes something plain, why it matters, or who
gets to decide; and as with much discussion of language, much more is at
stake than which words to use. In the case of plain English, language is a
"a mark of judiciousness, impartiality, and good sense," and "a symbol of
the struggle against totalitarianism" (Ibid.)

8   Angelou, M. (1969). *I Know Why the Caged Bird Sings*. New York:
Bantam.

9   I derive these five purposes from synthesizing applied linguistics and writing research, especially corpus linguistic analysis of patterns in a range of
English use, including the following:

Ädel, A. (2017). Remember that Your Reader Cannot Read Your Mind:
Problem/solution-oriented Metadiscourse in Teacher Feedback on
Student Writing, *English for Specific Purposes*, 45, 54–68.

Aull, B. (2019). A Study of Phatic Emoji Use in WhatsApp Communication,
Internet Pragmatics, 2(2), 206–32.

Aull, L. L. (2020). *How Students Write: A Linguistic Analysis*. New York:
Modern Language Association.

Aull, L. L., D. Bandarage, and M.R. Miller (2017). Generality in Student
and Expert Epistemic Stance: A Corpus Analysis of First-year, Upper-
level, and Published Academic Writing, *Journal of English for Academic
Purposes*, 26, 29–41.

Aull, L. L. and Z. Lancaster (2014). Linguistic Markers of Stance in
Early and Advanced Academic Writing: A Corpus-based Comparison,
Written Communication, 31(2), 151–83.

Bai, Q., Q. Dan, Z. Mu, and M. Yang (2019). A Systematic Review
of Emoji: Current Research and Future Perspectives, *Frontiers in
Psychology*, 10: https://doi.org/10.3389/fpsyg.2019.02221.

Barton, E. L. (1995). Contrastive and Non-Contrastive Connectives Metadiscourse Functions in Argumentation, *Written Communication*, 12(2), 219–39.

Barton, E. L. and G. Stygall (2002). *Discourse Studies in Composition.* Cresskill, NJ: Hampton Press.

Biber, D. (1988). *Variation across Speech and Writing.* Cambridge, Cambridge University Press. 1988.

Biber, D., et al. (2002). Speaking and Writing in the University: A Multidimensional Comparison, *TESOL Quarterly*, 36(1), 9–48.

Biber, D. and J. Egbert. (2018). *Register Variation Online.* Cambridge: Cambridge University Press.

Biber, D. and B. Gray. (2016). *Grammatical Complexity in Academic English: Linguistic Change in Writing.* Cambridge: Cambridge University Press.

Black, K. E. (2022). Variation in Linguistic Stance: A Person-Centered Analysis of Student Writing. *Written Communication*, 39(4), 531–563.

Brown, D. W. and C. C. Palmer (2015). The Phrasal Verb in American English: Using Corpora to Track Down Historical Trends in Particle Distribution, Register Variation, and Noun Collocations, in *Studies in the History of the English Language VI: Evidence and Method in Histories of English*, eds. M. Adams, L. J. Brinton and R. D. Fulk, 71–97. Berlin: Mouton de Gruyter.

Charles, M. (2006). The Construction of Stance in Reporting Clauses: A Cross-disciplinary Study of Theses, *Applied Linguistics*, 27(3), 492–518.

Crismore, A. (1983). *Metadiscourse: What it Is and how it Is Used in School and Non-school Social Science Texts*, in *Center for the Study of Reading.* Urbana-Champaign: University of Illinois Press.

Crismore, A. and R. Farnsworth (1990). *Metadiscourse in Popular and Professional Science Discourse*, in *The Writing Scholar: Studies in the Language and Conventions of Academic Discourse*, eds. A. Crismore and R., 45–68. Newbury Park, CA: Sage.

Crismore, A., R. Markkanen, and M.S. Steffensen. (1993). Metadiscourse in Persuasive Writing: A Study of Texts Written by American and Finnish University Students, *Written Communication*, 10(1), 39–71.

Crossley, S. A. (2020). Linguistic Features in Writing Quality and Development: An Overview, *Journal of Writing Research*, 11(3), 415–43.

Dixon, T., Egbert, J., Larsson, T., Kaatari, H., & Hanks, E. (2023). Toward an empirical understanding of formality: Triangulating corpus data with teacher perceptions. *English for Specific Purposes*, 71, 161–177.

Gawne, L. and G. McCulloch (2019). Emoji as Digital Gestures, *Language@ Internet*, 17(2).

Goźdź-Roszkowski, S. (2011). *Patterns of Linguistic Variation in American Legal English: A Corpus-based Study*. Bern, Switzerland: Peter Lang.

Gray, B. (2010). On the Use of Demonstrative Pronouns and Determiners as Cohesive Devices: A Focus on Sentence-initial This/these in Academic Prose, *Journal of English for Academic Purposes*, 9(3),167–83.

Gray, B. and D. Biber. (2012). Current Conceptions of Stance, in *Stance and Voice in Written Academic Genres*, eds. K. Hyland and C. S. Guinda, 15–33. London: Palgrave Macmillan.

Haas, C., Takayoshi, P., Carr, B., Hudson, K., & Pollock, R. (2011). Young people's everyday literacies: The language features of instant messaging. *Research in the Teaching of English*, 45(4): pp. 378–404.

Hardy, J. A. and E. Frigina (2016). Genre Variation in Student Writing: A Multi-dimensional Analysis, *Journal of English for Academic Purposes*, 22, 119–31.

Hardy, J. A. and U. Römer. (2013). Revealing Disciplinary Variation in Student Writing: A Multi-dimensional Analysis of the Michigan Corpus of Upper-level Student Papers (MICUSP), *Corpora*, 8(2), 183–207.

Harwood, N. (2009). An interview-based study of the functions of citations in academic writing across two disciplines. *Journal of pragmatics,* 41(3), 497–518.

Ho, V. (2018). Using Metadiscourse in Making Persuasive Attempts through Workplace Request Emails, *Journal of Pragmatics*, 134, 70–81.

Holmes, J. (1984). Modifying Illocutionary Force, *Journal of Pragmatics*, 8(3), 345–65.

Hyland, K. (1998). Persuasion and Context: The Pragmatics of Academic Metadiscourse, *Journal of Pragmatics*, 30(4), 437–55.

Hyland, K. (2004). *Disciplinary Discourses: Social Interactions in Academic Writing*. Ann Arbor: University of Michigan Press.

Hyland, K. (2005). Stance and Engagement: A Model of Interaction in Academic Discourse, *Discourse Studies*, 7(2), 173–92.

Hyland, K. (2005). *Metadiscourse: Exploring Interaction in Writing*. London: Continuum.

Hyland, K. and P. Tse (2004). *Metadiscourse in Academic Writing: A Reappraisal*, Applied Linguistics, 25(2): 156–77.

Kriaučiūnienė, R., La Roux, J., & Lauciūtė, M. (2018). Stance Taking in Social Media: the Analysis of the Comments About Us Presidential Candidates on Facebook and Twitter. *Verbum*, 9, 21–30.

Kuhi, D. and B. Behnam (2011). Generic Variations and Metadiscourse Use in the Writing of Applied Linguists: A Comparative Study and Preliminary Framework, *Written Communication*, 28(1), 97–141.

Lakoff, G. (1973). Hedges: A Study in Meaning Criteria and the Logic of Fuzzy Concepts, *Journal of Philosophical Logic*, 2(4), 458–508.

Larsson, T. (2019). Grammatical stance marking in student and expert production: Revisiting the informal-formal dichotomy. *Register Studies*, 1, 243–268.

Lee, C., & Barton, D. (2013). *Language online: Investigating digital texts and practices*. Abingdon, Oxfordshire: Routledge.

Lee, J. J. and N. C. Subtirelu (2015). Metadiscourse in the Classroom: A Comparative Analysis of EAP Lessons and University Lectures, *English for Specific Purposes*, 37, 52–62.

Li, T. and S. Wharton (2012). Metadiscourse Repertoire of L1 Mandarin Undergraduates Writing in English: A Cross-contextual, Cross-disciplinary Study, *Journal of English for Academic Purposes*, 11(4), 345–56.

McNamara, D. S., S. A Crossley, and P. M. McCarthy, (2010). Linguistic Features of Writing Quality, *Written Communication*, 27(1): 57–86.

Mao, L.R. (1993). I Conclude Not: Toward a Pragmatic Account of Metadiscourse, *Rhetoric Review*, 11(2): 265–89.

Mauranen, A. (2018). Second Language Acquisition, World Englishes, and English as a Lingua Franca (ELF), *World Englishes*, 37(1): 106–19.

McCulloch, G. (2020). *Because Internet: Understanding the New Rules of Language*. Harmondsworth: Penguin.

Mur-Duenas, P. (2011). An Intercultural Analysis of Metadiscourse Features in Research Articles Written in English and in Spanish, *Journal of Pragmatics*, 43(12), 3068-79.

Myers, G. (2013). Stance-taking and public discussion in blogs. In *Self-Mediation* (pp. 55–67). Routledge.

Myhill, D. (2008). Towards a Linguistic Model of Sentence Development in Writing, *Language and Education*, 22(5), 271–88.

Nesi, H. and S. Gardner (2012). *Genres across the Disciplines: Student Writing in Higher Education*. Cambridge: Cambridge University Press.

Römer, U. (2009). The Inseparability of Lexis and Grammar: Corpus Linguistic Perspectives, *Annual Review of Cognitive Linguistics*, 7(1), 140–62.

Rossen-Knill, D. (2011). Flow and the Principle of Relevance: Bringing our Dynamic Speaking Knowledge to Writing, *Journal of Teaching Writing*, 26(1), 39–67.

Silver, M. (2003). The Stance of Stance: A Critical Look at Ways Stance Is Expressed and Modeled in Academic Discourse, *Journal of English for Academic Purposes*, 2(4), 359–74.

Simpson, P. (1990). Modality in Literary-critical Discourse, in *The Writing Scholar: Studies in Academic Discourse*, ed. W. Nash. Newbury Park, CA: SAGE.

Squires, L. (2010). Enregistering Internet Language, *Language in Society*, 39(4), 457–92.

Swales, J. (1990). *Genre Analysis: English in Academic and Research Settings*. Cambridge: Cambridge University Press.

Swales, J. (2004). *Research Genres: Explorations and Applications*. Cambridge: Cambridge University Press.

Tannen, D., and A. M. Trester (eds.). (2013). *Discourse 2.0: Language and New Media*. Washington, DC: Georgetown University Press.

Thompson, S. E. (2003). Text-structuring Metadiscourse, Intonation and the Signalling of Organisation in Academic Lectures, *Journal of English for Academic Purposes*, 2(1), 5–20.

Triki, N. (2019). Revisiting the Metadiscursive Aspect of Definitions in Academic Writing, *Journal of English for Academic Purposes*, 37, 104–16.

Vande Kopple, W. (1985). Some Exploratory Discourse on Metadiscourse, *College Composition and Communication,* 36(1), 82–93.

Vande Kopple, W. J. (2012). The Importance of Studying Metadiscourse, *Applied Research on English Language*, 1(2): 37–44.

Widdowson, H. (2015). ELF and the Pragmatics of Language Variation, *Journal of English as a Lingua Franca* 4(2), 359–72.

Myth 2 You Can't Write That in School

[1] The Dissenters were so called because they refused to take oaths to Anglicanism required of all English university students and teachers by the Act of Uniformity in 1662.

[2] See a similar example in H. Blair, *Lectures on Rhetoric and Belles Lettres*. 1784: Robert Aitken, at Pope's Head in Market Street.

[3] This discussion focuses on language policies specifically, but many language policies also bear direct relationship to immigration debates and policies: For instance, more assimilationist immigration stances tend to mean more assimilationist language policies, whereas pluralist immigration stances and language policies more easily coexist; see: Fitzsimmons-Doolan, S. (2009), Is Public Discourse about Language Policy Really Public Discourse about Immigration? A Corpus-based Study, *Language Policy*, 8(4), 377–402. For a fuller discussion about language policy and immigration policy, see e.g., policies ibid., Eggington, W. and H. Wren (1997), *Language Policy: Dominant English, Pluralist Challenges* (Amsterdam; Philadelphia, PA: J. Benjamins), Ozolins, U. and M. Clyne (2001), Immigration and Language Policy, in *The Other Languages of Europe: Demographic, Sociolinguistic, and Educational Perspectives*, eds. G. Extra and D. Gorter (Clevedon: Multilingual Matters), 371–90; The Other Languages of Europe:

Demographic, Sociolinguistic, and Educational Perspectives, 2001. 118: p. 371; Conrick, M. and P. Donovan (2010), Immigration and Language Policy and Planning in Quebec and Canada: Language Learning and Integration, *Journal of Multilingual and Multicultural Development*, 31(4), 331–45; G. Valdés (1997), Bilinguals and Bilingualism: Language Policy in an Anti-immigrant Age, *International Journal of Society and Language*, 127, 25–52.

[4] Challenges include quality of instruction and student take-up of language study when it is no longer required. See a full UK Parliament 2021 report on languages in UK schooling here: https://lordslibrary.parliament.uk/foreign-languages-primary-and-secondary-schools/.

[5] From the *Las Vegas Sun*, excerpt from letter prohibiting languages other than English on the school bus from the Superintendent of the Esmeralda County School District, reported in "Students told to hold (native) tongue" by Timothy Pratt in December 2007: https://lasvegassun.com/news/2007/dec/19/students-told-to-hold-native-tongue/?_ga=2.9182262.2083529048.1643643237-220150693.1643643237.

Myth 3 You Can't Write That and Be Smart

[1] In this search conducted in January, 2022, some quizzes note their bias toward native English speakers. Some note different quizzes for types of intelligence, such as verbal or emotional intelligence. Example links appear below:

- Test Your Cognitive Skills!: www.test-iq.org/?gclid=Cj0KCQjw0KHBh DDARIsAFJ6UGizC0Rdq8WqouCuvEVZwjbOVFYCPQmpqu0D UUy3CktsvUMMLf_lcgoaArm7EALw_wcB.
- Find Out Where You Stand with our Verbal IQ test: www .psychologytoday.com/us/tests/iq/verbal-linguistic-intelligence-test.
- Have You Ever Wondered How Intelligent You Are Compared to Your Friends, Your Colleagues … and the Rest of the Nation?: www .bbc.co.uk/programmes/articles/2xhbqsm0NyPLfRzYqNl966M/how-intelligent-are-you.
- When You Complete a Free IQ Test You Will Get an Estimate of Your IQ Score or the Number of Questions You Answered Correctly: www.123test.com/iq-test/.
- An IQ Test Is an Assessment that Measures a Range of Cognitive Abilities and Provides a Score that Is Intended to Serve as a Measure of an Individual's Intellectual Abilities and Potential: www.verywellmind .com/how-are-scores-on-iq-tests-calculated-2795584.
- Online Assessment – USA Average IQ Score is 103.2: www.iqtestacademy .org/.

2   Additional links, about IQ test challenges, history, and writing and "sound-
    ing intelligent":

    • IQ Tests Are Known to Be Sensitive to Things like Motivation and
      Coaching: www.discovermagazine.com/mind/do-iq-tests-actually-measure-
      intelligence.
    • IQ Tests Have a Dark, Controversial History – But They're Finally Being
      Used for Good: www.businessinsider.com/iq-tests-dark-history-finally-
      being-used-for-good-2017-10.
    • Want to Sound Intelligent? Write Plainly and Simply: https://medium.com/
      swlh/want-to-sound-intelligent-write-plainly-and-simply-6d7acc5ddd71.
    • Science Explains Why People who Love Writing Are Smarter: https://
      iheartintelligence.com/love-writing-smarter/.

3   At this time, standardized testing was already used in China in order to
    rank and select, and written rather than oral tests were used in Prussia.
    Mann had visited Prussia and concluded that US students were not
    so well prepared, fueling his idea that they should begin taking written
    examinations.
4   Burt recommended his findings to audiences including teachers and law
    enforcement agents, even though some of his ideas were fanciful and
    speculative. Take, for instance, Burt's notion that "the near-sighted, or
    myopic perhaps because the things outside them look so blurred and indis-
    tinct, are peculiarly apt to be flung back upon their inner life; they brood
    and daydream," which brings to mind Oscar Wilde's Gwendolen in *The
    Importance of Being Earnest*, who says, "mamma, whose views on edu-
    cation are remarkably strict, has brought me up to be extremely short-
    sighted; it is part of her system; so do you mind my looking at you through
    my glasses?"
5   This four-domain model is based on research in progress with Norbert
    Elliot, and on Mislevy, R. (2018), *Sociocognitive Foundations of
    Educational Measurement*. (Abingdon, Oxfordshire: Routledge).
6   See a fuller history in Helen Patrick's "Examinations in English after
    1945" (www.cambridgeassessment.org.uk/news/examinations-in-england-
    after-1945-history-repeats-itself/) and in *Examining the World* (www
    .cambridgeassessment.org.uk/news/playlist/view/extracts-from-examining-
    the-world-playlist/) for Cambridge Assessment.

Myth 4 You Can't Write That on the Test

1   In the UK in 1820, if you were aged fifteen or older, you and your peers would
    have less than two years of education between you (van Leeuwen, B. and

J. van Leeuwen-Li (2015), *Average Years of Education.* IISH Datavers).
In the US in 1850, if you were a white student anywhere between five and
nineteen years old, you had about a 50–50 chance of being in school – and
if you were *not* white, your chances were almost 0 (Snyder, T. (1993), *120
Years of American Education: A Statistical Portrait.* US Department of
Education, Office of Educational Research and Improvement).

2   The shift from speaking to writing also happened outside of English-
medium higher education; for instance, the Baccalaureate examination
used for university admission established by Napoleon in 1808 shifted
from an oral to a written examination in 1830.

3   For more information on Morrill Act land seizures, treaties, and uses,
see Robert Lee and Tristan Ahtone's Land-Grab Universities Project:
www.hcn.org/issues/52.4/indigenous-affairs-education-land-grab-
universities.

4   Reported in Cambridge University News and Research, based on
Andrew Watts' research: www.cambridgeassessment.org.uk/news/how-
have-school-exams-changed-over-the-past-150-years/

5   In "Turn your papers over," Andrew Watts documents Amy's letter as
evidence of the similar "highs and lows" for past and present test takers.

6   See more examples from Cambridge assessment archives research here:
www.cam.ac.uk/research/features/playing-croquet-with-the-examiner-
he-was-much-like-other-people.

7   The answers are: adjective, and Beethoven, Wagner, Verdi.

8   *Correct writing* was rewarded in other ways, as well. In an example that
illustrates the four myths so far, Oxford University awarded scholarships
in 1870 for the best English essay on the topic "The reciprocal influence
on each other of National Character and National Language." *Oxford
University Gazette* (1870) *v.1-2 (1870–1872).*

9   See Accuplacer's exam candidate materials here: https://study.com/
academy/popular/accuplacer-writing-tips.html.

10 For an in-depth discussion of Microsoft Grammar Checker, see Anne
Curzan's *Fixing English.*

11 For instance, the University of Aberdeen in Scotland offered an 1880 class
in "English Language and Literature" said to cover "the higher Elements
of English Grammar; the Principles of Rhetoric, applied to English
Composition, and some portion of the history of English Literature."
Bain, A. (1866), *English Composition and Rhetoric: A Manual (rev.
American ed.).* New York: D. Appleton and Co.

12 For all of the proposals from the UK Department of Education and
Ofqual, see: www.gov.uk/government/consultations/proposed-changes-
to-the-assessment-of-gcses-as-and-a-levels-in-2022/proposed-changes-
to-the-assessment-of-gcses-as-and-a-levels-in-2022.

[13] See the following for more information on each examination task, where available:

- Cambridge Junior Examination 1858 task: www.cam.ac.uk/research/features/playing-croquet-with-the-examiner-he-was-much-like-other-people.
- Cambridge Examination for Women 1870 task: "You are requested to write an essay on *one* of the following subjects": (https://books.google.jo/books?id=oLYIAAAAQAAJ&printsec=frontcover&dq=university+oxford+women%27s+examination+paper&hl=en&sa=X&redir_esc=y#v=onepage&q=English%20examination&f=false).
- STAT 2009 task: There are two parts to this test, and four comments are offered for each part. You are required to produce two pieces of writing – one in response to a comment from Part A, and one in response to a comment from Part B. Part A is a more formal public affairs issue that invites argument. Part B is a less formal topic that invites more personal reflection. One hour is allocated for this test, with an additional five minutes reading time. (For these and other examples, see https://stat.acer.org/files/STAT_CIB.pdf.)
- Cambridge 2016 A-levels task: Julia Gillard makes an entry in her diary the night before she gives this speech. Write this entry (between 120 and 150 words), basing your answer closely on the material of the speech. The full writing exam can be found here: https://paper.sc/doc/5b4c363c6479033e61e6b725/, and this and other A-levels English exemplar writing examples can be found here: www.cambridgeinternational.org/Images/583260-cambridge-international-as-and-a-level-english-language-9093-paper-1-example-candidate-responses.pdf.
- IELTS 2022 task: "You should spend about 20 minutes on this task. The pie charts show the electricity generated in Germany and France from all sources and renewables in the year 2009. Summarize the information by selecting and reporting the main features and make comparisons where relevant. Write at least 150 words." (More detail can be found here: www.ieltsbuddy.com/sample-pie-chart.html.) For the full New Zealand IELTS information, on both the Academic Writing and General Writing exams, see: www.ielts.org/for-test-takers/test-format.

Myth 5 Chances Are, You Can't Write

[1] Example references include "Why Johnny Can't Write" in *Newsweek* in 1975; "Can't Write Can't Spell" in *The Age* in 2007; "Why Johnny Can't Write, and Why Employers are Mad" on NBC news in 2013, and "Why Kids Can't Write" in *The New York Times* in 2017.

2 For instance, two past CLA writing tasks asked students to (1) read documents about a plane and make a recommendation to a tech company about whether to purchase it; or (2) read documents about crime and make a recommendation to a mayor about the role of drug addicts in crime reduction.

3 For the full articles, see: www.washingtonpost.com/news/answer-sheet/wp/2017/04/27/why-so-many-college-students-are-lousy-at-writing-and-how-mr-miyagi-can-help/ and www.studyinternational.com/news/students-cant-write-properly-even-college-time-teach-expert/.

4 For the full article, see: www.smh.com.au/national/nsw/writing-wrongs-our-society-is-about-to-hit-a-literacy-crisis-20200917-p55wl7.html.

5 I was so flummoxed by how the *sophistication point* was used that I wrote an editorial in *Inside Higher Education* asking examiners to ignore it: www.insidehighered.com/admissions/views/2021/07/26/some-things-shouldnt-be-graded-ap-exams-opinion.

6 See the full article here: www.smh.com.au/national/how-does-grammar-help-writing-and-who-should-teach-it-20200917-p55wjc.html.

7 See more information on the scheme of assessment for AS- and A-Level English Language here: www.aqa.org.uk/subjects/english/as-and-a-level/english-language-7701-7702/scheme-of-assessment.

8 E.g. see the following AQA mark scheme example for the June 2020 "Writers' Viewpoints and Perspectives" paper: https://filestore.aqa.org.uk/sample-papers-and-mark-schemes/2020/november/AQA-87002-W-MS-NOV20.PDF.

9 These brief details are offered here: www.acer.org/au/towa/assessment-criteria.

10 See the full American Association of Colleges and Universities Written Communication VALUE Rubric here: https://d38xzozy36dxrv.cloudfront.net/qa/content/user-photos/Offices/OCPI/VALUE/Value-Rubrics-WrittenCommunication.pdf.

11 The metaphor of *control* in educational criteria and outcomes starts far earlier than tertiary education. The UK English primary curriculum includes emphasis on literature and an unnamed type of English throughout its criteria. The exception under "spelling, grammar" spells out the following: "Pupils should be taught to control their speaking and writing consciously and to use Standard English. They should be taught to use the elements of spelling, grammar, punctuation and 'language about language' listed." Uniquely, this example suggests *conscious* control, which implies conscious language awareness. (See more information about the UK primary school English curriculum here: www.gov.uk/government/publications/national-curriculum-in-england-english-programmes-of-study/national-curriculum-in-england-english-programmes-of-study.)

The US NAEP Writing Assessment criteria for primary and secondary schools include the expectation that "sentence structure is well controlled," and they emphasize context-specific appropriateness, e.g., "voice and tone are effective in relation to the writer's purpose and audience." But because all these criteria are framed by the NAEP's indication that higher education and workplace settings require "correct use of the conventions of standard written English," this register and dialect appear to be what the NAEP means by high-scored writing having "well controlled" sentence structure, voice, and tone, and "correct" grammar, usage, and mechanics. See the full Writing Framework for the 2011 NAEP here:

   https://www.nagb.gov/content/dam/nagb/en/documents/publications/frameworks/writing/2011-writing-framework.pdf.

12 The Framework is a consensus statement from several US organizations concerned with postsecondary writing. For all of the US Framework for Success in Postsecondary Writing outcomes, see https://lead.nwp.org/knowledgebase/framework-for-success-in-postsecondary-writing/.

13 The 2017 results were never released, and the next test is scheduled for 2030. See a 2022 overview by Natalie Wexler in Forbes here: https://www.forbes.com/sites/nataliewexler/2022/01/26/we-get-national-reading-test-results-every-2-years-writing-try-20/?sh=2474d1703b9d.

14 For instance, in the US Common Core State Standards materials: (www.corestandards.org/assets/Appendix_C.pdf), the first exemplary essay closes with the following statements: "Learning to dress for particular occasions prepares us for the real world. And teens have enough pressure already without having to worry about what they are wearing."

15 The Google Books Ngram Viewer, for instance, shows the predominance of *everyone * their* (e.g., *everyone in their, everyone for their*), which is much more common than phrases including *everyone * his or her*, which have been declining since 2010. (See the search at: https://books.google.com/ngrams/graph?content=everyone+*+their%2Ceveryone+*+his+or+her&year_start=1800&year_end=2019&corpus=en-2019&smoothing=3.)

16 The full writing exam includes fifteen minutes reading time and two hours to write four responses (in response to two readings). The full task of this example follows: Julia Gillard makes an entry in her diary the night before she gives this speech. Write this entry (between 120 and 150 words), basing your answer closely on the material of the speech.

   The full writing exam can be found here: https://paper.sc/doc/5b4c363c6479033e61e6b725/

   This and other A-Level English exemplar writing examples can be found here: https://www.cambridgeinternational.org/Images/583260-cambridge-international-as-and-a-level-english-language-9093-paper-1-example-candidate-responses.pdf

17 Students are recommended to take about twenty minutes on the task and to write at least 150 words (more detail can be found here: www .ieltsbuddy.com/sample-pie-chart.html.) For the full New Zealand IELTS information, on both the Academic Writing and General Writing exams, see: www.ielts.org/for-test-takers/test-format.

Myth 6 You Can't Write if You Didn't Write Well in High School

1 For the complete list of 2016 prompts, see: https://paper.sc/doc/5b4c363 c6479033e61e6b725/.
2 The NAPLAN also includes narrative tasks that require students to write a story. A recent example task begins this way: "Today you are going to write a narrative or story. The idea for your story is "The Box." What is inside the box? How did it get there? Is it valuable? Perhaps it is alive! The box might reveal a message or something that was hidden. What happens in your story if the box is opened?" For more information on the NAPLAN writing prompts and rubrics, see: www.nap.edu.au/naplan/writing.
3 See also more public-facing coverage of teacher challenges in the *Guardian* in April 2017: www.theguardian.com/education/2017/apr/29/ english-secondary-schools-facing-perfect-storm-of-pressures.
4 See, e.g., coverage in the *Guardian* in April 2017: www.theguardian .com/education/2017/apr/29/english-secondary-schools-facing- perfect-storm-of-pressures.
5 This is an overall rate, and attrition rates vary between private and public schools. See more information in the US National Association of Secondary School Principals (NASSP) January 2020 Principal Leadership Issue: www.nassp.org/publication/principal- leadership/volume-20/principal-leadership-january-2020/making- teachers-stick-january-2020/.
6 The article also notes that the news isn't all bad: "To date, the Government's Achievement Improvement Monitor (introduced in 2000), which rates the performance of school students against the National Literacy Benchmarks, indicates that improvement is at hand. In 2004, 97 per cent of year 3s, 93.4 per cent of year 5s and 96 per cent of year 7s met the benchmarks for writing set by the Ministerial Council on Education, Employment, Training and Youth Affairs. Figures for reading hovered around the high 80s and low 90s." See the full article here: www.theage .com.au/education/cant-write-cant-spell-20070226-ge4ap6.html.
7 See the full article here: www.macleans.ca/education/uniandcollege/ university-students-cant-spell/.
8 See the full blog post and comments here: www.cultofpedagogy.com/ grammar-spelling-errors/.

9   The use of AP courses and exams are also not equitable: access to these courses depends on schools and school districts. Students identifying as white are more likely to have access to AP courses, which are valued by colleges in student applications and can lend college credit, saving courses and money in college. In this way, courses that purport to take the place of college writing are part of "limited academic preparation by race/ethnicity" in the US (Arum, R. and J. Roksa, *Academically Adrift: Limited Learning on College Campuses*. Chicago: University of Chicago Press, 2011), and also send the inaccurate message that secondary and postsecondary writing are the same.

10 Corpus linguistic analysis is computer-aided analysis of lexical and grammatical patterns across corpora, or bodies of texts, of authentic language use. For more detail on the corpora and methods, see Aull, L. (2020), *How Students Write: A Linguistic Analysis*. New York: Modern Language Association; Aull, L. (2015), *First-year University Writing: A Corpus-based Study with Implications for Pedagogy*. London: Palgrave Macmillan; Aull, L. (2019), Linguistic Markers of Stance and Genre in Upper-level Student Writing, *Written Communication*, 36(2), 267–95; Aull, L. (2018), *Generality and Certainty in Undergraduate Writing Over Time*, in *Developing Writers in Higher Education: A Longitudinal Study*, ed. A. R. Gere. Ann Arbor, MI: University of Michigan Press. In particular, the three patterns discussed here were statistically significant patterns in A-graded writing by experienced postsecondary students in comparison with A-graded and ungraded writing by new college students.

11 Two linguistic patterns associated with cohesion in writing are cohesive words (or transition words/phrases) and cohesive moves (or rhetorical moves), described in more detail below.

- *Transition words* include a range of transitional words and phrases that show reformulations (e.g., *in other words, put another way*), addition (e.g., *furthermore, in addition*), cause and effect (e.g., *therefore*), and countering (e.g., *however*).

- *Rhetorical moves* are idea-steps that guide readers from what they know to what they don't know. These moves are larger than word-level transitions; They are used within and across paragraphs. For instance, academic writers often use three moves in their introductions to create a space for their research (J. Swales (1990), *Genre Analysis: English in Academic and Research Settings*. Cambridge Applied Linguistics Series., Cambridge; New York: Cambridge University Press. xi, 260.) Move 1 introduces the territory; move 2 introduces a gap in the territory; and move 3 occupies the gap, providing the writer's own contribution. See also: Ädel, A. (2014), Selecting Quantitative Data for Qualitative Analysis: A Case Study Connecting a Lexicogrammatical Pattern to Rhetorical Moves, *Journal of English for Academic Purposes*, 16, 68–80; Matsuda, P. and C. M. Tardy (2007), Voice in Academic Writing: The Rhetorical Construction of Author Identity in Blind Manuscript Review, *English for Specific Purposes*, 26, 235–49. For instance, academic writers often use three moves in their introductions to create a space for their research (Swales, J. (1990), *Genre Analysis: English in Academic and Research Settings*. Cambridge Applied Linguistics Series., Cambridge; New York: Cambridge University Press. xi, 260 p). Move 1 introduces the territory; move 2 introduces a gap in the territory; and move 3 occupies the gap, providing the writer's own contribution.

[12] Postsecondary writing also compresses information into noun phrases using nominalization. *Nominalization* is itself an example of nominalization: the word *nominalization* is a noun that refers to the process of nominalizing, or making a word into a noun. In another example, the word *industrialization* is a nominalization that refers to the process of bringing manufacturing to a place.

Myth 7 You Can't Get a Job if You Didn't Write Well in College

[1] Links to websites and articles in order of appearance:

- Penn State Smeal College of Business website (https://careerconnections .smeal.psu.edu/blog/2018/06/07/how-strong-writing-skills-benefit-your-career/)
- "Benefits of Writing for Students": Give a Grad a Go website and blog (www.giveagradago.com/news/2019/11/benefits-of-writing-for-students/ 448)
- Tulane University, School of Professional Advancement (https://sopa .tulane.edu/blog/importance-writing-skills-workplace)
- Forbes magazine article (www.forbes.com/sites/gretasolomon/2018/08/09/ why-mastering-writing-skills-can-help-future-proof-your-career/ ?sh=3f3187615831)
- Oregon State University blog (https://blog.pace.oregonstate.edu/the-importance-of-writing-in-the-workplace)

[2] This unsigned story, "The Lazy Lover: A Moral Tale," appeared in the March issue of the magazine in 1779.

[3] A partial example can be found in Scotland, where public schools prepared a larger part of the population for college. See Myers, D. (1983), *Scottish Schoolmasters in the Nineteenth Century: Professionalism and Politics*, in *Scottish Culture and Scottish Education, 1800–1980*, eds. W. M. Humes and H. M Paterson, 84. Edinburgh: John Donald.

⁴ See, e.g. 2020 data from the US Bureau of Labor Statistics (www
.bls.gov/careeroutlook/2020/data-on-display/education-pays
.htm), from the UK Government Labour Statistics (https://explore-
education-statistics.service.gov.uk/find-statistics/graduate-labour-
markets), and from the Australia Bureau of Statistics (www.abs.gov.au/
statistics/people/education/education-and-work-australia/latest-release).

⁵ For more information about the study, see https://newsroom.carleton
.ca/archives/2017/04/20/carleton-study-finds-people-spending-third-job-
time-email/ and Lanctot, A. M., *You've Got Mail, But Is It Important
And/Or Urgent?: An Investigation into Employees' Perceptions of Email*.
2019, doctoral dissertation, Carleton University.

⁶ See, e.g., tips for "not sounding silly" in emails to professors (www
.insidehighered.com/views/2015/04/16/advice-students-so-they-dont-
sound-silly-emails-essay) and etiquette tips for emails to lecturers/profes-
sors (www.usnews.com/education/blogs/professors-guide/2010/09/30/18-
etiquette-tips-for-e-mailing-your-professor and https://thetab.com/uk/
glasgow/2016/02/04/etiquette-emailing-lecturer-lecturer-8056).

⁷ See the full story here: www.bbc.com/news/business-58517083.

⁸ See the full article here: www.insidehighered.com/news/2022/12/09/
state-systems-group-plans-measure-and-promote-higher-ed-value?utm_
source=Inside+Higher+Ed&utm_campaign=37afa266f5-DNU_2021_
COPY_02&utm_medium=email&utm_term=0_1fcbc04421-37
afa266f5-236367914&mc_cid=37afa266f5&mc_eid=8be683a36c.

⁹ For coverage of research on discrepancies between college-pay and
postgraduate earnings, see, e.g., this 2021 *Washington Post* article: www
.washingtonpost.com/education/2021/11/01/college-degree-value-major/.

¹⁰ For the full text, please see: www.thebalancecareers.com/employee-letter-
and-email-examples-2059485.

¹¹ For the full text, see: www.uts.edu.au/sites/default/files/2018-01/
Management%20Decisions%20and%20Control%20%28Report
%20-%20Business%20Ver%2023.01.18%29_6.pdf.

Myth 8 You Can't Write That Because Internet

¹ This was, in fact, the first question someone asked me on a little island off
another little island off the coast of Honduras (if language was declining
because of the internet and texting), upon hearing I was an English language professor. That someone eventually became my life partner, which
goes to show that even the most compelling people learn this myth, and
also that there's hope for them.

² See the *Atlantic* article "The Internet Is Making Writing Worse" (www
.theatlantic.com/national/archive/2013/07/internet-making-writing-

worse/313199/) and the Pew Research Study (www.sciencedaily.com/releases/2020/01/200117085321.htm).

3 The full website offers advice and links with examples of what makes academic writing "formal," "objective," and "technical": www.sydney.edu.au/students/writing.html.

4 See the *Time* article: https://time.com/5629246/because-internet-book-review/.

5 See, for instance, coverage that describes the capability and popularity of ChatGPT and educators' concerns about it, on the BBC (www.bbc.com/news/technology-63861322), in *The New York Times* (www.nytimes.com/2023/01/16/technology/chatgpt-artificial-intelligence-universities.html), and in *The Sydney Morning Herald* (www.smh.com.au/national/this-month-the-world-changed-and-you-barely-noticed-20221214-p5c6en.html).

6 See, for instance, news coverage showing that internet use reduces study skills (www.sciencedaily.com/releases/2020/01/200117085321.htm) and news coverage discussing children and screen time (www.abc.net.au/news/2019-11-11/screen-time-and-impact-on-literacy/11681026?nw=0).

7 See the Pew Research Study (www.sciencedaily.com/releases/2020/01/200117085321.htm) and results from the first longitudinal study by the University of Massachusetts Dartmouth Center for Marketing Research (www.umassd.edu/media/umassdartmouth/cmr/studies-and-research/CollegePresidentsBlog.pdf).

8 Fun (family) fact: if you want to read about interpersonal emoji use in WhatsApp messages, read this study by my sister! Aull, B. (2019) A Study of Phatic Emoji Use in WhatsApp Communication, *Internet Pragmatics*, 2(2), 206–32.

9 The third most-liked tweet of 2021 is a kissing-face emoji accompanied by a selfie, tweeted by South Korean singer and songwriter Jungkook, member of the K-pop group BTS, with over 3.2 million likes. The most *retweeted* tweet of 2021 was also linked to BTS; the BTS group account tweeted the hashtags #StopAsianHate #StopAAPIHate. Both examples show the use of informal digital writing patterns, or emojis and hashtags, to convey interpersonal aims and to connect cohesively with other messages and language users.

10 Find the full irishtimes.com article in the newspaper's TV & Radio culture section (www.irishtimes.com/culture/tv-radio-web/harry-and-meghan-the-union-of-two-great-houses-the-windsors-and-the-celebrities-is-complete-1.4504502).

11 For the full *New York Times* article, see: www.nytimes.com/2021/04/19/well/mind/covid-mental-health-languishing.html

[12] See, e.g., klaviyo.com's top five campaigns here: www.klaviyo.com/blog/
top-email-and-sms-campaign-examples; see pure360.com's top 10 here:
https://www.pure360.com/a-look-back-10-emails-from-2021-that-were-
loving-and-why/.

[13] See the full article here: www.thelancet.com/article/S0140-6736(20)30183-
5/fulltext.

Conclusion: Writing Continuum, Language Exploration

[1] The full podcast about Haskell's book *Sounds Wild and Broken* can be
found here: https://theamericanscholar.org/the-sound-of-science/.

References

Introduction: The Writing We Actually Do

Curzan, A. (2014). *Fixing English: Prescriptivism and Language History*. Cambridge: Cambridge University Press.

Eggington, W. (1997). The English Language Metaphors We Plan by, in *Language Policy: Dominant English, Pluralist Challenges*, eds. W. Eggington and H. Wren, 29–46. Philadelphia, Pennsylvania: John Benjamins Publishing.

Graff, H. J. (2010). The Literacy Myth at Thirty. *Journal of Social History*, 4(3), 635–61.

Mills, J. (2020). Toward a Theory of Myth. *Journal for the Theory of Social Behaviour*, 50(4), 410–24.

Thurlow, C. (2006). From Statistical Panic to Moral Panic: The Metadiscursive Construction and Popular Exaggeration of New Media Language in the Print Media. *Journal of Computer-Mediated Communication*, 11(3), 667–701.

Zajko, V. and M. Leonard (2006). *Laughing with Medusa: Classical Myth and Feminist Thought*. Oxford: Oxford University Press.

Introduction: What Do We Do Instead?

Aull, B. and L. L. Aull (2021). "Write a Greeting for Your Email Here": Principles for Assessing Interpersonal Workplace Email Communication. *Journal of Writing Analytics*, 5 (1) 215–58.

Aull, L. L. (2020). *How Students Write: A Linguistic Analysis*. New York: Modern Language Association.

Biber, D. (1988). *Variation across Speech and Writing*. Cambridge, Cambridge University Press.

Biber, D. and J. Egbert (2018). *Register Variation Online*. Cambridge: Cambridge University Press.

Biber, D. and S. Conrad (2005). Register Variation: A Corpus Approach, in *The Handbook of Discourse Analysis*, eds. D. Tannen, H. E. Hamilton, and D. Schiffrin, 175–96. Hoboken, NJ: John Wiley & Sons.

Chafe, W. (1982). Integration and Involvement in Speaking, Writing, and Oral Literature, in *Spoken and Written Language: Exploring Orality and Literacy*, ed. D. Tannen, 35–54. Norwood, NJ: Ablex Publishing Corporation.

Clark, R. et al. (1990). Critical Language Awareness Part I: A Critical Review of Three Current Approaches to Language Awareness. *Language and Education*, 4(4), 249–60.

Davies, M. (2015). The Importance of Robust Corpora in Providing More Realistic Descriptions of Variation in English Grammar. *Linguistics Vanguard*, 1(1), 305–12.

Freire, P. (2000). *Pedagogy of the Oppressed*. 1970. Translated by Myra Bergman Ramos. New York: Continuum.

Hardy, J. A. and E. Friginal (2016). Genre Variation in Student Writing: A Multi-dimensional Analysis. *Journal of English for Academic Purposes*, 22, 119–31.

Hardy, J. A. and U. Römer (2013). Revealing Disciplinary Variation in Student Writing: A Multi-dimensional Analysis of the Michigan Corpus of Upper-level Student Papers (MICUSP). *Corpora*, 8(2), 183–207.

Hartig, A. J. and X. Lu (2014). Plain English and Legal Writing: Comparing Expert and Novice Writers. *English for Specific Purposes*, 33, 87–96.

Hyland, K. (2010). Constructing Proximity: Relating to Readers in Popular and Professional Science. *Journal of English for Academic Purposes*, 9(2), 116–27.

Jenkins, J. (2013). *English as a Lingua Franca in the International University: The Politics of Academic English Language Policy*. Abingdon, Oxfordshire: Routledge,

Johns, A. M (1997). *Text, Role, and Context: Developing Academic Literacies*. Cambridge: Cambridge University Press.

Lorés-Sanz, R. (2016). ELF in the Making? Simplification and Hybridity in Abstract Writing. *Journal of English as a Lingua Franca*, 5(1), 53–81.

Mauranen, A. (2012). *Exploring ELF: Academic English Shaped by Non-native Speakers*. Cambridge: Cambridge University Press.

McCulloch, G. (2019). *Because Internet: Understanding the New Rules of Language*. New York: Riverhead Books.

Milu, E. (2021). Diversity of Raciolinguistic Experiences in the Writing Classroom: An Argument for a Transnational Black Language Pedagogy. *College English*, 83(6), 415–41.

Shapiro, S. (2022). *Cultivating Critical Language Awareness in the Classroom*. Abingdon, Oxfordshire: Routledge.

Smitherman, G. (2017). Raciolinguistics, "Mis-education," and Language Arts Teaching in the 21st Century. *Language Arts Journal of Michigan*, 32(2), 3.

Swales, J. (1990). *Genre Analysis: English in Academic and Research Settings*. Cambridge; New York: Cambridge University Press.

Sword, H. (2012). *Stylish Academic Writing*. Cambridge, MA: Harvard University Press.

Introduction: But Shouldn't We Still Prioritize *Correct Writing*?

Anonymous (2016). Dear Student, I Just Don't Have Time to Mark your Essay Properly. In *the Guardian*, 20 May.

Biber, D. and B. Gray (2016). *Grammatical Complexity in Academic English: Linguistic Change in Writing*. Cambridge: Cambridge University Press.

Bourdieu, P. and J.-C. Passeron (1977). *Reproduction in Society, Culture, and Education*. Beverly Hills, CA: Sage.

Canagarajah, A. S. (2005). *Reclaiming the Local in Language Policy and Practice*. Mahwah, NJ: L. Erlbaum Associates.

Horner, B. et al. (2011). Language Difference in Writing: Toward a Translingual Approach. *College English*, 73(3), 303–21.

Matsuda, P. K. (2012). Let's Face It: Language Issues and the Writing Program Administrator. *Writing Program Administration*, 36(1), 141–64.

Miller, C. R. (1984). Genre as Social Action. *Quarterly Journal of Speech*, 70(2), 151–67.

Nesi, H. and S. Gardner (2012). *Genres Across the Disciplines: Student Writing in Higher Education*. Cambridge: Cambridge University Press.

Nevalainen, T. and E. C. Traugott (2016). *The Oxford Handbook of the History of English*. Oxford: Oxford University Press.

Swales, J. and C. Feak (2012). *Academic Writing for Graduate Students: Essential Tasks and Skills*. Ann Arbor, MI: University of Michigan Press.

Trachsel, M. (1987). *The History of College Entrance Examinations in English: A Record of Academic Assumptions about Literacy*. Austin, TX: The University of Texas at Austin.

Truss, L. (2004). *Eats, Shoots & Leaves: The Zero-Tolerance Approach to Punctuation*. Harmondsworth: Penguin.

1: Only One Kind of Writing Is Correct

Campbell, G. (1776). *The Philosophy of Rhetoric*: In two volumes. Edinburgh: W. Strahan; T. Cadell and W. Creech.

Head, F. H. (1883). What is a Liberal Education: An Address. Utica, MY:
    Ellis H. Roberts & Company Printers.
Hill, A. S. (1995). An Answer to the Cry for More English, in *The Origins
    of Composition Studies in the American College 1875–1925: A
    Documentary History*, ed. J. C. Brereton, 45–57. Pittsburgh, PA:
    University of Pittsburgh Press.
Newbolt, H. J., (1921). *The Teaching of English in England: Being the
    Report of the Departmental Committee Appointed by the President of
    the Board of Education to Inquire into the Position of English in the
    Educational System of England*. London: H. M. Stationery Office.

1: Context for the Myth

Ash, J. (1788). *Grammatical Institutes: or An Easy Introduction to Dr.
    Lowth's English Grammar*. A new edition. Revised, corrected and
    enlarged. London: Charles Dilly.
Baker, J. (2019). *An Introduction to English Legal History*. Oxford: Oxford
    University Press.
Bates, R. M. (1997). The English Primer – A Circular Journey.
    Internationale Schulbuchforschung, 19(3), 249–58.
Bex, T. and R. J. Watts (eds), *Standard English: the Widening Debate*.
    Abingdon, Oxfordshire: Routledge.
Bryson, B. and D. Case, (1990). *The Mother Tongue: English & How It Got
    that Way*. New York: W. Morrow.
Curzan, A. and M. Adams (2012). *How English Works: A Linguistic
    Instruction*. 3rd ed. Glenview, IL: Pearson Education Limited.
Downey, C. (1979). Introduction, in *Grammatical Institutes*, ed. J. Ash,
    Delmar, NY: Scholars' Facsimiles & Reprints.
Eggington, W. and H. Wren (1997). *Language Policy: Dominant English,
    Pluralist Challenges*. Vol. 83. Amsterdam: John Benjamins Publishing.
Fisher, A. (1770). *The Pleasing Instructor or Entertaining Moralist,
    Consisting of Select Essays, Relations, Visions, and Allegories Collected
    from… Eminent English Authors… to which are Prefixed New
    Thoughts on Education*. London: Robinson, and Newcastle: Slack.
Fisher, J. H. (1977). Chancery and the Emergence of Standard Written
    English in the Fifteenth Century. *Speculum*, 52(4), 870–99.
Flanders, J., (2020). *A Place for Everything: The Curious History of
    Alphabetical Order*. London: Picador.
Hammond, S. (1760). A complete and comprehensive spelling-dictionary
    of the English language, on the newest plan; for the use of
    young gentlemen, ladies, and others … By Samuel Hammond;
    Schoolmaster in Nottingham … Nottingham: Samuel Creswell.

Johnson, S. (1850). *A Dictionary of the English Language: In which the Words Are Deduced from Their Originals; and Illustrated in Their Different Significations by Examples from the Best Writers.* London: Henry G. Bohn.

King, R. P. (2018). The Draconian Dictionary Is Back, in *The Atlantic*, August 5.

Kitzhaber, A. (1963). *Themes, Theories and Therapy: The Writing of College Students.* New York: McGraw-Hill Company.

Lang, B. (1982). Strunk, White and Grammar as Morality. *Soundings*, 65(1), 23–30.

Lowth, R. (1776). *A Short Introduction to English Grammar: With Critical Notes.* London: J. Dodsley.

Lynch, J. (2009). *The Lexicographer's Dilemma: The Evolution of 'Proper' English, from Shakespeare to South Park.* New York: Bloomsbury Publishing USA.

   (2021). A Place for Everything: The Curious History of Alphabetical Order by Judith Flanders. *Dictionaries: Journal of the Dictionary Society of North America,*. 42(1), 281–5.

Martin, P. (2019). *The Dictionary Wars.* Princeton: Princeton University Press.

Massing, M. (2018). *Fatal Discord: Erasmus, Luther, and the Fight for the Western Mind.* New York: HarperCollins.

Miller, T. P. (1997). *The Formation of College English: Rhetoric and Belles Lettres in the British Cultural Provinces.* Pittsburgh, PA: University of Pittsburgh Press.

Murray, L. (1979 [1795]). *English Grammar, Adapted to the Different Classes of Learners.* London: Scolar Press.

Scragg, D. G. (1974). *A History of English Spelling.* vol. 3. Manchester: Manchester University Press.

Swift, J. (1969 [1712]). *A Proposal for Correcting, Improving and Ascertaining the English Tongue,* ed. R. C. Alston. Menston.

Tieken-Boon van Ostade, I. (2000). Of Norms and Networks: The Language of Robert Lowth, in the Eleventh International Conference on English Historical Linguistics, Santiago de Compostela.

Ulman, H. L. (1990). Discerning Readers: British Reviewers' Responses to Campbell's Rhetoric and Related Works. Rhetorica: A Journal of the History of Rhetoric, 8(1), 65–90. https://doi.org/10.1525/rh.1990.8.1.65.

Upward, C. and G. Davidson (2011). *The History of English Spelling*, vol. 26. Hoboken, NJ: John Wiley & Sons.

van Ostade, I.T.-B. (2010). *The Bishop's Grammar: Robert Lowth and the Rise of Prescriptivism.* Oxford: Oxford University Press.

Vorlat, E., (1959). The Sources of Lindley Murray's "The English Grammar." *Leuvense Bijdragen*, 48, 108–25.

Webster, N. (1962 [1828]). From the Preface to An American Dictionary
    of the English Language, in *Dictionaries and "That" Dictionary: A*
    Casebook on the Aims of Lexicographers and the Targets of Reviewers,
    eds. J. Sledd and W. B. Ebbitt., 32–5. Chicago: Scott Foresman.
Webster, N. (1790). *The American Spelling Book*, vol. 1. Worcester, MA:
    Isaiah Thomas.

1: Consequences of the Myth

Baker, J. T. (1899). Correct English: How to Use It, in *Correct English*
Ball, C. E. and D. M. Loewe (eds.) (2017). *Bad Ideas About Writing*.
    Morgantown, WV: West Virginia University Libraries Digital
    Publishing Institute.
Brown, D. W. (forthcoming). Dictionaries, Language Ideologies, and
    Language Attitudes*, in Cambridge Handbook of the Dictionary*.
    Cambridge: Cambridge University Press.
Cameron, D. (2012). *Verbal Hygiene*. Abingdon, Oxfordshire: Routledge.
Clark, B. (2012). 15 Grammar Goofs That Make You Look Silly, on
    Copyblogger: https://copyblogger.com/grammar-goofs/.
Eliot, C. W. (1888). Can School Programs Be Shortened and Enriched?
    Atlantic Monthly, 1012, 250–8.
Gee, J. P. (2007). *Social Linguistics and Literacies: Ideology in Discourses*.
    Abingdon, Oxfordshire: Routledge.
Gould, C. (1987). Josephine Turck Baker, 'Correct English,' and the
    Ancestry of Pop Grammar. *The English Journal*, 76(1) 22–7.
Graham, S. and T. Santangelo, (2014). Does Spelling Instruction Make
    Students Better Spellers, Readers, and Writers? A Meta-analytic
    Review. *Reading and Writing*, 27(9), 1703–43.
Horner, W.B., (1990). The Roots of Modern Writing Instruction: Eighteenth-
    and Nineteenth-century Britain. *Rhetoric Review*, 8(2), 322–45.
Lang, B., (2020). Strunk, White, and Grammar as Morality, in *Writing and*
    the Moral Self, 11–18, Abingdon, Oxfordshire: Routledge.
Lippi-Green, R., (1994). Accent, Standard Language Ideology, and
    Discriminatory Pretext in the Courts. *Language in Society*, 23(2),
    163–98.
Miller, E. L. (1900). Literary Study and Character Formation. *The School*
    Review, 8(5), 285–91.
Pattanayak, A. (2017). There is One Correct Way of Writing and Speaking,
    in *Bad Ideas About Writing*, eds. Ball, C. E. and D. M. Loewe,
    82–7. Morgantown, WV: West Virginia University Libraries Digital
    Publishing Institute.
Pei, M. (1967). *The Story of the English Language*. New York: HarperCollins.

Pullum, G. K. (2009). 50 Years of Stupid Grammar Advice. *The Chronicle of Higher Education*, 55(32), B15.

Reynolds, T. (2005). Selling College Literacy: The Mass-market Magazine as Early 20th-Century Literacy Sponsor. *American Periodicals: A Journal of History & Criticism*, 15(2), 163–77.

Roberts, S. (2009). The 'Elements of Style' Turns 50, in *The New York Times*, April 29.

Vorlat, E. (1999). *On the Originality of Lindley Murray's Prescriptive Canon. Thinking English Grammar*. Leuven/Paris: Peeters.

Wallraff, B. (2015). Improve Your Writing to Improve Your Credibility, in *Harvard Business Review*, July 29.

Zachrisson, R. E. (1931). Four Hundred Years of English Spelling Reform. *Studia neophilologica*, 4(1), 1–69.

1: Closer to the Truth

Ädel, A. (2006). *Metadiscourse in L1 and L2 English*. vol. 24. Amsterdam: John Benjamins Publishing.

Aull, L. L. (2015). *First-year University Writing: A Corpus-based Study with Implications for Oedagogy*. London: Palgrave Macmillan.

Baron, D. (2009). *A Better Pencil: Readers, Writers, and the Digital Revolution*. Oxford: Oxford University Press.

Biber, D. and B. Gray, (2010). Challenging Stereotypes about Academic Writing: Complexity, Elaboration, Explicitness. *Journal of English for Academic Purposes*, 9(1), 2–20.

Biber, D. et al. (2002). Speaking and Writing in the University: A Multidimensional Comparison. *TESOL Quarterly*, 36(1), 9–48.

Groom, N. (2009). Phraseology and Epistemology in Academic Book Reviews: A Corpus-driven Analysis of Two Humanities Disciplines, in *Academic Evaluation*, 122–39, New York: Springer.

Hyland, K. and C.S. Guinda (2012). *Stance and Voice in Written Academic Genres*. New York: Springer.

McNamara, D. S. (2013). The Epistemic Stance between the Author and Reader: A Driving Force in the Cohesion of Text and Writing. *Discourse Studies*, 15(5), 579–95.

McWhorter, J. (2022). Blackness and Standard English Can Coexist. Professors, Take Note, in *The New York Times*, May 3.

Pratt, R. A. (2017). *Selma's Bloody Sunday: Protest, Voting Rights, and the Struggle for Racial Equality*. Baltimore, MD: Johns Hopkins University Press.

Römer, U. and S. Wulff (2010). Applying Corpus Methods to Written Academic Texts: Explorations of MICUSP. *Journal of Writing Research*, 2(2), 99–127.

Tagliamonte, S. A. and D. Denis (2008). Linguistic Ruin? LOL! Instant Messaging and Teen Language. *American Speech*, 83(1), 3–34.

Thompson, G. (2001). Interaction in Academic Writing: Learning to Argue with the Reader. *Applied Linguistics*, 22(1), 58–78.

Waldron, S., C. Wood, and N. Kemp (2017). Use of Predictive Text in Text Messaging over the Course of a Year and its Relationship with Spelling, Orthographic Processing and Grammar. *Journal of Research in Reading*, 40(4), 384–402.

2: You Can't Write that in School

Clarendon Report (1864). In Report of Her Majesty's Commissioners appointed to inquire into the Revenues and Management of Certain Colleges and Schools, and the Studies Pursued and Instruction Given Therein. London: H.M.S.O.

Defoe, D. and K. D. Bülbring (1890). *The Compleat English Gentleman.* London: Folcroft Library Editions.

Jenkins, R. (2018). We Must Help Students Master Standard English. *The Chronicle of Higher Education*, April 10.

Rae, J. (1982). The Decline and Fall of English Grammar. *The Observer*, February 7.

2: Context for the Myth

Anderson, R. D. and P. A. Lee, (1995). *Education and the Scottish People, 1750–1918.* Oxford: Oxford University Press.

Bain, A. (1866). *English Composition and Rhetoric.* London: Longmans.

Blair, H., (1965 [1784]). *Lectures on Rhetoric and Belles Lettres.* Published by Robert Aitken, at Pope's Head in Market Street, reprinted 1965. Carbondale, IL: Southern Illinois University Press.

Cambridge, University of, Local Examination Syndicate (UCLES). (1883). Examiner Bound Volume Report 1883. Cambridge Assessment Archives & Heritage. Cambridge, UK: Cambridge Assessment.

Conrick, M. and P. Donovan (2010). Immigration and Language Policy and Planning in Quebec and Canada: Language Learning and Integration. *Journal of Multilingual and Multicultural Development*, 31(4), 331–45.

De Bellaigue, C. (2018). *Home Education in Historical Perspective: Domestic Pedagogies in England and Wales, 1750–1900.* Abingdon, Oxfordshire: Routledge.

Devon Commission (1847). *Digest of Evidence Taken Before Her Majesty's Commissioners of Inquiry into the State of the Law and Practice in Respect to the Occupation of Land in Ireland*. Part I.

Eggington, W. and H. Wren, (1997). *Language Policy: Dominant English, Pluralist Challenges*. Amsterdam; Philadelphia, PA: J. Benjamins.

Fitzsimmons-Doolan, S. (2009). Is Public Discourse about Language Policy Really Public Discourse about Immigration? A Corpus-based Study. *Language Policy*, 8(4), 377–402.

Franklin, B. (1931). Observations Relative to the Intentions of the Original Founders of the Academy in Philadelphia, in *Educational Views of Benjamin Franklin*, ed. T. Woody. New York: McGraw-Hill Book Company.

Graff, H. J. (1979). The Literacy Myth: Literacy and Social Structure in the Nineteenth-century City. New York: Academic Press.

Hodson, J. (2006). The problem of Joseph Priestley's (1733–1804) descriptivism. *Historiographia Linguistica*, 33(1–2), 57–84.

Leibowitz, A. H. (1974). Language as a Means of Social Control: The United States Experience. Paper presented at the Annual Meeting of the World Congress of Sociology (Eighth) in Toronto, Canada.

Logan, D. (1979). Universities in the Commonwealth. *Journal of the Royal Society of Arts*, 127(5279), 700–17.

London, University of. (1838–43). Examination and Matriculation Papers. London.

Miller, T. P. (1990). Where Did College English Studies Come From? *Rhetoric Review*, 9(1), 50–69.

Monaghan, E. J. (1991). Family Literacy in Early 18th-Century Boston: Cotton Mather and His Children. *Reading Research Quarterly*, 26(4), 342–70.

Mugglestone, L. (2003). *Talking proper: The rise of accent as social symbol*. Oxford: Oxford University Press.

Ozolins, U. and M. Clyne (2001). Immigration and Language Policy, in *The Other Languages of Europe: Demographic, Sociolinguistic, and Educational Perspectives*, eds. G. Extra and D. Gorter, 371–90. Clevedon: Multilingual Matters and European Cultural Foundation.

Pavlenko, A. (2002). We Have Room for But One Language Here: Language and National Identity in the US at the Turn of the 20th Century. *Multilingua*, 21(2–3), 163–96.

Popular Education in England, vols. I to VI. London: HMSO.

Priestley, J. (1772). *A Course of Lectures on Oratory and Criticism*. London: J. Johnson.

Raftery, D., J. McDermid, and G. E. Jones (2007). Social Change and Education in Ireland, Scotland and Wales: Historiography on Nineteenth-century Schooling. *History of Education*, 36(4–5), 447–63.

Reinhold, M. (1968). Opponents of Classical Learning in America during the Revolutionary Period. *Proceedings of the American Philosophical Society*, 112(4), 221–34.

Robbins, S. (2002)."The Future Good and Great of our Land": Republican Mothers, Female Authors, and Domesticated Literacy in Antebellum New England. *The New England Quarterly*, 75(4), 562–91.

(2004). *Managing Literacy, Mothering America: Women's Narratives on Reading and Writing in the Nineteenth Century.* Pittsburgh, PA: University of Pittsburgh Press.

Sack, S. (1962). Liberal Education: What Was it? What Is it? *History of Education Quarterly*, 2(4), 210–24.

Spack, R. (2002). *America's Second Tongue: American Indian Education and the Ownership of English, 1860–1900.* Lincoln, NE: University of Nebraska Press.

Suto, I., and T. Oates (2021). High-stakes Testing after Basic Secondary Education: How and Why Is it Done in High-performing Education Systems? Cambridge Assessment Research Report. Cambridge: Cambridge Assessment.

The Royal Commission on the State of Popular Education in England [Newcastle Commission], Parliamentary Papers, 1861, XXI, pp. 293–328; in English Historical Documents, XII(1), 1833–1874, ed. by G. M. Young and W. D. Hancock (New York, NY: Oxford University Press, 1956), pp. 891–97.

Valdés, G. (1997). Bilinguals and Bilingualism: Language Policy in an Anti-immigrant Age. *International Journal of Society and Language*, 127, 25–52.

van Leeuwen, B. and J. van Leeuwen-Li (2015). *Average Years of Education.*, IISH Dataverse: hdl. handle. net/10622/KCBMKI.

Woody, T. (1920). *Early Quaker Education in Pennsylvania.* New York: Teachers College, Columbia University.

2: Consequences of the Myth

Anderson, M. (2015). The Costs of English-only Education, *The Atlantic*, November 2.

Arnet, C. et al. (1994). Teaching Children How to Discriminate. Paper presented at NWAVE Conference, Stanford University, Palo Alto, CA.

Baldwin, J. (1979). If Black English Isn't a Language, Then Tell Me, What Is? in *The New York Times*, July 29.

Baron, D. (1990). *The English-only Question: An Official Language for Americans?* New Haven, CT: Yale University Press.

(2014). America's War on Language, on The Web of Language blog, September 3.

Baynes, C. (2019). Government "Deported 7,000 Foreign Students after Falsely Accusing Them of Cheating in English Language Tests." *The Independent*, June 14.

Bianco, J. L. (1997). English and Pluralistic Policies: The Case of Australia, in *Language Policy Dominant English, Pluralist Challenges*, eds. W. Eggington and H. Wren, 107–20. Amsterdam; Philadelphia, PA: J. Benjamins.

Bourne, J. (1997). "The Grown-ups Know Best": Language Policy-Making in Britain in the 1990s, in *Language Policy: Dominant English, Pluralist challenges*, eds. W. Eggington and H. Wren, 49–65. Amsterdam; Philadelphia, PA: J. Benjamins.

Clements, G. and M. J. Petray, (2021). *Linguistic Discrimination in US Higher Education: Power, Prejudice, Impacts, and Remedies*. Abingdon, Oxfordshire: Routledge.

Davila, B. (2016). The Inevitability of "Standard" English: Discursive Constructions of Standard Language Ideologies. *Written Communication*, 33(2), 127–48.

Duff, P. A. and D. Li (2009). Indigenous, Minority, and Heritage Language Education in Canada: Policies, Contexts, and Issues. *Canadian Modern Language Review*, 66(1), 1–8.

Dyste, C. (1989). Proposition 63: The California English Language Amendment. *Applied Linguistics*, 10(3), 313–30.

Gardiner-Garden, J. (1999). *From Dispossession to Reconciliation*. Research Paper 27. 1998–99. Canberra: Parliament of Australia.

Judd, E. L. (1987). The English Language Amendment: A Case Study on Language and Politics. *TESOL Quarterly*, 21(1), 113–35.

Kirkland, E. S. (1883). *Speech and Manners for Home and School*. Chicago: Jansen, Mcclurg & Company.

Kohler, M. (2017). *Review of Languages Education Policies in Australia*. Report commissioned by the Multicultural Education and Languages Committee (MELC). Adelaide: Government of South Australia.

Launspach, S. (2021). Conflicting Ideologies: Language Diversity in the Composition Classroom, in *Linguistic Discrimination in US Higher Education*, eds. G. Clements and M. J. Petray, 55–73. Abingdon, Oxfordshire: Routledge.

Mac Síthigh, D. (2018). Official Status of Languages in the United Kingdom and Ireland. *Common Law World Review*, 47(1), 77–102.

Macedo, D. (2000). The Colonialism of the English-Only Movement. *Educational Researcher*, 29(3), 15–24.

Marshall, D. F. (1988). *Foreign Reactions to American Concerns about the English Only Amendment, in TESOL.*, paper presented at the Annual Meeting of the Teachers of English to Speakers of Other Languages (TESOL) in Chicago, Illinois, March 8–13, 1988.

May, S. (2005). Bilingual/immersion Education in Aotearoa/New Zealand: Setting the Context. *International Journal of Bilingual Education and Bilingualism*, 8(5), 365–76.

McAuliffe, M. and A. Triandafyllidou. (2022). 1 Report Overview: Technological, Geopolitical and Environmental Transformations Shaping Our Migration and Mobility Futures. *World Migration Report*, 2022(1), e00022.

Metz, M. H. (1989). Real School: A Universal Drama amid Disparate Experience. *Politics of Education Association Yearbook*, 4(5), 75–91.

Mislevy, R. and N. Elliot (2020). Ethics, Psychometrics, and Writing Assessment: A Conceptual Model, in *After Plato: Rhetoric, Ethics, and the Teaching of Writing*, 143–62. Logan, UT: Utah State University Press.

Nunberg, G. (1990). What the Usage Panel Thinks, in *The State of the Language*, eds. C. Ricks and L. Michaels, 467–82. Los Angeles: University of California Press.

Odell, L., D. Goswami, and A. Herrington (1983). The Discourse-based Interview: A Procedure for Exploring the Tacit Knowledge of Writers in Nonacademic Settings, in *Research on Writing: Principles and Methods*, eds. P. Mosenthal, L. Tamor, and S. A. Walmsley, 221–236. London: Longman.

Rae, J. (1982). The Decline and Fall of English Grammar, in *The Observer*, February 7.

Rafael, V. L. and M. L. P. Pratt (2021). Introduction. *American Quarterly*, 73(3), 419–37.

Ramirez, M. (2016). Dual-language Learning Programs on the Rise. *The Education Digest*, 81(8), 26.

Shapiro, S. (2014). "Words That You Said Got Bigger": English Language Learners' Lived Experiences of Deficit Discourse. *Research in the Teaching of English*, 48(4), 386–406.

Silber, J. R. (1977). *The Need for Elite Education*, in Harper's, June.

Simpson, J., J. Caffery, and P. McConvell (2009). Gaps in Australia's Indigenous Language Policy: Dismantling Bilingual Education in the Northern Territory. Australian Institute of Aboriginal and Torres Strait Islander Studies (AIATSIS) Discussion Paper 24: https://aiatsis .gov.au/sites/default/files/research_pub/simpson-caffery-mcconvell-dp24-indigenous-language-policy_0_3.pdf.

Smitherman, G. (1998). Ebonics, King, and Oakland: Some Folk Don't Believe Fat Meat Is Greasy. *Journal of English Linguistics*, 26(2), 97–107.

Tyack, D. and W. Tobin (1994). The "Grammar" of Schooling: Why Has It Been so Hard to Change? *American Educational Research Journal*, 31(3), 453–79.

Vickers, S. et al. (2021). Split Infinitives: the English "Rule" that Refuses to Quietly Die, in the *Guardian*, Letters page, July 1.

Wilder, L. and J. Wolfe (2009). Sharing the Tacit Rhetorical Knowledge of the Literary Scholar: The Effects of Making Disciplinary Conventions Explicit in Undergraduate Writing about Literature Courses. *Research in the Teaching of English*, 44(2), 170–209.

Wiley, T. G. and M. Lukes (1996). English-only and Standard English Ideologies in the US. *TESOL Quarterly*, 30(3), 511–35.

2: Closer to the Truth

Hill, A. S., L. R. Briggs, and B. S. Hurlbut (1896). *Twenty Years of School and College English*. Cambridge, MA: Harvard University.

House, J. (2012). English as a Lingua Franca and Linguistic Diversity. *Journal of English as a Lingua Franca*, 1(1), 173–5.

UDLR (1996). Universal Declaration of Linguistic Rights: www.egt.ie/udhr/udlr-en.html.

3: You Can't Write that and Be Smart

Burt, C. (1925). *The Subnormal School Child*. New York: Appleton.

Mann, H. (1845). Boston Grammar and Writing Schools. *The Common School Journal*, 7(21–3), 321–68.

Mosley, M. (2020). *The Great British Intelligence Test*, BBC webpage: www.bbc.co.uk/programmes/articles/5tFHwWMgg9VbrHT9kvGlFqd/the-great-british-intelligence-test.

3: Context for the Myth

Behizadeh, N. and G. Engelhard, Jr. (2011). Historical View of the Influences of Measurement and Writing Theories on the Practice of Writing Assessment in the United States. *Assessing Writing*, 16(3), 189–211.

Binet, A. and T. Simon (1916). *The Development of Intelligence in Children*. Baltimore, MD: Williams & Wilkins.

Boring, E. G. (1923). Intelligence as the Tests Test it. *New Republic*, 36(1923), 35–7.

Brigham, C. C. (1923). *A Study of American Intelligence*. Princeton, NJ; Oxford: Princeton University Press; Oxford University Press.

Burt, C. (1914). The Measurement of Intelligence by the Binet Tests: Part II. *The Eugenics Review*, 6(2), 140–52.

Cohen, A. S. (2016). Harvard's Eugenics Era. *Harvard Magazine*, 118(4), 48–52.

Eliot, C. W. (1869). Addresses at the Inauguration of Charles William Eliot as President of Harvard College. October 19. Cambridge, MA: Sever and Francis.

(1898). *Educational Reform: Essays and Addresses*. New York: The Century Co.

Hammond, J. (2019). *Composing Progress in the United States: Race Science, Social Justice, and the Rhetorics of Writing Assessment, 1845–1859*. Ann Arbor, MI: University of Michigan Press.

Hillegas, M. (1912). Scale for the Measurement of Quality in English Composition by Young People: The Location of the Zero Point for English Composition. *Teachers College Record*, 13(4), 12–14.

Hudelson, E. (1923). The Development and Comparative Values of Composition Scales. *The English Journal*, 12(3), 163–8.

Johnson, F. W. (1913). The Hillegas-Thorndike Scale for Measurement of Quality in English Composition by Young People. *The School Review*, 21(1), 39–49.

Kayfetz, I. (1914). A Critical study of the Hillegas Composition Scale. *The Pedagogical Seminary*, 21(4), 559–77.

Leslie, M. (2000). The Vexing Legacy of Lewis Terman. *Stanford Magazine*, July/August.

Logan, S. W. (2008). *Liberating Language: Sites of Rhetorical Education in Nineteenth-Century Black America*. Carbondale, IL: Southern Illinois University Press.

Lunsford, A. A. (1986). The Past and Future of Writing Assessment, in *Writing Assessment: Issues and Strategies*, eds. K. L. Greenberg, H. S. Wiener, and R. A. Donovan, 1–12. New York: Longman.

Mann, H. (1887). *A Few Thoughts for a Young Man*. Boston, MA: Lee and Shepard.

Messerli, J. (1972). *Horace Mann: A Biography*. New York: Knopf.

New England Association of Teachers of English (1913). *The Hillegas Scale*. Leaflet no. 104. Cambridge, MA: New England Association of Teachers of English.

Reese, W. J. (2013). *Testing Wars in the Public Schools*. Cambridge, MA: Harvard University Press.

Spearman, C. (1904). "General Intelligence," Objectively Determined and Measured. *The American Journal of Psychology*, 15(2), 201–92.

Stoddard, W. (1916). A Comparison of the Hillegas and Harvard-Newton Scales in English Composition. *The Pedagogical Seminary*, 23(4), 498–501.

Stout, D. and S. Stuart (1991). E. G. Boring's Review of Brigham's A Study of American Intelligence: A Case-Study in the Politics of Reviews. *Social Studies of Science*, 21(1), 133–42.

Terman, L. M. (1916). *The Measurement of Intelligence: An Explanation of and a Complete Guide for the Use of the Stanford Revision and Extension of the Binet-Simon Intelligence Scale*. Boston, MA: Houghton Mifflin company.

Thorndike, E. L. (1904). *An Introduction to the Theory of Mental and Social Measurements*. New York: Teacher's College, Columbia University.

   (1913). Notes on the Significance and Use of the Hillegas Scale for Measuring the Quality of English Composition. *The English Journal*, 2(9), 551–61.

Yerkes, R. M. (1923). Foreword, in *A Study of American Intelligence*, ed. C. C. Brigham, i–viii. Princeton; London: Princeton University Press; Oxford University Press.

3: Consequences of the Myth

Cohen, A. S. (2016). *Imbeciles: The Supreme Court, American Eugenics, and the Sterilization of Carrie Buck*. Harmondsworth: Penguin.

Connors, R. J. and A. A. Lunsford (1988). Frequency of Formal Errors in Current College Writing, or Ma and Pa Kettle Do Research. *College Composition and Communication*, 39(4), 395–409.

Elliot, N. (2005). *On a Scale: A Social History of Writing Assessment in America*. Bern, Switzerland: Peter Lang.

Goddard, H. H. (1912). *The Kallikak Family: A Study in the Heredity of Feeble-mindedness*. London: Macmillan.

Gould, S. J. (1996). *The Mismeasure of Man*. New York: W. W. Norton & Company.

Hamp-Lyons, L. (2007). The Impact of Testing Practices on Teaching, in *International Handbook of English Language Teaching*, eds. J. Cummins and C. Davison, 487–504. New York: Springer.

Lombardo, P. A. (2003). Facing Carrie Buck. *The Hastings Center Report*, 33(2), 14–17.

Mislevy, R. J. (2018). *Sociocognitive Foundations of Educational Measurement*. Abingdon, Oxfordshire: Routledge.

Russell, J. E. (1903). The Educational Value of Examinations for Admission to College. *The School Review*, 11(1), 42–54.

Ulrich, L. T. (1999). Harvard's Womanless History. *Harvard Magazine*, 102, 50–9.

Walsh, C. (2012). Hard-earned Gains for Women at Harvard. *Harvard Gazette*, 4, 26.

Wright, K. (2017). Inventing the "Normal" Child: Psychology, Delinquency, and the Promise of Early Intervention. *History of the Human Sciences*, 30(5), 46–67.

3: Closer to the Truth

Dryer, D. B. (2015). Writing Is Unnatural, in *Naming What We Know: Threshold Concepts of Writing Studies*, eds. L. Adler-Kassner and E. Wardle, Denver, CO: University Press of Colorado.

Locust, C. (1988). Wounding the Spirit: Discrimination and Traditional American Indian Belief Systems. *Harvard Educational Review*, 58(3), 315–31.

Mercer, J.R., (2022). *Labeling the Mentally Retarded: Clinical and Social System Perspectives on Mental Retardation.* Los Angeles: University of California Press.

Mislevy, R. J. (1997). Postmodern Test Theory, in *Transitions in Work and Learning: Implications for Assessment*, National Research Council. Washington, D.C.: National Academic of Sciences National Research Council.

Perelman, L. C. (2013). Critique of Mark D. Shermis & Ben Hammer, Contrasting State-of-the-art Automated Scoring of Essays: Analysis. *Journal of Writing Assessment*, 6(1), 1–10.

Royster, J. J., (1996). When the First Voice You Hear Is not Your Own. *College Composition and Communication*, 47(1), 29–40.

Samuda, R. J. (1998). *Psychological Testing of American Minorities: Issues and Consequences.* Thousand Oaks, CA: Sage.

Schuster, C., (1990). The Ideology of Literacy: A Bakhtinian Perspective, in *The Right to Literacy*, eds. A. A. Lunsford, H. Moglen, and J. Slevin, 225–32. New York: The Modern Language Association.

Von Stumm, S. and R. Plomin (2015). Socioeconomic Status and the Growth of Intelligence from Infancy through Adolescence. *Intelligence*, 48, 30–6.

4: You Can't Write that on the Test

Bardell, G. S., G. M. Forrest, and D. Shoesmith (1978). *Comparability in GCE: A Review of the Boards' Studies; 1964–1977.* Joint Matriculation Board.

Burt, C. (1945). The Reliability of Teachers' Assessments of the Pupils. *British Journal of Educational Psychology*, 15(2), 80–92.

Crofts, J. M. and D. C. Jones (1928). *Secondary School Examination Statistics: Prefaced by a Simple Introduction to Statistical Methods.* London: Longmans, Green and Company, Limited.

Tattersall, K., (2007). A Brief History of Policies, Practices and Issues Relating to Comparability: Techniques for Monitoring the Comparability of

Examination Standards, 43–96: https://assets.publishing.service.gov.uk/
government/uploads/system/uploads/attachment_data/file/487051/2007-
comparability-exam-standards-d-chapter2.pdf.

4: Context for the Myth

Barker, D. G. (1967). The History of Entrance Examinations. *Improving
College and University Teaching*, 15(4), 250–3.

Berlin, J. (1984). *Writing Instruction in Nineteenth-century American
Colleges*. Carbondale, IL: Southern Illinois University Press.

Connors, R. J. (1997). *Composition-Rhetoric: Backgrounds, Theory, and
Pedagogy*. Pittsburgh, PA: University of Pittsburgh Press.

Goldin, C. and L. F. Katz, (1999). The Shaping of Higher Education:
The Formative Years in the United States, 1890 to 1940. *Journal of
Economic Perspectives*, 13(1), 37–62.

Hearnshaw, F. J. C. (1929). *The Centenary History of King's College,
London, 1828–1928*. London: G. G. Harrap.

Johnson, D. (2016). Can You Answer These Questions From the Original
SAT?, in Time, June 20.

Jones, G. A. (2014). An Introduction to Higher Education in Canada, in
Higher Education Across Nations, eds. K. M. Joshi and S. Paivandi,
vol. 1, 1–38. Delhi: B. R. Publishing.

Levine, S. (2019). A Century of Change in High School English
Assessments: An Analysis of 110 New York State Regents Exams,
1900–2018. *Research in the Teaching of English*, 54(1), 31–57.

Mann, H. (1854). *Dedication of Antioch College, and Inaugural Address of
Its President, Hon. Horace Mann: With Other Proceedings*. Yellow
Springs, Boston: A. S. Dean.

Morris, G. P. (1900). Twenty-five Years of Woman's Higher Education:
An Interview with President L. Clark Scelye of Smith College, in
Congregationalist (1891–1901), 404. Boston: American Periodicals
Series II.

Snyder, T. D. (1993). *120 Years of American Education: A Statistical
Portrait*. Washington, DC: US Department of Education, Office of
Educational Research and Improvement.

Stedman, L. C. (2008). The NAEP Long-term Trend Assessment:
A Review of its Transformation, Use, and Findings. Paper
Commissioned for the 20th Anniversary of the National Assessment
Governing Board 1988–2008.

Stray, C., (2001). The Shift from Oral to Written Examination: Cambridge
and Oxford 1700–1900. *Assessment in Education: Principles, Policy &
Practice*, 8(1), 33–50.

Trachsel, M. (1992). *Institutionalizing Literacy: The Historical Role of College Entrance Examinations in English*. Carbondale, IL: Southern Illinois University Press.

University of Cambridge Local Examinations Syndicate, (1893). English Composition Examiner Report.

(1904). Forty-Sixth Annual Report of the Local Examinations,

(1913). English Composition Examiner Report. p. xvii.

(2008). How Have School Exams Changed over the Past 150 Years?

Vaughan, G. B. (1985). *The Community College in America: A Short History*. Revised. Washington, DC: American Association of Community and Junior Colleges.

Watts, A. (2008). Cambridge Local Examinations 1858–1945, in *Examining the World: A History of the University of Cambridge Local Examinations Syndicate*, ed. S. Raban, 36–71. Cambridge: Cambridge University Press.

(2008). Turn Your Papers Over. *History Today*, 58(8).

Webb, S. (1902). London University: A Policy and a Forecast. *The Nineteenth Century and After: A Monthly Review*, 51(304), 914–31.

4: Consequences of the Myth

Anderson, P., et al., (2015). The Contributions of Writing to Learning and Development: Results from a Large-scale Multi-institutional Study. *Research in the Teaching of English*, 50(2), 199–235.

Applebee, A. and J. Langer (2011). "EJ" Extra: A Snapshot of Writing Instruction in Middle Schools and High Schools. *The English Journal*, 100(6), 14–27.

Arum, R. and J. Roksa (2011). *Academically Adrift: Limited Learning on College Campuses*. Chicago, IL: University of Chicago Press.

Aull, L. L. (Forthcoming). Attention to Language in Composition. *Composition Forum*.

Bain, A., (1866). *English Composition and Rhetoric: A Manual* (rev. American ed.). New York: D. Appleton and Co.

Beaufort, A. (2007). *College Writing and Beyond: A New Framework for University Writing Instruction*. Logan, UT: Utah State University Press.

Blodget, A. (2019). It's Time to End Timed Tests, in *Education Week*, September 30.

Brereton, J. (1996). *The Origins of Composition Studies in the American College, 1875–1925*. Pittsburgh, PA: University of Pittsburgh Press.

Burt, C. (1921). Mental and Scholastic Tests. Report by the Education Officer Submitting Three Memoranda by Mr. Cyril Burt. London: P. S. King and Son Ltd.

(1945). The Reliability of Teachers' Assessments of their Pupils. *British Journal of Educational Psychology*, 15(2), 80–92.

Carter, D., J. Manuel, and J. Dutton (2018). How Do Secondary School English Teachers Score NAPLAN?: A Snapshot of English Teachers' Views. *Australian Journal of Language and Literacy*, 41(3), 144–54.

Connors, R. J. (1999). Composition History and Disciplinarity, in *History, Reflection, and Narrative: The Professionalization of Composition, 1963–1983*, eds. M. Rosner, B. Boehm, and D. Journet. Stamford, CT: Ablex Publishing.

Connors, R., Lisa S. Ede & Andrea A. Lunsford. (1984). "The Revival of Rhetoric in America." Essays on Classical Rhetoric and Modern Discourse. Ed. Connors, Ede & Lunsford. Carbondale: Southern Illinois Univ. Press, 1984: 1–15

Cook-Gumperz, J., ed. (2006). *The Social Construction of Literacy.* Cambridge: Cambridge University Press.

Dance, C. (2017). An Oxford Exam from 1884, from Dance's Historical Miscellany: www.danceshistoricalmiscellany.com/an-oxford-exam-from-1884/.

Gannon, S. (2019). Teaching Writing in the NAPLAN Era: The Experiences of Secondary English Teachers. *English in Australia*, 54(2), 43–56.

Haswell, R. H. (2012). Methodologically Adrift. *College Composition and Communication*, 63(3), 487–91.

Locke, T. (2010). *Beyond the Grammar Wars. A Resource for Teachers and Students on Developing Language Knowledge in English/Literacy Classroom.* Abingdon, Oxfordshire: Routledge.

Luce-Kapler, R. and D. Klinger (2005.) Uneasy Writing: The Defining Moments of High-stakes Literacy Testing. *Assessing Writing*, 10(3), 157–73.

MacDonald, S. P. (2007). The Erasure of Language. *College Composition and Communication*, 58(4), 585–625.

Moore, C. (2011). History of the English Language in the English Department: Past and Present, in *Contours of English and English Language Studies, eds.* M. Adams and A. Curzan, 157–67. Ann Arbor, MI: University of Michigan Press.

Oxford University Gazette (1870). Oxford University Gazette. Vols.1–2 (1870–1872).

Ross, A. (2001). What is the Curriculum? In *Developing Pedagogy: Researching Practice*, ed. J. Collins, J. Soler and K. Insley, 122–31. London: Paul Chapman.

Sternberg, R. J. (2007). Who Are the Bright Children? The Cultural Context of Being and Acting Intelligent. *Educational Researcher*, 36(3), 148–55.

(2022). The Search for the Elusive Basic Processes Underlying Human Intelligence: Historical and Contemporary Perspectives. *Journal of Intelligence*, 10(2):28: https://doi.org/10.3390/jintelligence10020028.

UK Government (2021). Proposed Changes to the Assessment of GCSEs, AS and A Levels in 2022. Updated September 30, 2021: www.gov.uk/government/consultations/proposed-changes-to-the-assessment-of-gcses-as-and-a-levels-in-2022/proposed-changes-to-the-assessment-of-gcses-as-and-a-levels-in-2022.

Watts, A. (2008). Cambridge local examinations 1858–1945. Examining the World: A History of the University of Cambridge Local Examinations Syndicate, pps 36–71.

Watts, A. (2019). *School Certificate Examinations in England, 1918–1950. A Historical Investigation of the Formation and Maintenance of a National Examination System: Examination Boards, Teachers and the State*: https://doi.org/10.17863/CAM.43215.

Winterowd, W. R. (1998,). *The English Department: A Personal and Institutional History*. Carbondale, IL: Southern Illinois University Press.

Zwick, R. (2017). *Who Gets In?: Strategies for Fair and Effective College Admissions*. Cambridge, MA: Harvard University Press.

4: Closer to the Truth

Ädel, A., (2008). Involvement Features in Writing: Do Time and Interaction Trump Register Awareness? in *Linking up Contrastive and Learner Corpus Research*, 35–53. Leiden: Brill Publishing.

Au, K. H. (2006). *Multicultural Issues and Literacy Achievement*. Mahwah, NJ: L. Erlbaum Associates.

Aull, L.L., (2017). Corpus Analysis of Argumentative Versus Explanatory Discourse in Writing Task Genres. *Journal of Writing Analytics*, 1(1), 1–47.

(2019). Linguistic Markers of Stance and Genre in Upper-level Student Writing. *Written Communication*, 36(2), 267–95.

Bejar, I. I. (2017). A Historical Survey of Research Regarding Constructed-response Formats, in *Advancing Human Assessment*, eds. R. E. Bennett and M. von Davier, 565–633. Cham, Switzerland: Springer.

Cambridge, University of. (1870). Examination for Women. Examination Papers, with Lists of Syndics and Examiners: https://archive.org/details/examinationforw00unkngoog/page/n7/mode/2up.

Coates, H. (2007). Developing Generalizable Measures of Knowledge and Skill Outcomes in Higher Education. Paper delivered at the Proceedings of AUQF2007: Evolution and Renewal In Quality Assurance, Hobart, Australia, July 11–13, 2007.

Deane, P., T. O'Reilly, S-F. Chao, and K. Dreier (2018). Writing Processes in Short Written Responses to Questions Probing Prior Knowledge. *ETS Research Report Series*, 2018(1), 1–30.

Dilnot, C. (2016). How Does the Choice of A-level Subjects Vary with Students' Socio-economic Status in English State Schools? *British Educational Research Journal*, 42(6), 1081–1106.

Ede, L. S. and A. A. Lunsford (1990). *Singular Texts/Plural Authors: Perspectives on Collaborative Writing*. Carbondale, IL: Southern Illinois University Press.

Elgin, S. H. (1976). Why "Newsweek" Can't Tell us Why Johnny Can't Write. *The English Journal*, 65(8), 29–35.

Elliot, N. (2016). A Theory of Ethics for Writing Assessment. *Journal of Writing Assessment*, 9(1), 1–29.

Gere, A. R. et al. (2013). Local Assessment: Using Genre Analysis to Validate Directed Self-Placement. *College Composition and Communication*, 4(64), 605–33.

Huot, B. and M. M. Williamson (1997). Rethinking Portfolios for Evaluating Writing, in *Situating Portfolios: Four Perspectives*, eds. K. B. Yancey and I. Weiser. Logan, UT: Utah State University Press.

Judy, S. (1977). On Second Thought: Reviewing the SAT Decline. *The English Journal*, 66(8), 5–7.

Kamenetz, A. (2015). *The Test: Why Our Schools are Obsessed with Standardized Testing – But You Don't Have to Be*. New York: PublicAffairs.

Kelly-Riley, D. and N. Elliot (2014). The WPA Outcomes Statement, Validation, and the Pursuit of Localism. *Assessing Writing*, 21, 89–103.

Labov, W. and J. Waletzky (1997). Narrative Analysis: Oral Versions of Personal Experience. *Journal of Narrative and Life History*, 7(1–4), 3–38.

Lunsford, A. A. (2013). Our Semi-literate Youth? Not So Fast. Report. Stanford University: www.stanford.Edu/group/ssw/cgi-bin/materials/OPED_Our_Semi-Literate_Youth.Pdf.

Lunsford, A. A., J. Fishman, and W. M. Liew. (2013). College Writing, Identification, and the Production of Intellectual Property: Voices from the Stanford Study of Writing. *College English*, 75(5), 470–92.

Marini, J.P., et al. (2019). Validity of SAT® Essay Scores for Predicting First-Year Grades. New York: College Board.

Mary, B., M. Wade, and P. Sarah (2004). Assessment as Opportunity: A Conversation with Brian Huot. *Issues in Writing*, 14(2), 94–115.

Olinghouse, N. G., S. Graham, and A. Gillespie (2015). The Relationship of Discourse and Topic Knowledge to Fifth Graders' Writing Performance. *Journal of Educational Psychology*, 107(2), 391–406.

Perelman, L. (2012). Construct Validity, Length, Score, and Time in Holistically Graded Writing Assessments: The Case against Automated Essay Scoring (AES). In *International Advances in Writing Research: Cultures, Places, Measures*, eds. C. Bazerman et al., 121–31. Fort Collins, CO: WAC Clearinghouse.

Poe, M. and N. Elliot, (2019). Evidence of Fairness: Twenty-five Years of Research in Assessing Writing. *Assessing Writing*, 42, 100418.

Poe, M., N. Eliot, J. A. Gogan, Jr., and T. G. Nurudeen, Jr. (2014). The Legal and the Local: Using Disparate Impact Analysis to Understand the Consequences of Writing Assessment. *College Composition and Communication*, 65(4), 588–611.

Robinson, J. A. (1981). Personal Narratives Reconsidered. *The Journal of American Folklore*, 94(371), 58–85.

Rothman, T. and M. Henderson, (2011). Do School-based Tutoring Programs Significantly Improve Student Performance on Standardized Tests? *RMLE Online*, 34(6), 1–10.

Smith, K. G., K. Girdharry, and C. W. Gallagher (2021). Writing Transfer, Integration, and the Need for the Long View. *College Composition and Communication*, 73(1), 4–26.

Snyderman, M. and S. Rothman (1987). Survey of Expert Opinion on Intelligence and Aptitude Testing. *American Psychologist*, 42(2), 137.

Von Stumm, S. et al. (2020). Predicting Educational Achievement from Genomic Measures and Socioeconomic Status. *Developmental Science*, 23(3), e12925.

Yancey, K. B. and I. Weiser (eds.) (1997). *Situating Portfolios: Four Perspectives*. Logan, UT: Utah State University Press.

Zwick, R. (2019). Assessment in American Higher Education: The Role of Admissions Tests. *The Annals of the American Academy of Political and Social Science*, 683(1), 130–48.

5: Chances Are, You Can't Write

Baker, J. (2020). Writing Wrongs: "Our Society Is About to Hit a Literacy Crisis," in *The Sydney Morning Herald*, September 19.

Clare, J. (2002). New Cambridge Students "Can't Write English," in *The Telegraph*, July 16.

Fahey, G. (2020). Wrestling the Writing Decline Key to Education Improvement, *The Canberra Times*, September 20: www.cis.org.au/commentary/opinion/wrestling-the-writing-decline-key-to-education-improvement/.

Sheils, M. (1975). Why Johnny Can't Write, in Newsweek, December 8: www.leetorda.com/uploads/2/3/2/5/23256940/why_johnny_cant_write__newsweek_1975___1_.pdf.

Wilce, H. (2006). University Students: They Can't Write, Spell or Present an Argument, in The Independent, May 24.

5: Context for the Myth

Aull, L.L (2021). What AP Scorers Shouldn't Grade, in *Inside Higher Education*, July 25.

Benjamin, R., et al., (2009). *Returning to Learning in an Age of Assessment: Introducing the Rationale of the Collegiate Learning Assessment*. New York: CAE.

Boyd, R. (1993). Mechanical Correctness and Ritual in the Late Nineteenth-Century Composition Classroom. *Rhetoric Review*, 11(2), 436–55.

Farkas, G. (2011). *American Journal of Sociology*, 117(3), 1000–2.

McConnell, K. D. (2011). Review of "Academically Adrift." *Research & Practice in Assessment*, 6, 40–2.

5: Consequences of the Myth

Association of American Colleges and Universities (2009). Written Communication VALUE Rubric: wpacouncil.org/files/framework-for-success-postsecondary-writing.pdf.

Curzan, A. (2009.) Says Who? Teaching and Questioning the Rules of Grammar. *PMLA*, 124(3), 870–9.

Council of Writing Program Administrators, the National Council of Teachers of English, and the National Writing Project. (2011). Framework for Success in Postsecondary Writing: wpacouncil.org/files/framework-for-success-postsecondary-writing.pdf.

Gee, J. P. (2002). Literacies, Identities, and Discourses. *Developing Advanced Literacy in First and Second Languages: Meaning with Power*, 159–75.

Lankshear, C. and M. Knobel (2003). *New Literacies: Changing Knowledge and Classroom Learning*. Maidenhead: Open University Press.

Minnis, M. (1994). Toward a Definition of Law School Readiness, in *Sociocultural Approaches to Language and Literacy: An Interactionist Perspective*, eds. V. John-Steiner, C. P. Panofsky and L. W Smith, 347–90. Cambridge: Cambridge University Press.

Ohmann, R. (2003). *Politics of Knowledge: The Commercialization of the University, the Professions, and Print Culture*. Middletown, CT: Wesleyan University Press.

Sternberg, R. J. (2015). Successful Intelligence: A Model for Testing Intelligence beyond IQ Tests. *European Journal of Education and Psychology*, 8(2), 76–84.

Williams, B. T. (2007). Why Johnny Can Never, Ever Read: The Perpetual
   Literacy Crisis and Student Identity. *Journal of Adolescent & Adult
   Literacy*, 51(2), 178–82.

5: Closer to the Truth

Applebee, A. et al. (1990). *The Writing Report Card, 1984–88: Findings
   from the Nation's Report Card*. Princeton, NJ: National Assessment of
   Educational Progress.
Aull, L. L., D. Bandarage and M. R. Miller (2017). Generality in Student
   and Expert Epistemic Stance: A Corpus Analysis of First-year,
   Upper-level, and Published Academic Writing. *Journal of English for
   Academic Purposes*, 26, 29–41.
Brereton, J. (2012). A Closer Look at the Harvard Entrance Examinations
   in the 1870s, in *Writing Assessment in the 21st Century: Essays in
   Honor of Edward M. White*, eds. N. Elliot and L. Perelman, 31–43.
   New York: Hampton Press.
Brown, D. W. and L. L. Aull (2017). Elaborated Specificity versus
   Emphatic Generality: A Corpus-Based Comparison of Higher-and
   Lower-Scoring Advanced Placement Exams in English. *Research in
   the Teaching of English*, 51(4), 394–417.
Cook, Margaret, plus editors. (2007). Can't Write Can't Spell…, in The
   Age, February 26.
Godstein, D. (2017). Why Kids Can't Write, in *The New York Times*,
   August 2.
Haswell, R. and N. Elliot (2019). *Early Holistic Scoring of Writing: A Theory,
   a History, a Reflection*. Logan, UT: Utah State University Press.
James, C. L. (2008). Electronic Scoring of Essays: Does Topic Matter?
   Assessing Writing,. 13(2), 80–92.
Kellaghan, T. and V. Greaney (2019). *Public Examinations Examined*.
   Washington, DC: The World Bank.
Lunsford, A. A. and K. J. Lunsford (2008). "Mistakes Are a Fact of
   Life": A National Comparative Study. *College Composition and
   Communication*, 59(4), 781–806.
National Association for College Admission Counseling and National
   Association of Student Financial Aid Administrators (2022). Toward
   a More Equitable Future for Postsecondary Access.
National Center for Education Statistics. (2019). National Assessment
   of Educational Progress 2017 Writing, May 10: https://nces.ed.gov/
   nationsreportcard/writing/2017writing.aspx.
Stedman, L. C., I. V. Mullis, and M. Timpane, (1998). An Assessment of
   the Contemporary Debate over US Achievement. *Brookings Papers
   on Education Policy*, (1), 53–121.

6: You Can't Write if You Didn't Write Well in High School

Applebee, A. and J. Langer (2011). *The National Study of Writing Instruction: Methods and Procedures*. Albany, NY: Center on English Learning & Achievement.

6: Context for the Myth

Applebee, A. N. and J. A. Langer (2011). "EJ" Extra: A Snapshot of Writing Instruction in Middle Schools and High Schools. *The English Journal*, 100(6), 14–27.
  (2013). *Writing Instruction that Works: Proven Methods for Middle and High School Classrooms*. New York: Teachers College Press.
Aull, L. L. (2015). Connecting Writing and Language in Assessment: Examining Style, Tone, and Argument in the US Common Core Standards and in Exemplary Student Writing. *Assessing Writing*, 24, 59–73.
  (2018). Generality and Certainty in Undergraduate Writing Over Time, in *Developing Writers in Higher Education: A Longitudinal Study*, ed. A. R. Gere. Ann Arbor, MI: University of Michigan Press.
Aull, L. L. and Z. Lancaster (2014). Linguistic Markers of Stance in Early and Advanced Academic Writing: A Corpus-based Comparison. *Written Communication*, 1(33), 151–83.
Bernstein, S. N. and E. Lowry (2017). The Five-paragraph Essay Transmits Knowledge, in *Bad ideas About Writing*, eds. C. E. Ball and D. M. Loewe, 214–19. Morgantown, WV: West Virginia University Libraries Digital Publishing Institute.
Borman, G. D. and N. M. Dowling (2008). Teacher Attrition and Retention: A Meta-analytic and Narrative Review of the Research. *Review of Educational Research*, 78(3), 367–409.
Cambridge Assessment and Research. (2008). "How have school exams changed over the past 150 years?" Accessed July 2022. www.cambridgeassessment.org.uk/news/how-have-school-exams-changed-over-the-past-150-years/.
Clark, I. L. and A. Hernandez (2011). Genre Awareness, Academic Argument, and Transferability. *The WAC Journal*, 22, 65–78.
Geiger, T. and M. Pivovarova (2018). The Effects of Working Conditions on Teacher Retention. *Teachers and Teaching*, 24(6), 604–25.
Gibbons, S. (2019). "Death by PEEL?" The Teaching of Writing in the Secondary English Classroom in England. *English in Education*, 53(1), 36–45.
Graham, S. (2019). Changing How Writing Is Taught. *Review of Research in Education*, 43(1), 277–303.

Hillocks, G., (2002). *The Testing Trap: How State Writing Assessments Control Learning.* New York: Teachers College Press.

Kiuhara, S. A., S. Graham, and L. S. Hawken (2009). Teaching Writing to High School Students: A National Survey. *Journal of Educational Psychology*, 101(1), 136–60.

Kobrin, J. L., H. Deng, and E. J. Shaw (2011). The Association between SAT Prompt Characteristics, Response Features, and Essay Scores. *Assessing Writing*, 16(3), 154–69.

Macbeth, K. P. (2010). Deliberate False Provisions: The Use and Usefulness of Models in Learning Academic Writing. *Journal of Second Language Writing*, 19(1), 33–48.

Mason, S. and C. P. Matas (2015). Teacher Attrition and Retention Research in Australia: Towards a New Theoretical Framework. *Australian Journal of Teacher Education (Online)*, 40(11), 45–66.

Melzer, D. (2009). Writing Assignments across the Curriculum: A National Study of College Writing. *College Composition and Communication*, 61(2), W240–W261.

Ronfeldt, M., S. Loeb, and J. Wyckoff (2013). How Teacher Turnover Harms Student Achievement. *American Educational Research Journal*, 50(1), 4–36.

Sahlberg, P. (2009). A Short History of Educational Reform in Finland. White Paper, April.

See, B. H., R. Morris, S. Gorard, and D. Kokotsaki (2020). Teacher Recruitment and Retention: A Critical Review of International Evidence of Most Promising Interventions. *Education Sciences*, 10(10), 262–307.

Soliday, M. (2002). *The Politics of Remediation: Institutional and Student Needs in Higher Education.* Pittsburgh, PA: University of Pittsburgh Press.

Sutcher, L., L. Darling-Hammond, and D. Carver-Thomas (2016). *A Coming Crisis in Teaching? Teacher Supply, Demand, and Shortages in the US.* Palo Alto, CA: Learning Policy Institute.

Thaiss, C. and T. M. Zawacki (2006). *Engaged Writers Dynamic Disciplines: Research on the Academic Writing Life.* Porstmouth, NH: Heinemann.

6: Consequences of the Myth

Biber, D. and S. Conrad (2019). *Register, Genre, and Style.* Cambridge University Press.

Devitt, A. J. (2007). Transferability and Genres, in *The Locations of Composition*, eds. C. J. Keller and C. R. Weisser, 215–27. Albany, NY: State University of New York Press.

Driscoll, D. L. et al. (2020). Genre Knowledge and Writing Development: Results from the Writing Transfer Project. *Written Communication*, 37(1), 69–103.

Jarratt, S., K. Mack, A. Sartor, and S. E. Watson (2007). *Pedagogical Memory and the Transferability of Writing Knowledge: An Interview-based Study of UCI Juniors and Seniors.* Irvine, CA: University of California.

Miller, S. (1991). *Textual Carnivals: The Politics of Composition.* Carbondale, IL: Southern Illionois University Press.

Rounsaville, A., R. Goldberg, and A. Bawarshi (2008). From Incomes to Outcomes: FYW Students' Prior Genre Knowledge, Meta-cognition, and the Question of Transfer. *WPA: Writing Program Administration*, 1(32), 97–112.

Sullivan, P., (2015). The UnEssay: Making Room for Creativity in the Composition Classroom. *College Composition and Communication*, 67(1), 6–34.

Wardle, E. (2009). "Mutt Genres" and the Goal of FYC: Can We Help Students Write the Genres of the University? *College Composition and Communication*, 60(4), 765–89.

Wingate, U. and C. Tribble (2012). The Best of Both Worlds? Towards an English for Academic Purposes/Academic Literacies Writing Pedagogy. *Studies in Higher Education*, 37(4), 481–95.

6: Closer to the Truth

Ädel, A. (2014). Selecting Quantitative Data for Qualitative Analysis: A Case Study Connecting a Lexicogrammatical Pattern to Rhetorical Moves. *Journal of English for Academic Purposes*, 16, 68–80.

Adler-Kassner, L. and E. Wardle (2015). *Naming What We Know: Threshold Concepts of Writing Studies.* Denver, CO: University Press of Colorado.

Adler-Kassner, L. and P. O'Neill (2010). *Reframing Writing Assessment to Improve Teaching and Learning.* Logan, UT: Utah State University Press.

Anson, C. M. (2016). The Pop Warner Chronicles: A Case Study in Contextual Adaptation and the Transfer of Writing Ability. *College Composition and Communication*, 67(4), 518–49.

Bazerman, C. et al. (2018). *The Lifespan Development of Writing.* Urbana, IL: National Council of Teachers of English.

Brown, D. W. and L. L. Aull (2017). Elaborated Specificity vs. Emphatic Generality: A Corpus-Based Comparison of Higher and Lower

Scoring Advanced Placement Exams in English. *Research in the Teaching of English*, 51(4), 394–417.

Cheng, A. (2007). Transferring Generic Features and Recontextualizing Genre Awareness: Understanding Writing Performance in the ESP Genre-based Literacy Framework. *English for Specific Purposes*, 26(3), 287–307.

Fischer, K. W. and T. R. Bidell (2006). Dynamic Development of Action, Thought, and Emotion, in *Theoretical Models of Human Development: Handbook of Child Psychology*, eds. W. Damon and R. M. Learner, vol. I, 313–99. New York: Wiley.

Granville, S. and L. Dison (2005). Thinking about Thinking: Integrating Self-reflection Into an Academic Literacy Course. *Journal of English for Academic Purposes*, 4(2), 99–118.

Halliday, M. A. K. and R. Hasan (1976). *Cohesion in English*. London: Longman.

Hyland, K. (2005). Stance and Engagement: A Model of Interaction in Academic Discourse. *Discourse Studies,*. 7(2), 173–92.

James, M. A. (2014). Learning Transfer in English-for-Academic-Purposes Contexts: A Systematic Review of Research. *Journal of English for Academic Purposes*, 14, 1–13.

Jarratt, S. C., K. Mack, A. Sartor, and S. E. Watson (2009). Pedagogical Memory: Writing, Mapping, Translating. *Writing Program Administration*, 33(1–2), 46–73.

Keen, J. (1997). Grammar, Metalanguage, and Writing Development. *Teacher Development*. 3(1), 431–45.

Lancaster, Z. (2016). Do Academics Really Write This Way? A Corpus Investigation of Moves and Templates in "They Say/I Say." *College Composition and Communication*, 67(3), 437–64.

Macken-Horarik, M. (2009). Navigational Metalanguages for New Territory in English: The Potential of Grammatics. *English Teaching: Practice and Critique*, 8(3), 55–69.

Matsuda, P. K. and C. M. Tardy, (2007). Voice in Academic Writing: The Rhetorical Construction of Author Identity in Blind Manuscript Review. *English for Specific Purposes*, 26(2), 235–49.

Meizlish, D., D. LaVaque-Manty, and N. Silver (2013). Think Like/Write Like, in *Changing the Conversation About Higher Education*, ed. R. Thompson. Lanham, MD: Rowman & Littlefield.

Negretti, R. (2012). Metacognition in Student Academic Writing. *Written Communication,*. 29(2), 142–79.

Parkinson, J. (2017). The Student Laboratory Report Genre: A Genre Analysis. *English for Specific Purposes*, 45, 1–13.

Ritter, K. (2009). *Before Shaughnessy: Basic Writing at Yale and Harvard, 1920–1960*. Carbondale, IL: Southern Illinois University Press.

7: You Can't Get a Job if You Didn't Write in College

Dias, P., A. Freedman, P. Medway, and A. Parr (2013). *Worlds Apart: Acting and Writing in Academic and Workplace Contexts*. Abingdon, Oxfordshire: Routledge.

Dursun, A., J. K. Morris, and A. Ünaldı (2020). Designing Proficiency-oriented Performance Tasks for the 21st-century Workplace Written Communication: An Evidence-centered Design Approach. *Assessing Writing*, 46 (October).

Schneider, B. and J.-A. Andre (1973) (2005). University Preparation for Workplace Writing: An Exploratory Study of the Perceptions of Students in Three Disciplines. *The Journal of Business Communication*, 42(2), 195–218.

Spilka, R. (1998). *Writing in the Workplace: New Research Perspectives*. Carbondale, IL: Southern Illinois University Press.

7: Context for the Myth

Aley, R. (1915). "The College and the Freshman." *School and Society*, 2(31), 152–4.

Anson, C. M. and L. L. Forsberg (1990). Moving Beyond the Academic Community: Transitional Stages in Professional Writing. *Written Communication*, 7(2), 200–31.

Aull, L. L. and V. Ross (2020). From Cow Paths to Conversation: Rethinking the Argumentative Essay. *Pedagogy: Critical Approaches to Teaching Literature, Language, Composition, and Culture*, 20(1), 21–34.

Barnard, H. C. (1947). *A Short History of English Education from 1760 to 1944*. London: University of London Press.

Bazerman, C. et al., eds. (2009). *Traditions of Writing Research*. Abingdon, Oxfordshire: Routledge.

Bizzell, P. (1992). *Academic Discourse and Critical Consciousness*. Pittsburgh Series in Composition, Literacy, and Culture. Pittsburgh, PA: University of Pittsburgh Press.

Brown, P. and S. C. Levinson (1987). *Politeness: Some Universals in Language Usage*. Cambridge: Cambridge University Press.

Burstein, J., N. Elliot, and H. Molloy (2016). Informing Automated Writing Evaluation using the Lens of Genre: Two Studies. *Calico Journal*, 33(1), 117–41.

Chambers, W. (1876). Getting On, in Chambers's *Journal of Popular Literature, Science, and Arts*, June, 353–5.

Cox, M., C. Ortmeier-Hooper, and K. E. Tirabassi (2009). Teaching Writing for the "Real World": Community and Workplace Writing. *English Journal*, 98(5), 72–80.

Eliot, C. W. (1915). Educational Evolution. *School and Society*, 1(1), 1–13.

Engle, J. (2007). Postsecondary Access and Success for First-generation College Students. *American Academic*, 3(1), 25–48.

Finkenstaedt-Quinn, S. A., M. Petterson, A. R. Gere, and G. V. Schultz (2021). Praxis of Writing-to-Learn: A Model for the Design and Propagation of Writing-to-Learn in STEM. *Journal of Chemical Education*, 98(5), 1548–55.

Graff, H. J. (1991). *The Literacy Myth: Cultural Integration and Social Structure in the Nineteenth Century*. Piscataway, NJ: Transaction Publishers.

Gubala, C., K. Larson, and L. Melonçon (2020). Do Writing Errors Bother Professionals? An Analysis of the Most Bothersome Errors and How the Writer's Ethos Is Affected. *Journal of Business and Technical Communication*, 34(3), 250–86.

Gutierrez, K. (2017). Editor's Introduction: Assessing the Value of Experiential Learning in Community-Engaged Projects. *Open Words: Access and English Studies*, 10(1), 1–6.

Jansen, F. (2012). The Putative Email Style and its Explanations: Evidence from Two Effect Studies of Dutch Direct Email Letters and Direct Marketing Emails. *Language@ Internet*, 9(2).

Lanctot, A. M. (2019). *You've Got Mail, But Is It Important And/Or Urgent?: An Investigation into Employees' Perceptions of Email*. Doctoral thesis. Carleton University.

McCulloch, G. (2020). *Because Internet: Understanding the New Rules of Language*. New York: Riverhead Books.

Meloncon, L. and S. Henschel (2013). Current State of US Undergraduate Degree Programs in Technical and Professional Communication. *Technical Communication*, 60(1), 45–64.

Mirel, B. (1996). Writing and Database Technology: Extending the Definition of Writing in the Workplace. Electronic Literacies in the Workplace: Technologies of Writing, 91–112.

Moral and Entertaining Magazine editors (1779). The Lazy Lover: A Moral Tale, in *The Moral and Entertaining Magazine*.

Myers, D. 1800. (1980). Scottish Schoolmasters in the Nineteenth Century: Professionalism and Politics, in *Scottish Culture and Scottish Education, 1800–1980*, eds. W. M. Humes and H. M. Paterson. Edinburgh: John Donald.

Nevins, A. (1962). *The Origins of the Land-grant Colleges and State Universities: A Brief Account of the Morrill Act of 1862 and its Results*. Washington, DC: Civil War Centennial Commission.

Ochsner, R. and J. Fowler (2004). Playing Devil's Advocate: Evaluating the Literature of the WAC/WID Movement. *Review of Educational Research*, 74(2), 117–40.

Pigg, S. and A. Berger (2020). Still "Worlds Apart"? Early-Career Writing Learning as a Cross-Field Opportunity. *College English*, 82(5), 507–14.

Rogers, P. (2009). The Contributions of North American Longitudinal Studies of Writing in Higher Education to our Understanding of Writing Development, in *Traditions of Writing Research*, ed. C. Bazerman, et al., Abingdon, Oxfordshire: Routledge.

Rosebury, K. G. (1902). Inaugural Address of the Earl of Rosebery, K. G., to the University of Glasgow, November 16, 1900. *The Edinburgh Review,* 195(399), 58–78.

Sherrill, J. E. (1879). *The Normal Teacher*. Danville, IN: J. E. Sherrill.

Skovholt, K., A. Grønning, and A. Kankaanranta (2014). The Communicative Functions of Emoticons in Workplace E-mails. *Journal of Computer-Mediated Communication*, 19(4), 780–97.

Stuckey-French, N. (2011). *The American Essay in the American Century*. Columbia, MI: University of Missouri Press.

Waldvogel, J. (2007). Greetings and Closings in Workplace Email. *Journal of Computer-Mediated Communication*, 12(2), 456–77.

7: Consequences of the Myth

Beason, L. (2001). Ethos and Error: How Businesspeople React to Errors. *College Composition and Communication*, 53(1), 33–64.

Defazio, J., J. Jones, F. Tennant, and S. A. Hook (2010). Academic Literacy: The Importance and Impact of Writing across the Curriculum – A Case Study. *Journal of the Scholarship of Teaching and Learning*, 10(2), 34–47.

Krugman, P. (2022). Wonking Out: Education Has Less to Do with Inequality than You Think, in *The New York Times*, April 29.

Penrose, A. M. (2002). Academic Literacy Perceptions and Performance: Comparing First-generation and Continuing-generation College Students. *Research in the Teaching of English*, 36(4), 437–61.

Singletary, M. (2015). College Costs Aren't Always Worth it, Alumni say, So Think before Borrowing, in *The Washington Post*, September 30.

7: Closer to the Truth

Al Hilali, T. S. and J. McKinley, (2021). Exploring the Socio-contextual Nature of Workplace Writing: Towards Preparing Learners for the Complexities of English L2 Writing in the Workplace. *English for Specific Purposes*, 63(3), 86–97.

American Management Association (2019). AMA Critical Skills Survey: Workers Need Higher-level Skills to Succeed in the 21st Century.

Bargiela-Chiappini, F., C. Nickerson, and B. Planken (2013). What is Business Discourse?, in *Business Discourse*, eds. Bargiela-Chiappini, F., C. Nickerson, and B. Planken, 3–44. New York: Springer.

Ede, L. S. and A. A. Lunsford (1992). *Singular Texts/Plural Authors: Perspectives on Collaborative Writing*. Carbondale, IL: Southern Illinois University Press.

Paré, A. (2002). Keeping Writing in its Place: A Participatory Action Approach to Workplace Communication, in *Reshaping Technical Communication*, eds. B. Mirel and R. Spilka, 75–98. Abingdon, Oxfordshire: Routledge.

Stafford, J. (1974). At This Point in Time, TV Is Murdering the English Language, in *The New York Times*, September 15: www.nytimes .com/1974/09/15/archives/at-this-point-in-time-tv-is-murdering-the-english-language.html.

Storch, N. (2005). Collaborative Writing: Product, Process, and Students' Reflections. *Journal of Second Language Writing*, 14(3), 153–73.

8: You Can't Write that Because Internet

Clark, L. (2012). Text Message Slang "Invading GCSEs and A-levels" as Teenagers Abandon Basic Grammar and Punctuation, in the *Daily Mail*, October 23.

Grace, A., et al. (2015). Undergraduates' Attitudes to Text Messaging Language Use and Intrusions of Textisms into Formal Writing. *New Media & Society*, 17(5), 792–809.

Guardian Staff, (1978). Further Uses of Literacy, in the *Guardian*. https:// theguardian.newspapers.com/search/?query=further%20uses%20 of%20literacy&dr_year=1978-1978.

John, A. (2013). The Internet Is Making Writing Worse, in *The Atlantic*, July 17.

Media, C. S. (2015). *The Common-sense Census: Media Use by Tweens and Teens*. Vancouver, BC: British Columbia Teachers' Federation.

Shuy, R. W. (1976). *Confronting the Literacy Crisis*. Washington, DC: Department of Health, Education and Welfare, National Institute of Education.

8: Context for the Myth

Bennett, K. (2009). English Academic Style Manuals: A Survey. *Journal of English for Academic Purposes*, 8(1), 43–54.

Dewey, J. (1927). *The Public and Its Problems* (Athens, OH: Swallow Press).

Eisenstein, E. L. (1980). *The Printing Press as an Agent of Change*, vol. 1. Cambridge: Cambridge University Press.

Lee, J. J., T. Bychkovska, and J. D. Maxwell (2019). Breaking the Rules? A Corpus-based Comparison of Informal Features in L1 and L2 Undergraduate Student Writing. *System*, 80, 143–53.

Murray, D. E. (2000). Changing Technologies, Changing Literacy Communities? *Language Learning & Technology*, 4(2), 39–53.

Thompson, C. (2009). Clive Thompson on the New Literacy. *Wired*, 17(9), August 24.

Thurlow, C. (2006). From Statistical Panic to Moral Panic: The Metadiscursive Construction and Popular Exaggeration of New Media Language in the Print Media. Journal of Computer-Mediated Communication, 11(3), 667–701.

8: Closer to the Truth

Aull, B. (2019). A Study of Phatic Emoji Use in WhatsApp Communication. *Internet Pragmatics*, 2(2), 206–32.

Carr, N. (2008) Is Google Making us Stupid? *The Atlantic*, August 15.

Crystal, D. (2010). The Changing Nature of Text, in *Text Comparison and Digital Creativity: The Production of Presence and Meaning in Digital Text Scholarship*, eds. W. T. van Peursen, E. Thoutenhoofd, and A. van der Weel, 229–51. Leiden: Brill.

DeKay, S. H. (2012). Interpersonal Communication in the Workplace: A Largely Unexplored Region. *Business Communication Quarterly*, 75(4), 449–52.

Gray, B. (2010). On the use of Demonstrative Pronouns and Determiners as Cohesive Devices: A Focus on Sentence-initial This/these in Academic Prose. *Journal of English for Academic Purposes*, 9(3), 167–83.

Herring, S. C. (2013). Relevance in Computer-mediated Conversation, in *Handbook of Pragmatics of Computer-mediated Communication*, eds. S. C. Herring, D. Stein and T. Virtanen, 245–68. Berlin: Mouton de Gruter.

Hougaard, T. T. and M. Rathje (2018). Emojis in the Digital Writings of Young Danes, in *Jugendsprachen/Youth Languages: Aktuelle Perspektiven internationaler Forschung/Current Perspectives of International Research*, ed. A. Ziegler, 773–806. Berlin: De Gruyter.

Huang, C. et al. (2020). Clinical Features of Patients Infected with 2019 Novel Coronavirus in Wuhan, China. *The Lancet*, 395(10223), 497–506.

Kuznekoff, J. H., S. Munz, and S. Titsworth (2015). Mobile Phones in the Classroom: Examining the Effects of Texting, Twitter, and Message Content on Student Learning. *Communication Education*, 64(3), 344–65.

Lorenz-Spreen, P., B. M. Mønsted, P. Hövel, and S. Lehmann (2019). Accelerating Dynamics of Collective Attention. *Nature Communications*, 10(1), 1759.

May, K. E. and A. D. Elder (2018). Efficient, Helpful, or Distracting? A Literature Review of Media Multitasking in Relation to Academic Performance. *International Journal of Educational Technology in Higher Education*, 15(1), 1–17.

McWhorter, J. (2016). The Linguistic Evolution of "Like," *The Atlantic*, November 25.

Murphy, C. (2020). Before Zuckerberg, Gutenberg. *The Atlantic*, 325(1), 22–4.

Pinker, S. (2015). *The Sense of Style: The Thinking Person's Guide to Writing in the 21st Century*. Harmondsworth: Penguin.

Shepherd, R. P. (2018). Digital Writing, Multimodality, and Learning Transfer: Crafting Connections between Composition and Online Composing. *Computers and Composition*, 48, 103–14.

Steinbrich, P. (2014). Perceptual Salience of Academic Formulas in Academic Writing, in *Language Skills: Traditions, Transitions and Ways Forward*, eds. H. Chodkiewicz and M. Trepczyńska, 343–365. Cambridge: Cambridge University Press.

Sutherland, K., C. Davis, U. Terton, and I. Visser (2018). University Student Social Media Use and its Influence on Offline Engagement in Higher Educational Communities. *Student Success*, 9 (2), 13–24.

Sword, H. (2012). *Stylish Academic Writing*. Cambridge, MA: Harvard University Press.

Tagg, C. (2013). Scraping the Barrel with a Shower of Social Misfits: Everyday Creativity in Text Messaging. *Applied Linguistics*, 34(4), 480–500.

Thurairaj, S., E. P. Hoon, S. S. Roy, and P. K. Fong (2015). Reflections of Students' Language Usage in Social Networking Sites: Making or Marring Academic English. *Electronic Journal of E-learning*, 13(4), 301–15.

Vanderplank, R. (2010). Déjà Vu? A Decade of Research on Language Laboratories, Television and Video in Language Learning. *Language Teaching*, 43(1), 1–37.

Whitman, W. (1885). Slang in America. *The North American Review*, 141(348), 431–5.

9: Conclusion

Baker-Bell, A. (2020). *Linguistic Justice: Black Language, Literacy, Identity, and Pedagogy.* Abingdon, Oxfordshire: Routledge.

Crosthwaite, P. and K. Jiang (2017). Does EAP Affect Written L2 Academic Stance? A Longitudinal Learner Corpus Study. *System*, 69, 92–107.

Perryman-Clark, S. M. (2013). African American Language, Rhetoric, and students' Writing: New Directions for SRTOL. *College Composition and Communication*, 64(3), 469–95.

Reiff, M.J. and A. Bawarshi (2011). Tracing Discursive Resources: How Students Use Prior Genre Knowledge to Negotiate New Writing Contexts in First-Year Composition. *Written Communication*, 28(3), 312–37.

Shapiro, S. (2022). *Cultivating Critical Language Awareness in the Writing Classroom.* Abingdon, Oxfordshire: Routledge.

Storch, N. and J. Tapper, (2009). The Impact of an EAP Course on Postgraduate Writing. *Journal of English for Academic Purposes*, 8(3), 207–23.

Index